Pictorial Dictionary
of
British 19th Century
FURNITURE DESIGN

Introduction by Edward Joy

An Antique Collectors' Club Research Project

© 1977 The Antique Collectors' Club
World copyright reserved

Reprinted 1984, 1986, 1989, 1994

ISBN 0 902028 47 2

British Library Cataloguing-in-Publication Data
A catalogue record for this book is available from the British Library

Printed in England on Consort Royal Satin from Donside Mills, Aberdeen,
by the Antique Collectors' Club Ltd., 5 Church Street, Woodbridge, Suffolk IP12 1DS

Antique Collectors' Club

The Antique Collectors' Club was formed in 1966 and now has a five figure membership spread throughout the world. It publishes the only independently run monthly antiques magazine *Antique Collecting* which caters for those collectors who are interested in widening their knowledge of antiques, both by greater awareness of quality and by discussion of the factors which influence the price that is likely to be asked. The Antique Collectors' Club pioneered the provision of information on prices for collectors and the magazine still leads in the provision of detailed articles on a variety of subjects.

It was in response to enormous demand for information on 'what to pay' that the price guide series was introduced in 1968 with the first edition of *The Price Guide to Antique Furniture* (completely revised, 1978 and 1989), and a book which broke new ground by illustrating the more common types of antique furniture, the sort that collectors could buy in shops and at auctions rather than the rare museum pieces which had previously been used (and still to a large extent are used) to make up the limited amount of illustrations in books published by commercial publishers. Many other price guides have followed, all copiously illustrated, and greatly appreciated by collectors for the valuable information they contain, quite apart from prices. The Antique Collectors' Club also publishes other books on antiques, including horology and art reference works, and a full book list is available.

Club membership, which is open to all collectors, costs little. Members receive free of charge *Antique Collecting*, the Club's magazine (published ten times a year), which contains well-illustrated articles dealing with the practical aspects of collecting not normally dealt with by magazines. Prices, features of value, investment potential, fakes and forgeries are all given prominence in the magazine.

Among other facilities available to members are private buying and selling facilities, the longest list of 'For Sales' of any antiques magazine, an annual ceramics conference and the opportunity to meet other collectors at their local antique collectors' clubs. There are over eighty in Britain and more than a dozen overseas. Members may also buy the Club's publications at special pre-publication prices.

As its motto implies, the Club is an amateur organisation designed to help collectors get the most out of their hobby: it is informal and friendly and gives enormous enjoyment to all concerned.

For Collectors – By Collectors – About Collecting

The Antique Collectors' Club, 5 Church Street, Woodbridge, Suffolk

Contents

Acknowledgements

The work on this book was started in 1971 when Clive Wainwright of the Victoria and Albert Museum drew up a list of the contemporary pattern books, drawings and illustrated references from contemporary sources.

Jeremy Cooper of Sotheby's very generously advised on the categories used in this pictorial approach though the final format is our responsibility. Tricia Kessler worked long, hard and intelligently on the research side, spending many hours tracing references, checking likely sources, and attempting to locate material.

The staff of the Victoria and Albert Museum Library were kind and patient as were librarians, book sellers and other sources we troubled.

A succession of photographers laboured to take the photographs often, following the rules of the institutions in which they worked, without artificial light. Some were amateur, some professional, and the results had to be touched up by a small army of illustrators who not only made good the flaws in photography but also indistinct areas in the original printing.

Commander Horncastle patiently set about the mammoth task of separating some 5,000 illustrations into their various headings.

For information on the furniture designs after 1860 we are much indebted to the researches of Pauline Agius whose book *British Furniture 1880-1915* is shortly to be published by The Antique Collectors' Club.

After the book had been set out in proof form Edward Joy very kindly put at our disposal his great knowledge of nineteenth century British furniture and provided a most valuable introduction and commentary upon the various sources used. He also provided a useful chronology of key dates.

It is a sad reflection on the economics of publishing that the position has now been reached that specialist projects such as this book are no longer viable. In 1971 it had a hope of making commercial sense. In 1977 it is on a par with Robinson Crusoe's first canoe.

June 1977

Introduction

This *Dictionary* is planned to show the complete range of Victorian furniture in illustrations drawn from contemporary sources. Also shown are the antecedents of the Victorian era, when classical taste, already established in this country for over a century and a half, still held sway before it was submerged beneath the 'Battle of the Styles'. There are also illustrations of the immediate post-Victorian developments, including the first stirrings of the Modern Movement, so that the whole story covers the period 1800 to 1914.

The sources quoted are drawn from as wide a field as possible and are set out in general chronological sequence. The illustrations represent the work of individual architects, professional furniture designers, artists and working craftsmen and of the compilers of trade manuals, firms' catalogues and encyclopaedias. All types of furniture are shown to demonstrate the great variety and complexity of Victorian pieces, from the most expensive to the relatively cheap and from the most fashionable to the strictly utilitarian, designed, that is, for the homes of the well-to-do as well as for smaller houses and even cottages.

Examination of the illustrations will enable readers to compare the commercial productions, the run-of-the-mill pieces, with those which gained special prominence at exhibitions and also with those which were attempts to seek renewed interpretations of traditional design through an understanding of the past. Thus one can see the difference between, on the one hand, the commercial productions in fashionable styles, which usually did no more than add stylistic trimmings to pieces of standard forms, and, on the other, the carefully thought out designs which embodied progressive thinking related to contemporary social conditions.

Recent research into nineteenth century material, following and promoting interest in Victorian furniture, means that we can now approach the subject with much more confidence and availability of information. We can trace the origin and development of Victorian styles and recognise the progressive designers. The period has been sadly neglected in the past. We now know that the best Victorian furniture, in both design and craftsmanship, can bear comparison with that of the Georgian period. It is a special source of satisfaction to know that foreign designers were keenly interested, particularly after 1850, in the work of the best English designers whose influence was sometimes greater abroad than at home.

Since the *Dictionary* is pictorial, a very simplified classification of furniture has been adopted, based on shape and form, with visual impact in mind. The furniture has been divided into broad groups; each group is then subdivided into categories as well as, in some cases, into easily identifiable features. This means that pieces which are normally sorted out into many different types may all be found under one main heading. Under 'Shelves', for instance, are all kinds of shelved furniture (consoles, dumb waiters, stands, canterburys, whatnots, etc.), as well as bookshelves, corner shelves, etc. 'Couches' as a general term includes sofas, ottomans, settees, settles, benches and hall seats. 'Screens' includes pole and cheval screens as well as bedroom and similar screens.

It was felt that keeping to simple groupings would prove more helpful than trying to catch up with the vast multiplicity of names, often adopted as trade labels, with romantic-sounding titles usually culled from the medieval period (prompted, it seems in many cases, by the novels of Sir Walter Scott) which the Victorians were particularly fond of inventing. 'Dressoir', for example, was a favoured term for a sideboard for twenty years after Talbert popularised it at the 1862 Exhibition. The term was then discarded, as were many other similar titles which were not inherently descriptive and bore little relation, if any, to the piece concerned. It is true that some terms have persisted, like Henry Shaw's 'Glastonbury' chair, mistakenly thought to have belonged to the last Abbot of Glastonbury, and 'grandfather' clock which John Gloag has traced to a popular song of 1878. Some names, such as 'Sutherland' table, are clearly here to stay, but others of the Victorian period, in view of what has been noted and of the partiality of the antique trade for adopting its own unauthorised nomenclature, are best ignored.

At the end of the text on individual designers or firms in the section on The Designers and Design Books references are made to select examples of furniture. Figures refer to page numbers of illustrations in this *Dictionary*. In a work of such magnitude, prepared as it was over seven years, it is almost inevitable that mistakes occur, and we are aware of minor errors which have crept in. While irritating, none of these in any way affect either individual groupings or the work as a whole, and we would be glad to hear any suggestions for improvement.

Key dates in 19th Century British Furniture History

1802   Thomas Sheraton's *Drawing Book* (with *Appendix*), reissue of original 1791-94 edition, establishes the 'Sheraton style' of light, graceful and compact furniture, and links the earlier phase of English neo-classicism (Adam and Hepplewhite) with the later (Regency) phase.

1807   Thomas Hope's *Household Furniture* is the basis of the Regency interpretation of neo-classicism with its furniture designs closely related to models from antiquity. At the same time Hope's use of symbolic decoration points the way to early Victorian symbolism.

1808   George Smith's *Household Furniture* popularises Hope's interpretation but lacks his scholarship; the basis of the late Regency style.

1820-30   Beginning of the 'Battle of the Styles'. The final phase of classicism competes with historical revivals. Richard Brown's *Rudiments*, 1820, carries symbolic decoration much further and introduces rounded and heavier forms to furniture. In contrast, P. and M.A. Nicholson's *Practical Cabinet Maker*, 1826, strongly reaffirms classical ('Grecian') taste. George Smith's *Guide* 1826, illustrates designs in Grecian, Etruscan, Egyptian, Roman, Gothic and Louis Quatorze styles and admits that his designs of 1808 are now 'wholly obsolete'.

1833   J.C. Loudon's *Encyclopaedia* confirms that the four prevailing fashionable styles are the Grecian, Gothic, Tudor ('Elizabethan') and Louis Quatorze, all generally interpreted by adding appropriate stylistic ornament to standard forms of furniture.

1835   A.W.N. Pugin's *Gothic Furniture of the Fifteenth Century* reveals real understanding of the Gothic style and marks the beginning of reformist Gothic. Constructional details are often fully revealed as an integral part of the design and proof of honest craftsmanship. This was to be an important influence in progressive furniture design later, but Pugin's reforms are delayed by contemporary preoccupation with other revivals

c.1835-60   Proliferation of historical revivals; general trend towards rounded forms and carved decoration. Richard Bridgens's *Furniture with Candelabra,* 1838, emphasises Elizabethan style, with its two main features of strapwork and spiral turning (the latter a late Stuart element). Thomas King popularises the 'Old French Style' (a mixture of all *ancien régime* styles) in a number of publications, advocating machine carving. Henry Whitaker's *Treasury of Designs,* 1847, has designs in at least seven principal styles, including the Renaissance. Henry Lawford adds touches of originality in the 'Naturalistic Style'. Abundance of upholstery reflects the universal search of comfort in furniture.

1851   The Great Exhibition confirms the triumph of historicism and encourages elaborate and symbolic decoration. 'Exhibition' furniture, both in 1851 and later in 1862, though not typical of everyday production and subject to growing criticism, nevertheless continues to influence trade production through publications devoted to the grander exhibits, notably by J. Braund, J.B. Waring, H. Lawford and G.W. Yapp.

1862   International Exhibition, London, has first public exhibition of the work of Morris and Company (founded 1861) and the first display in Europe of Japanese arts and crafts.

c.1865	Philip Webb designs 'workaday' oak furniture for Morris and Company who begin production of their 'Sussex' chair.
c.1868	Beginning of Art Furniture; reformist designs obscured by ill-adapted commercial output illustrated in the growing number of trade catalogues. Two important elements are progessive Gothic furniture and ebonised furniture, with straight lines, slender turned supports, spindle galleries and painted panels, typified in T.E. Collcutt's cabinet at the London Exhibition, 1871. Rounded forms and carving now replaced by rectilinear forms and painted decoration.
1867	Bruce Talbert's *Gothic Forms* illustrates reformist 'Early English' Gothic furniture of framed construction, low-relief carving, inlaid and pierced decoration and bold hinges. In contrast William Burges designs furniture of sturdy construction decorated with paintings and insets of later medieval inspiration.
1868	C.L. Eastlake's *Hints on Household Taste* displays simpler versions of panelled early-English furniture and has wide following in the United States.
1877	William Watt's trade catalogue publishes the designs of E.W. Godwin in Anglo-Japanese style, grouping solid and void in functional rectilinear simplicity. Japanese and other oriental influence predominant in the products of Liberty's, founded in Regent Street in 1875.
1870s	Revival of Georgian and Queen Anne styles prompted by Wright and Mansfield's prize-winning cabinet in Adam style at the Paris Exhibition, 1867.
1882	Foundation of the Century Guild by A.H. Mackmurdo; beginning of the Arts and Crafts Movement formed of guilds and societies devoted to the hand crafts. These combine in 1888 in the Arts and Crafts Exhibition Society to hold displays of their work. The Movement influenced by the ideals of William Morris whose company plays a prominent part in it.
c.1890	Morris and Company, however, under their new designer, George Jack, show Georgian influences in their marquetry furniture, in strong contrast to their earlier oak pieces.
1893	Cotswold School, off-shoot of Arts and Crafts Movement, founded by Ernest Gimson and the Barnsley brothers, with the aim of making furniture in the best traditions of English rural craftsmanship, directly inspired by Morris's teachings.
1895	Samuel Bing's Art Nouveau shop opens in Paris and gives its name to the new style, current throughout Europe, based on waving and sinuous lines of natural forms, free from historical precedents. Liberty's prominent in adopting the new style which has leading interpreters in C.R. Mackintosh and C.A.F. Voysey. Commercial debasement gives rise to the 'Quaint' style.
1896	Death of William Morris. Ambrose Heal, who had joined his family firm of Heal and Son in 1893, becomes its chief furniture designer and produces furniture in full accord with the Arts and Crafts Movement with which the firm is closely linked.
1896	Heal's famous catalogue reintroduces simple wooden bedsteads.
1900	Ambrose Heal wins Silver Medal for bedroom suite at the Paris Exhibition.

Contemporary sources quoted in the Dictionary

The dates of the publication of nineteenth century books and catalogues of furniture designs give rise to certain difficulties.

Some design books are known to have had a number of reissues, especially those of the first half of the century, but the dates of these and even, in some cases, of their first editions, are often as obscure as the personalities of the designers themselves. Thomas King, for example, was a prolific producer of design books (it is still not clear whether he was author or publisher), yet the dates of his first editions and of their reissues remain so far largely a mystery. Again, what is now accepted as the date of a first edition may well turn out to be a reissue. Recent evidence, for instance, points to an earlier edition (undiscovered) of R. Bridgens's *Furniture with Candelabra*, 1838.

Later in the century some firms continued to issue the same catalogues year after year without dates, so that what may be considered as referring to the furniture of a particular year may equally apply to a decade (or more) earlier or later. While all this indicates a strong conservative element in Victorian taste, much work clearly remains to be done to establish a precise chronology of publication.

A certain latitude (normally with approximate dates of later editions in mind) has been adopted in the *Dictionary* to give dates at which the designs concerned can be said to reflect faithfully the prevailing standards of taste.

1802	**T. Sheraton.** Appendix to *The Cabinet-Maker and Upholsterer's Drawing Book.*
1804	**T. Sheraton.** *The Cabinet-Maker, Upholsterer and General Artist's Encyclopaedia.*
1808	**G. Smith.** *A Collection of Designs for Household Furniture and Interior Decoration.*
1822	**R. Brown.** *The Rudiments of Drawing Cabinet and Upholstery Furniture.*
1823	*The London Chairmakers' and Carvers' Book of Prices.*
1825	**H. Whitaker.** *Designs of Cabinet and Upholstery Furniture in the Most Modern Style.*
1826	**P. and M.A. Nicholson.** *The Practical Cabinet-Maker, Upholsterer and Complete Decorator.*
1826	**G. Smith.** *The Cabinet-Maker and Upholsterer's Guide, Drawing Book and Repository.*
1826	**C.H. Tatham.** *Etchings of Ancient Ornamental Architecture* (fourth edition).
1829	**T. King.** *The Modern Style of Cabinet Work Exemplified* (second revised, improved edition, 1835; *Supplementary Plates to The Modern Style of Cabinet Work Exemplified,* c.1840).
1830	**T. King.** *Designs for Carving and Gilding.*

The Designers and Design Books

THOMAS SHERATON(1751-1806)

The designs begin with those of the last of the famous Georgian trinity of craftsmen-designers, Chippendale, Hepplewhite and Sheraton, who have given their names to the styles of the 'golden age' of English furniture. Sheraton, who was trained as a craftsman but did not have a workshop of his own and made a poor living by giving drawing lessons — no piece of furniture made by him has ever been identified — was perhaps the most technically accomplished of the trinity in his drawings, as befitted his profession, and the most original in his designs. He carried Hepplewhite's interpretation of Robert Adam's neo-classicism a stage further towards light and delicate furniture, with a genius for designing multi-purpose pieces which incorporated mechanical gadgets — a reflection of the current interest not only in small, compact and often portable furniture needed to offset the pressure on living space following the population explosion after 1780, but also in mechanical devices engendered by the increasing pace of the Industrial Revolution.

Sheraton's designs were a bridge between the two main phases of neo-classicism: Adam's graceful forms which obviously caught much of the spirit of the rococo, and the stricter archaeological interpretation of ancient furniture, based on close research, of which Thomas Hope was the chief exponent. Sheraton's most influential book, the one which created the 'Sheraton style', was the *Cabinet-Maker and Upholsterer's Drawing Book*, first published in parts between 1791 and 1794. The designs shown in the *Dictionary* below are from the *Appendix* to the *Drawing Book* in the 1802 reissue.

Sheraton's *Cabinet Dictionary* of 1803, perhaps more strictly a manual for practising craftsmen than a pattern book, shows evidence of the new archaeological approach to furniture in its designs of the Grecian couch and its illustrations of the new Regency features of animal monopodia, lion masks and lion paw feet, simulated bamboo legs and concave chair legs anticipating the 'sabre' legs of the early nineteenth century. Sheraton also left an unfinished work, *The Cabinet-Maker, Upholsterer and General Artists's Encyclopaedia*, compiled between 1804 and the year of his death, 1806. This book marks a sad decline from his original work, suggests an unbalanced mind and forecasts the wider aberrations of early Victorian design. The *Encyclopaedia* did, however, contain the earliest recorded designs of the Regency interpretation of Egyptian taste applied to furniture.

For typical Sheraton pieces see dressing tables, 32; cabinets, 84; chairs, 211; desks, 344. Compare Sheraton's earlier chairs with those in his *Encyclopaedia*, 190.

C.H. TATHAM (1772-1842)

The architect, Henry Holland (1745-1806), worked for the Prince of Wales and his coterie of Whig aristocrats whose prime source of inspiration was France, where the new classical taste had taken root. Holland's mastery of Graeco-Roman details was largely due to the drawings of Charles Heathcote Tatham, who had been employed in Holland's office and in 1794 was sent to Italy for three years to supply the architect with sketches from original sources. The result was the publication in 1799 of Tatham's *Etchings of Ancient Ornamental Architecture*, reissued in 1810.

For examples see survey of Tatham's *Etchings*, 255-6.

A selection of Thomas Hope's classical

T. HOPE (1768-1831)

Thomas Hope stands apart from other designers of the Georgian period. He was a wealthy connoisseur and collector who had travelled extensively throughout the Mediterranean world to study ancient remains. His fine collection of antiquities was mainly housed in his London home in Duchess Street. In 1807 appeared *Household Furniture and Interior Decoration executed from Designs by Thomas Hope* which was fundamentally a guide book to Hope's collection. It made the Duchess Street house into one of the show places of London and has established Hope's reputation as the great interpreter of pure classical forms.

Hope took meticulous care to make his drawings, and consequently his furniture, as close to ancient models as possible. His book was to have much influence on other designers in the first quarter of the century. But one can now legitimately have second thoughts concerning Hope's reputation. There is a good case for seeing him also as a precursor of Victorianism, for his designs include a considerable amount of symbolic ornament which is so often considered a particular Victorian innovation.

Hope's standing clearly owes much to the fact that his death coincided so closely with 1830, the end of the Georgian era and a date accepted as the concluding date of 'antique' English furniture. Apart from the artificiality of such dating — and in 1830, it must be remembered, Hope's publication was almost twenty five years old — the symbolism on his furniture was criticised, and in some cases derided, by contemporaries. After Hope came a divided world of furniture styles, the advance guard of the historical revivals competing with the rear-guard of classicism.

designs from Household Furniture. Courtesy Victoria and Albert Museum.

Drawing-room designed by Thomas Hope. The drawings on this and the facing page are from Hope's Household Furniture. Courtesy Victoria and Albert Museum.

The Egyptian room by Thomas Hope. The chair and couch on the facing page can be seen in this drawing.

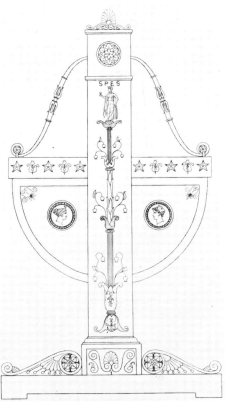

Cradle with emblems of night.

Chimney piece.

Round monopodium with inlay designs, by Hope. Courtesy Victoria and Albert Museum.

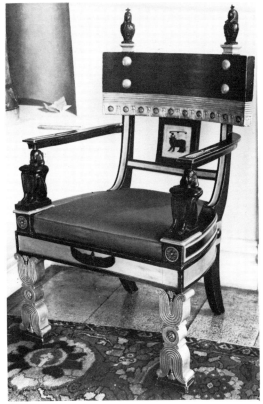

Egyptian style chair and couch designed by Thomas Hope. Courtesy Faringdon Collection Trust.

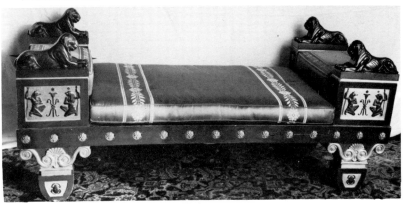

GEORGE SMITH

Hope's designs were put into general circulation by George Smith, the author of a pattern book which quickly followed Hope's publication and had practically the same title: *A Collection of Designs for Household Furniture and Interior Decoration, 1808*. Little so far is known about Smith's career. He was a practising craftsman who claimed, without justification it seems, to be upholsterer to the Prince of Wales. There is certainly much emphasis on upholstery in his book, a concession to the growing interest in this branch of interior decoration which was largely due to the increasing output of materials from the factories. This was to be of importance for furniture design, not only in the attempt to relate curtains and window cornices to the various styles which were beginning to affect furniture but also in the thicker padding which was being applied to seats of all kinds with consequent influence on their design.

Smith took over many of the classical features of Hope's designs. He makes great use of animal monopodia on a variety of pieces, tables, sideboards, chairs and sofas, for instance, of double lotus leaves meeting centrally in legs and stretchers, of winged feet on tables and cabinets, of console supports on tables and seats, and of varied fashionable decorative ornaments such as stars and bolt heads. His chairs in general adopt the straight lines which were considered to have been the distinguishing mark of ancient furniture, thus failing to continue the use of contrasting curves which were such an attractive feature of the 'Trafalgar' chair. His *Household Furniture* undoubtedly kept classical types of furniture very much alive, as did the reissue of Tatham's *Etchings* in 1810. But Smith could not possibly match the scholarship which gave precision to many of Hope's designs.

Smith also paid great attention to Gothic designs; indeed his book of 1808 presents more illustrations of this style than any previous publication. He claims that Gothic produced "a more abundant variety of ornaments and forms than can possibly be obtained in any other style", and he proceeds to apply his Gothic decoration to every kind of furniture. Herein the fundamental error of designing furniture in historical revivals becomes clear. Smith's designs are not Gothic at all; they simply show furniture of current fashionable forms with the addition of Gothic ornament — pierced quatrefoils, crockets, pinnacles, pointed arches, etc. copied from medieval buildings.

Smith's *Cabinet-Maker and Upholsterer's Guide* of 1826, with 153 plates, shows what had happened within two decades, for it illustrates interiors in Grecian, Egyptian, Etruscan, Roman, Gothic and Louis Quatorze styles while the author admits that his designs of 1808 are now wholly obsolete owing to the rapid change in taste and the difficulty of finding new forms. Smith's furniture is now heavy and clumsy and its decoration coarser, though the *Guide*, accepted as the exemplar of late Regency taste, was to have some influence in America as well as in England.

Examples of 1808 designs: 18, 19; Gothic bed, 20; monopodia, 147, 156, 168, 541; winged feet, 176; double lotus link, 273 (top left); winged monopodia, 427. For 1826 designs, 33, 52, 114, 124, 136, 344 (compare with Sheraton designs on same page).

Drawing room chairs in profile from Smith's Collection of Designs for Household Furniture and Interior Decoration, 1808. Courtesy Victoria and Albert Museum.

RICHARD BROWN

In 1820 Richard Brown issued his *Rudiments of Drawing Cabinet and Upholstery Furniture*, a popular work quickly followed by a second and enlarged edition in 1822. Brown, who called himself 'an architect and professor of perspective' had published a work on perspective in 1815, and over a long period, from 1804 to 1828, exhibited architectural drawings at the Royal Academy. In his *Rudiments* he not only makes much use of symbolic ornament but introduces the rounded forms which were to be the most important structural elements in early Victorian furniture. The main reason for this change was the growing insistence among all classes on comfort in furniture and the fittings of the home, a natural development in an age which accepted the principle that people were entitled to enjoy the abundant and cheap products of industry as a reward for their labours.

Brown's Rudiments 1822

Brown pays lip service to Hope and there is much of Hope's inspiration in his classical designs, including reference to Egyptian and Etruscan, as well as Greek and Roman styles. To these Brown adds Gothic and Moresque. It is in symbolic decoration that he shows the other side of Hope's influence. He advocates the use of a wide variety of flowers, leaves and plants for ornament, drawn from "every tree of the forest and flower of the valley", and he particularly encourages the use of English varieties. It is in decoration that he displays a certain whimsical imagination which sometimes approaches the absurd. He suggests that a dressing table should have decoration of plants which produce perfumes, with the addition of fig leaves "to denote the dress of our first parents". Sofas should be decorated with symbols of comfort, the couch flower, for instance, and heartsease. Another suggestion is to have the figure of Narcissus on a cheval glass "to show our folly in being too much in love with our own persons".

In general Brown's furniture designs display a tendency towards heaviness as well as rotundity. Use is made of curved edges and scrolled supports. The top rails of dining-room and drawing-room chairs take the form of curved yokes. It is noticeable that the central pillar supports of dining tables are now much thicker, and rest on a square platform base with round feet. The stumpy turned foot is found on sofas. There is much more turned work on structural members, on chair legs, for example, which are now straight and no longer of sabre form. In short, in these forms as in decoration, Brown shows, seventeen years before Victoria's accession, features which are essentially early Victorian in character.

Brown 1822

Examples: 29, 147, 427, 453.

PETER and MICHAEL ANGELO NICHOLSON (1765-1844 and c.1796-1842)

In direct contrast to Brown's *Rudiments*, the two Nicholsons, father and son, published a book in 1826 (this is the date on the title page though some plates are dated 1827) which reaffirmed total adherence to Grecian forms so strongly supported by Hope. This was *The Practical Cabinet-Maker, Upholsterer and Complete Decorator*. Peter Nicholson, the elder, was of Scottish extraction and worked in his early years as a cabinet-maker before branching into a career as architect and mathematician. He made special contribution to the study of building materials and the use of scientific means of construction, on which he published several works. His son, Michael Angelo, was responsible for most of the eighty one plates in *The Practical Cabinet-Maker* and seems to have designed many of the pieces. The book was a success and was reissued as late as 1846. This is convincing proof that the traditional classical style still had many adherents.

The introduction to the book maintains that the illustrations are taken "from the purest classical models" of the period "when the arts and sciences were in the very zenith of perfection". Thus the Grecian taste is stressed, though there are also designs in the Egyptian style (these include some of the last Regency interpretations of this style) and even some in the Gothic. Some designs are clearly based on Hope's.

P. & M.A. Nicholson 1826

The Nicholsons were also influenced by contemporary fashions in furniture. Like Brown, they illustrate chairs with yoke-shaped top rails which end in spiral volutes. Scrolls of classical form employing acanthus and honeysuckle decoration appear on the pediments of case furniture (wardrobes, cabinets, bookcases, etc.) and on the backs of sideboards and sofas. Tables with circular and octagonal tops are related to the later, and not earlier, Regency types. But as on the whole the Nicholsons come out so strongly in favour of the classical, their book must have helped considerably to continue the best features of Regency furniture into the next decade or two.

Examples: 6, 43, 71, 184, 214, 267, 317, 491, 428; Gothic, 136.

THE LONDON CHAIRMAKERS' AND CARVERS' BOOK OF PRICES

All the books so far cited were published within the Georgian period and indicate the growing division between the old and the new. Changes were obvious but were bound to be slow. Most of the practising craftsmen in the second quarter of the century had been trained in the classical tradition and radical changes required a new generation of workers. Conservatism in furniture design was encouraged also by the trade publications which fixed craftsmen's wages. The example illustrated in the *Dictionary* is *The London Chairmakers' and Carvers' Book of Prices* (1823 edition; originally published in 1802). By arrangement between employers and workers, prices were fixed for the making of all the components of furniture and for carving and other forms of decoration. This system was of obvious advantage to both sides as it led to smooth industrial relations but it inevitably led to the repetition of standard patterns.

Examples: 14, 177-8; chair components (in Hepplewhite, Sheraton and Regency styles), 213-4.

London Chairmakers' 1823

ACKERMANN'S REPOSITORY OF ARTS

An excellent contemporary guide to Regency taste can be found in Ackermann's *Repository of Arts* which was published in monthly parts between 1809 and 1828. Most numbers contained a coloured plate of fashionable furniture. The *Repository's* taste was catholic. Classicism naturally predominated in the earlier issues, but also shown (September, 1817) was the first recorded illustration of the new 'Elizabethan' style, then examples of Egyptian pieces, and, between 1825 and 1827, a long run of Gothic designs which were published as a whole in 1827 (Pugin's Gothic Furniture — see section on A.W.N. Pugin, infra).

JOHN C. LOUDON (1783-1843)

It seems strange at first view that after 1830 so much inspiration should be sought in the furniture of the medieval and Tudor periods, but there were many reasons for this. The long-accepted standards of the eighteenth century were being challenged. In 1844 a clergyman wrote in the scholarly journal, the *Quarterly Review*, clearly confident that he was voicing the opinion of many of his readers,

Loudon 1833

that "the century we live in is not more remarkable for its railways and marvels of science than for a reaction from preceding barbarism in matters of taste". Attention was turned to periods which were regarded as the sources of truly national styles; antiquarian research concentrated on medieval and Tudor architecture and resulted in a growing amount of accurate information; both the Anglicans (in the Tractarian Movement) and the Roman Catholics (after the Emancipation Act of 1829) looked back to pre-Reformation England; and there was great interest aroused by the romantic literature of the time, particularly by Scott's novels. In the rapidly changing conditions of the nineteenth century there was perhaps a natural tendency to cling to the apparent stability of a more remote past.

The changes of the time were first set out in a remarkable publication, Loudon's *Encyclopaedia of Cottage, Farm and Villa Architecture and Furniture*, first issued in 1833 and reissued many times until as late as 1867. Loudon, another Scot, was a prolific compiler of books, encyclopaedias and magazines dealing with a variety of subjects, all praising self-help. As its title indicates, the *Encyclopaedia*, with over 1,100 pages and 2,000 engravings, is a mine of information on the homes and furnishings of all classes, in contrast to earlier pattern and similar books which had the upper and middle classes mainly in mind. New materials, including metals for furniture, mechanical devices (particularly applied to invalid furniture), methods of staining and graining wood are all described and illustrated, with emphasis, in most cases, on functional forms which can at the same time provide comfort.

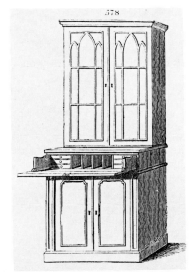

Loudon 1833

In a well-known passage Loudon describes the four fashionable furniture styles of his day as the Grecian, Gothic, Tudor and Louis Quatorze, the last-named being the only style of the eighteenth century to receive attention. These fashions, soon to proliferate, may be said really to have begun the 'Battle of the Styles' which was to divide architects and designers into opposing camps. The Grecian, except in a few examples, was losing the purity of Hope's strict interpretation and was becoming what has been termed 'sub-classical'. Gothic was a growing force but 'Gothic' furniture, as has been seen, was still no more than stock pieces. Some dealers tackled the problem by acquiring genuine old Gothic fragments (panels, carved work, etc.) to make up into their own versions of medieval furniture, thus creating many a puzzle for present-day collectors. The 'Tudor' furniture of the time, usually called 'Elizabethan', was even stranger, for one of its most characteristic features was spiral turning which was not Elizabethan at all but late Stuart in origin. These lapses are explained by the fact that art history was then in its infancy and designers were very ready to put their own versions of the past into print. The Louis Quatorze style differed from the preceding in that its decoration did, in this case, form an essential part of the construction of furniture and was not merely a decorative addition. This particular revival demonstrated the continuation of French influence which had for so long been a potent factor in the development of English furniture, and when the restored Bourbon monarchy revived the styles of the *ancien régime* in France after 1815 their example was rapidly followed in England. But here again there was much confusion, for though the Louis Quatorze style was essentially one of baroque interpretation, the English adherents of the style often added considerable rococo ornament of the Louis Quinze period, and indeed the features became so mixed that the general description of the 'Old French Style' was frequently used. The *Encyclopaedia* had enormous influence, not only in England, but also in America and as far away as Australia. It had no less than eleven later editions. It treated every aspect and all types of buildings, from villas to cottages, with analytical notes which display, on the whole, a remarkable objectivity. It differs from most previous books of the kind in devoting attention to cheap, utilitarian furniture. Nothing else in print of the time gives us such a detailed account of the early Victorian household.

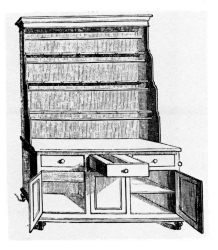

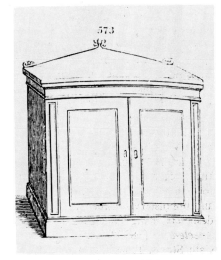

Loudon 1833

Examples: Metal, 1, 256, 486; Gothic, 178, 258; Elizabethan, 237; for range of designs, 7, 14, 22, 29, 85, 114, 144, 431.

RICHARD BRIDGENS

The Elizabethan style was given special prominence in a book designed by Richard Bridgens — *Furniture with Candelabra and Interior Decoration*. The date usually given to this book is 1838, but there seems to have been an earlier (undiscovered) edition in 1833. Richard Bridgens, about whom little is known, was an architect who exhibited at the Royal Academy between 1813 and 1826 and was engaged for a time on restoration work at Aston Hall, Birmingham. As his book has no text we have no clue to his own views on his designs. The plates, which are coloured, are presented in collaboration with Henry Shaw who in 1836 published a valuable book, *Specimens of Ancient Furniture* (reissued as late as 1866) which shows examples from early times based on a study of actual pieces and provided much information for the Elizabethan revival.

Bridgens's book has fifty nine plates of which eight are Gothic, twenty four Grecian, and twenty seven Elizabethan. Interspersed with engravings of Tudor furniture in a number of old houses, the Elizabethan designs show the author's attempts to relate the style to modern pieces such as chairs, a bookcase, chest of drawers, sideboard, cellaret, occasional table, window seat, etc. There is much use of strapwork ornament, easily applied to such furniture. Elizabethan chairs incorporate strapwork carving and demonstrate the common error of the time in having Stuart features of tall backs, turned legs and spirally turned uprights. The Grecian plates also show a certain amount of confusion for they include a 'marqueterie centre table' with a circular top decorated with marquetry of English, not classical, flowers. Bridgens was clearly intent on taking full advantage of the prevailing interest in this Elizabethan furniture and he shows only passing interest in the Gothic.

Examples: Strapwork, 125, 142; Elizabethan chairs, 190-1; Gothic, 258; Elizabethan pieces, 279, 286, 295, 508; Elizabethan and Gothic sideboards, 430.

The 'Glastonbury' chair drawn by Henry Shaw from the Specimens of Ancient Furniture, 1836. Courtesy Victoria and Albert Museum.

THOMAS KING

Siegfried Giedion has called the nineteenth century that of the 'reign of the upholsterer'. Upholsterers often also took the title of 'Decorators', a term which became very fashionable among leading London firms who undertook the complete decorating and furnishing of a house. Coupled with the proliferation of styles this emphasis on upholstery which, as we have seen, resulted in the rounded forms and the heavy padding of seating furniture and an increase in the number of such pieces, helped to break down the traditional arrangement of reception rooms in which space had been the overriding consideration and furniture was set in an orderly system against the walls. Hence the typical Victorian interior of lush hangings, multi-patterned wall papers and a multitude of pieces of furniture scattered around the room; familiar to older people who can remember their grandparents' homes and to those who have seen such interiors either reconstructed in museums or in those Victorian houses which have been preserved with their contents.

But the Victorian interior was clearly presaged before the Queen's accession in the designs of Thomas King who called himself, significantly, "an upholsterer of forty five years' experience" and published a number of pattern books of furniture and upholstery between 1829 and about 1840. Like so many other contemporary designers, King remains a shadowy figure. One of his books, *The Upholsterer's Accelerator* (1833?), lists some twelve publications by him and gives his address in Gate Street, Lincoln's Inn Fields, London. There is no doubt about the popular appeal of his works, for his best-known production, *The Modern Style of Cabinet Work Exemplified,* first published in 1829, followed by a new and improved edition

T.King 1829

in 1835, was reissued unaltered as late as 1862 — another testimony to the conservatism of early Victorian taste. Moreover, *Supplementary Plates to the Modern Style* (1840), added twenty eight plates with sixty eight new designs to the seventy two plates and 227 designs of the 1835 edition. King was a devotee of French revivals, announcing in the *Modern Style* that "as far as possible the English style is carefully blended with Parisian taste". His later works continue to emphasise this 'Old French Style' and one of them, the undated *French Designs* has eighteen plates "displaying the French taste for elegance and lightness". One point King makes very clear; this French style could be executed cheaply and rapidly, for the gilded parts required carving only in gold scrolls and massive foliage, while enrichments such as mouldings, borders and rosettes could be done in composition ornament. This cheapness of production, it can be added, was also an important reason why strapwork ornament and the Elizabethan style were so popular.

King's furniture designs rarely achieve the lightness which he associated with the Old French Style. Many pieces, tables of all kinds, wash-stands and teapoys in particular, stand on solid bases ('blocks') and these betray increasingly heavy forms. Larger pieces, wardrobes, sideboards, commodes, etc., have a cresting usually of carved honeysuckle or acanthus. Scrollwork decorates the top rails of drawing-room chairs which often have rounded backs. Even more scrollwork of interlaced curves appears in the designs in the *Supplementary Plates*, applied in this case to furniture (a firescreen, bed, flower stand, 'fancy' occasional tables, etc.) which are not included in the *Modern Style*. King by no means neglects the classical style; there are designs in contemporary versions of Grecian taste. There are also Gothic designs for a hall chair and bookcases (halls and libraries were considered very suitable for Gothic treatment).

Examples: Elizabethan, 8, 23, 24, 33, 191, 483, 492; Grecian, 100, 113, 124, 142, 483, 492; French, 33, 156, 168, 217-8, 295, 432-4, 442-4; Gothic, 89; wash-stand, solid base, 71; scrolled crests, 53; scroll tops, chairs, 217-8; blocks, 482; legs, all styles, 517.

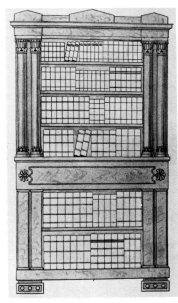
Modern Style Exemplified 1829

HENRY WOOD, JOHN TAYLOR, HENRY LAWFORD AND W. TOMS

These four designers may be taken to represent general trade production at about the mid-century.

Wood, who called himself a 'decorative draughtsman', of Percy Street, London, was particularly intent on designing pieces for upholstering in Berlin woolwork. This kind of work, introduced from Germany, had become increasingly popular since the beginning of the century as it could be done cheaply at home. Housewives bought patterns on square paper and copied them stitch by stitch in coloured wools on square-mesh canvas. The fashion was at its height between about 1820 and 1860. Wood published *Eighteen Plates for Berlin Woolwork* and other pattern books on the subject, all undated but probably between 1840-50. His *Cheval and Pole Screens* reminds us of the universal use in Victorian times of this type of furniture, now obsolete, designed to keep the heat of large coal fires from becoming too uncomfortable for those sitting near them. Wood's other designs show his special fondness for tall chairs with fully upholstered backs, some with spiral uprights, which were typical Elizabethan drawing-room examples of the time.

John Taylor, upholsterer, had been an employee of the well-known London firm of George Oakley and had his own upholstery business near Covent Garden. He had contributed a number of designs to the *Repository of Arts* between 1821 and 1824. The designs in his *Upholsterer's and Cabinet Maker's Pocket Assistant* are so typical of furniture designs of the 1850s that they are placed at that date in the dictionary, although the book was probably published slightly earlier, and c.1825 has been suggested. Taylor's designs show the usual mixture of styles and he made early use of foliate cresting on sofas and sideboards, and of peg-top and bun feet, heavily turned on tables and cabinets.

T. King 1835

Henry Wood 1848

Henry Lawford, describing himself as an "architectural designer and lithographer", published his *Chair and Sofa Manufacturer's Book of Designs* about 1845. His versions of seating furniture in historical styles are not particularly distinguished except in one respect. There are examples among them of what may be considered a relatively original early Victorian style marked by abundant upholstery, rounded forms and much use of naturalistic carving, all dictated by considerations of comfort. Historical borrowings are obvious but their treatment shows a certain independent approach. The tentative title of the 'Naturalistic Style' has been to this type of furniture, which is often of novel form, but it must be stressed that the study of its exact nature is still in its infancy and awaits further research.

W. Toms, a "carver in general", demonstrates in his *36 New, Original and Practical Designs for Chairs* that by 1840 the established features of chairs in the dining- and drawing-rooms of many households included curved backs, often of balloon shape, with carved ornament and buttoned upholstery, turned and carved front legs and curved back legs.

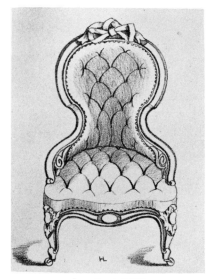

Lawford 1855

Examples: Henry Wood: 158, 179, 193-4; Elizabethan chair, spiral, 169; tall-backed chairs, 262; rounded forms, 454.

Examples: John Taylor: upholstery, 24-5; crests, 55; all types of chairs, 224; for general range, 91, 100, 125, 136, 150, 179, 300-2, 436-7.

Examples: Henry Lawford: 'Naturalistic' style, 150-1, 303; tall-backed chairs, 184, 195.

Examples: W. Toms: balloon-backs, 192, 219.

HENRY WHITAKER

For a study of fashionable styles just before the Great Exhibition of 1851 there is no better record than Henry Whitaker's *The Practical Cabinet-Maker and Upholsterer's Treasury of Designs*, 1847. Though Whitaker was the most versatile and informative of the designers of his day, little, again, is known about him. His reputation was an established one for his designs were executed for the Queen at Osborne and for a number of distinguished clients, including the Marquis of Exeter and the Dukes of Devonshire and Northumberland. Moreover, his earlier works give us an interesting guide to the evolution of styles after 1825. In that year he published *Designs of Cabinet and Upholstery Furniture in the Most Modern Style* in which the current classical forms begin to show a tendency towards elaborate ornament in rather heavily carved foliate scroll work. Yet shortly after this, in 1827, he published *Five Etchings from the Antique* which though not applied to furniture design, were accurate drawings of antique ornament which echo Tatham's search for the purest classical forms.

Whitaker 1825

Classicism, however, is only a small element of the *Treasury of Design*. Its title page lists no less than seven styles – Grecian, Italian, Renaissance, Louis Quatorze, Gothic, Tudor and Elizabethan – to which, for good measure are added two designs in the text in 'Francis I' style. Grecian and Gothic are relegated to a very minor role; of the twenty seven parts of the book, each containing four plates and each plate often having several designs, by far the greater number are devoted to the Italian and the Elizabethan. The Louis Quatorze style is described as "thoroughly worn out" but this is a hasty judgement, as French influence was to be continued by the many French craftsmen who emigrated to work in England either freely or as refugees after the political troubles in France in 1848 and 1851 (with a further influx after 1870). "At present", writes Whitaker, "the Renaissance and the Italian divide the fashionable world." Like Thomas King, Whitaker is preoccupied with achieving results at as little cost as possible ("beauty may be obtained as cheaply as ugliness") and he attempts to prove that this can include a wide variety of fitments such as chimney pieces, stair railings, window cornices and draperies, grates, wall papers, even china and silver, though he is chiefly concerned with furniture. With reference to the design of an Elizabethan sideboard, he admits that it is perhaps richer than utility requires, "were it not for the carving companies who very much now facilitate the bosting of carvings" (bosting — or boosting — referring to the general outline of the wood which was prepared ready for the carver's detailed work).

Whitaker's designs are typical of the time in adding the appropriate ornament to standard forms to distinguish the styles. This decoration could be easily transferred from one piece of furniture to another or even, with suitable modifications, to parts of the room; the pattern of marquetry on a table top, for instance, could be applied to a ceiling.

The Renaissance style was the newcomer to the scene and was to be prominent at the 1851 Exhibition. It illustrates how designers, in their constant search for new styles, were ransacking the post-classical centuries and working their way into early modern history. The Renaissance style also had an appealing novelty, for the very word — Renaissance — was of recent coinage and was attracting the attention of scholars.

The best contemporary account of the situation is to be found in an essay by R.N. Wornum, *The Exhibition as a Lesson in Taste,* which won a prize of 100 guineas awarded by the editors of the *Art-Journal Illustrated Catalogue of the Great Exhibition.* Wornum, later to become Keeper of the National Gallery, was as enthusiastically pro-Renaissance as he was anti-Gothic. But he divided the Renaissance into the 'Cinquecento' and the 'Mixed Cinquecento or Renaissance', the line between them being drawn at about 1550. The earlier phase, the Cinquecento, was 'the culminating style in Ornamental Art' and thus purer than the later Renaissance style. This was an arbitrary decision even for a leading scholar of the period, and needless to say, meant little to Whitaker and other designers who were simply concerned with embellishments and not forms. It is often impossible in some cases to distinguish their Renaissance furniture from their Elizabethan.

Whitaker's Renaissance designs are marked by ornament consisting of either a mixture of fruit, flowers, foliage, human masks and birds or pendants, arches, lions' heads and scrolls supposedly taken from Italian sources.

Examples: Classical, 33; (1825), 100, 135; (1847), 142; Louis Quatorze, 486, 509; Elizabethan, 486, 509, 434-5; Renaissance, 434-5, 373.

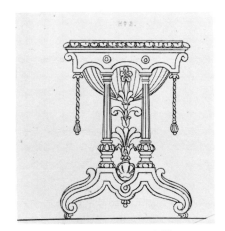

Henry Whitaker 1847

Henry Whitaker's carved mahogany table designed for the Conservative Club, 1844.
Courtesy Victoria and Albert Museum.

A.W.N. PUGIN (1812-1852)

A retrospective glance is now essential, for among the many books on styles appeared one which is now regarded as the first reformist manifesto of the post-Georgian era. This was *Gothic Furniture in the Style of the Fifteenth Century* by A.W.N. Pugin, published in 1835. Pugin is one of the most fascinating figures of the nineteenth century. In the course of his short and frantically crowded life as architect, designer, lecturer and writer, he designed many churches and secular buildings and a vast range of their contents, including those in the New Houses of Parliament, rebuilt after the disastrous fire of 1834. His career began at the early age of fifteen when he designed Gothic furniture for Windsor Castle under the general direction of his father, A.C. Pugin. In 1827 Ackermann published twenty seven designs of Gothic furniture which had appeared previously in the *Repository of Arts*. This publication *(Pugin's Gothic Furniture)* is now convincingly held to represent the work of A.W.N. Pugin, though for long it was assumed to be his father's. Pugin was later very critical of this early work, referring to the "enormities in the furniture" which he designed for Windsor Castle because he had failed to grasp the true meaning of Gothic. The turning point came in 1835 when he was converted to Roman Catholicism and set out with incredible energy to study and apply the fundamental principles of Gothic medieval art. In 1841 he published *The True Principles of Pointed or Christian Architecture* in which he laid down the two basic rules of design: "1st, that there should be no features about a building which are not necessary for convenience, construction and propriety; 2nd, that all ornament should consist of enrichment of the essential construction". Only Gothic architecture, he maintained, obeyed these rules

In *Gothic Furniture of the Fifteenth Century* these principles are applied to furniture. Many of the pieces illustrated in superb detail are clearly too large for normal domestic use but simpler pieces, tables, stools, chairs, chests, a screen and a prie-dieu, could be adapted for commercial production. Pugin's ornament was taken from nature, based on the flowers and foliage of medieval carving which he later illustrated in his *Floriated Ornament* of 1849, a book intended to correct the lifeless copies of so much contemporary Gothic decoration.

Pugin organised the Medieval Court at the Great Exhibition. He, more than anybody else, was responsible for the Gothic revival of the later Victorian period.

In one other respect he made a most important contribution to Victorian design. This was in revealing the structural framework of furniture, a feature of medieval joinery which was quite contrary to established cabinet-making practice. In panelled furniture, for instance, the pegs which secure the mortise and tenon joints are clearly shown. This not only made the constructional details an attractive form

Above: 'Fashionable Chairs' from the Repository of Arts (Ackermann), September 1817. The top chair is Elizabethan. Courtesy Victoria and Albert Museum.

Left: Marquetry walnut table, c.1847 by Pugin for Abney Hall. Courtesy Victoria and Albert Museum.

of decoration but proved the honesty and skill of the craftsman. This open display came to be accepted by many of the most progressive designers of the later part of the century, though Pugin's reforms were inevitably slow in their effects in the conditions of the day.

Examples: *Passim* for a comprehensive selection from *Gothic Furniture of the Fifteenth Century.*

Below left: Pugin's cabinet designed for Abney Hall, Cheshire, c.1847. Courtesy City of Salford Art Gallery and Museum.

Below: Oak cabinet designed by Pugin, exhibited at the Great Exhibition 1851. Courtesy Victoria and Albert Museum.

THE GREAT EXHIBITION 1851

One long-held view of the furniture shown at the Great Exhibition can be dealt with at once. Until recently the exhibits were considered to be typical of the furniture then in general use. Once 1830 became so firmly established as the terminus of antique furniture, little attention was paid to the following two decades until the appearance of the mass of illustrative material connected with the 1851 Exhibition. This seemed to confirm the drastic decline in standards of design after 1830. Yet one has now only to compare the normal products of furniture firms as seen in their pattern books and other records with their exhibits to recognise that the latter were prestige pieces made for the special occasion. Exhibitors inevitably fell into the temptation of over-elaborating their pieces and these were bound to be imitated.

See under Braund and Yapp for examples of Exhibition furniture.

Above: Carved and marquetry walnut chair with porcelain portrait of Prince Albert, designed and made by Henry Eyles for the Great Exhibition of 1851. Courtesy Victoria and Albert Museum.

Left: Carved oak table, designed and made by Henry Eyles for the Great Exhibition, 1851. Courtesy Victoria and Albert Museum.

BLACKIE'S CABINET-MAKER'S ASSISTANT

The immediate effect of the Great Exhibition on furniture design was to confirm the historical approach of the previous decades with renewed search for novelty inculcated by the Exhibition. These effects can be seen in Blackie's *Cabinet-Maker's Assistant*, 1853. This is in three sections. The first two follow the traditional methods of earlier publications, such as that of the Nicholsons, in presenting a treatise on geometry and drawing followed by practical observations on cabinet-making, including a technical description of the thirty nine most popular woods used by the trade, directions for the most economical methods of construction, and sections on veneering and carving. The third section is a trade manual. It has 101 plates dealing with furniture of every kind preceded by sixty three pages of description with instructional hints designed for practical use both by individual cabinet-makers and by larger firms.

The book had over 400 trade subscribers from all parts of the country. Most of these, over 200, were in London (they included Smee and Son and Bielefeld, leading producer of papier mâché) but there was substantial support from Glasgow, Liverpool, Manchester, Sheffield, Birmingham, Preston and Dundee and occasional subscribers from places as far apart as Penzance, Falkirk, Worcester and Lancaster. There was thus a wide distribution throughout England and Scotland, suggesting that the designs were extensively copied or adapted.

The authorship is anonymous but evidence points to P. Thomson whose signature appears on the plates and who later, c.1860, published under his own name *The Cabinet-Maker's Sketchbook* with the note 'Author of *The Cabinet-Maker's Assistant*'.

Among Blackie's plates are examples from the Great Exhibition, indicating a desire to keep up-to-date and a search for novelty. Novelty is indeed stressed, for there are plates devoted to such unusual pieces as 'Fret Rails and Clock for Steam-Boat Cabins', and 'Portable Bed-Chair and Ottoman Seat', and the very first sentence of the preface echoes Smith's lament of 1826 by stating that "Every one connected with Cabinet-Making is aware of the difficulty of obtaining good and novel Designs for Furniture". But while much of the furniture in Blackie's publication is well made with good materials and is often attractive enough, it firmly keeps to established precedent. If 1851 had any lessons for reformist designers it was going to be some time before they received attention.

One point is certainly made: most of the designs are in the Elizabethan style, proving that its two main features, strapwork (fretwork) and spiral turning had recommended themselves to the trade for their rapidity and cheapness of production. There are concessions to Louis Quinze rococo taste, now generally referred to as the 'Louis Style', mixed as usual with baroque elements of Louis Quatorze. There is one example of the Moorish or Alhambra style, and one example, a bedstead, in medieval style. The last is a commercial rendering of Pugin's designs. Whatever the style, the old error persists in simply signifying it by the appropriate ornament. The preface is quite frank about this in a passage worth quoting: "Whenever such designs are obtained, everyone is equally aware how comparatively easy it is to adapt them to the kind of work required; they may, in fact, be multiplied indefinitely, by engrafting the decoration of one on the forms of another". There were, of course, the occasional experiments encouraged by the exhibits of 1851. One plate, for example, shows six 'National Emblem Chairs', decorated with carved roses, thistles or shamrock, furnishing "a striking example of how much originality may be produced from most familiar objects when treated in a true artistic spirit".

Blackie 1859

Examples: Elizabethan crests, 92-3, chairs, 197, hall stands, 356; 'national' chairs, 185; range of styles: chairs, 243; sideboards, 437; tables, 485, 511, 520.

WILLIAM SMEE AND SONS

William Smee of 6 Finsbury Pavement, London, mentioned above as a subscriber to Blackie's *Cabinet-Maker's Assistant*, was founder of a business which was prominent in the Victorian period for its catalogues of which *Designs for Furniture*, 1850-55, is a typical example. These catalogues were quite different from previous publications of furniture designs and set a fashion which was to be followed for the rest of the century. The firm carried on both wholesale and retail business; it ranks as one of the largest wholesalers of the mid-century. The printed catalogues were aimed at the middle-class market and the result was that furniture shopkeepers from all parts of the country could sell orders to their customers from them or buy pieces for their own stocks. The title page of *Designs for Furniture* states that supplies were "always kept ready for sale at their Cabinet and Upholstery Manufactory and Warerooms". It is known that in at least one case, and there are probably more to add to this (for the custom became generally accepted), the Smee and Sons name and address, which appeared on a printed sheet inside the back cover and not on the title page of the catalogue, was replaced by those of another shopkeeper who thus advertised the furniture as his own.

The catalogue has 374 pages of line engraved drawings. There is no text or introduction but the drawings have brief descriptions with references to alternative woods and modes of decoration, and space is left for prices to be inserted accordingly. The catalogue covers an immense range in current styles from suites for bedrooms, dining-rooms and drawing-rooms to chairs and tables and down to towel horses, trays, and hat, umbrella and dress stands. The furniture seems to have been designed and made for the most part by the firm, but it appears that some pieces may have been made by other manufacturers and included in the catalogue without acknowledgement.

Smee and Sons earned a reputation for furniture of good quality — the best pieces in the catalogue are labelled 'Superior'. The firm exhibited at many exhibitions, beginning with the Great Exhibition, then in Paris in 1855 (where the furniture was described by M.D. Wyatt as "strong and soundly made but inelegant"), in London in 1862, and in Paris again in 1867 and 1878. They are known to have furnished completely a house in Victoria, Australia, in 1859. Among the professional designers on their staff later was the distinguished E.W. Godwin, whose work is examined below (see *Watt's Catalogue*, 1877).

The mid-century pieces remain practical interpretations of the popular historical styles, Greek (among the specialities were bedsteads in 'Modern Greek' style), Roman, Gothic, French and Elizabethan. Spiral-turned legs and back uprights were found on the 'vesper' chair, of the fashionable prie-dieu type, with low seat and tall back. Another example of this type, 'stuffed in stripes', but without spiral turning, is called the 'Devotional Chair'.

The Victoria and Albert Museum has a large collection of pen drawings of c.1850 from the firm's records, and these obviously form the basis of the *Designs for Furniture*. In some of these drawings parts of furniture (e.g. legs and feet), are shown in different forms in the same design to appeal to the buyer's particular fancy.

Examples: Simpler types: 15, 56, 113, 115; chairs: round-backed and upholstered, 158-9, balloon-back and Elizabethan, 195, 223, devotional type, 262; sideboards, classical and rococo, 436; davenports, 349.

W.Smee & Sons 1850

J.B. WARING

The International Exhibition in London in 1862 was not only the largest of its kind held in Britain in the nineteenth century (it was larger than the Great Exhibition but could hardly match the latter's prestige), but was also to have significant influence on furniture and interior decoration, for it introduced the work of William Morris to the public and, for the first time in Europe, included exhibits from Japan. The importance of these two developments, however, remained largely hidden except to the discerning few, for, following the examples of the Great Exhibition and the Paris Exhibition of 1855, popular fancy was still caught by elaborate ornament, particularly in carving and marquetry.

No publication of the time is clearer testimony to this than J.B. Waring's *Masterpieces of Industrial Art and Sculpture at the International Exhibition*, issued in 1863 following the International Exhibition of 1862. This was a massive publication in three heavy volumes with 300 coloured plates providing a magnificent record of the outstanding exhibits, including many examples of furniture. It was perhaps inevitable that the 'masterpieces' should be the most spectacular pieces, foreign as well as British. The English text — a full page was devoted to each illustration — was written by Waring himself and was accompanied by a French translation.

Waring's background explains his preoccupation with artistic adornment. He was trained as an architect but rarely practised. He travelled extensively in Italy, France and Spain to study architecture and works of art. He had some skill as an artist; he had been a student at the Royal Academy and in 1843 was awarded the Society of Arts medal for architectural decoration. He published a number of books, sometimes jointly with other architects, with, for instance, T.R. Macquoid (who designed Holland and Sons' prize-winning bookcase at the 1851 Exhibition) in their *Architectural Art in Italy and Spain*, 1850, and with M.D. Wyatt in guide books, 1854, to the newly erected Crystal Palace at Sydenham. Waring was also intimately concerned with the organisation of exhibitions. After preliminary experience with the Manchester Exhibition of 1857 he was appointed superintendent of the architectural gallery and of the classes for furniture, earthenware, glass, goldsmiths' work and objects used in architecture at the 1862 Exhibition. In 1868 he was Chief Commissioner of the Leeds Exhibition of works of art.

The *Masterpieces* reveal Waring's treatment of furniture as works of art. His admiration centred on the use of ornament, admirably suited of course for illustration in colour. He was in no sense a designer of furniture or a critic of contemporary fashions.

Examples: 1862 Exhibition cabinets by W. Burges and Norman Shaw, 87 (top left); exhibition sideboards, 456-7.

Above: Painted oak cabinet with inlay, designed by Norman Shaw for the International Exhibition, 1862. Courtesy Victoria and Albert Museum.

Right: Burges' painted cupboard and secretaire, made for the International Exhibition, 1862. Courtesy Victoria and Albert Museum.

JOHN BRAUND AND HENRY LAWFORD

Two further books popularised exhibition furniture. John Braund, an "artist in design", of 5, George Street, Portman Square, London, produced *Illustrations of Furniture* in 1858. Nothing appears to be known about his background, but the contents of the book are clearly revealed on the title page for, in addition to furniture, it includes "candelabra and musical instruments from the Great Exhibitions, London and Paris, with examples of similar articles from royal palaces and noble mansions". Elaboration is again the keynote, with distinct touches of Renaissance and Elizabethan ornament, covering a comprehensive selection of pieces. There are no original designs.

Henry Lawford, whose earlier work has been referred to, fell under the paramount French influence at the 1862 Exhibition, one result of which was to renew a particular fashion in the mid-Victorian period for marquetry and buhl work. In 1856 Lawford published *The Cabinet of Practical, Useful and Decorative Furniture Designs* in which, among designs in current Elizabethan, Gothic and rococo taste, and some views of interiors, appear twenty nine coloured plates of marquetry and buhl work. These coloured plates are repeated in *The Cabinet of Marquetry, Buhl and Inlaid Woods* designed by Henry Lawford. There is no date on the title page but the dedication is dated May, 1870. The designs confirm the fashion for these revived decorative techniques, and some outstanding marquetry furniture was produced by leading London firms, among which one can single out Jackson and Graham and Holland and Sons. It was, however, a revival with a difference, for while earlier work of this kind had been mainly due to foreign craftsmen, by the 1870s English craftsmen were producing their own pieces and were credited with being able to compete on terms of equality with continental firms.

Examples: Braund *passim* for exhibition (1851, 1855) furniture. For Lawford's buhl work and marquetry: cabinets, 127-8; desks, 347; tables, 521.

Lawford 1867

LORENZO BOOTH

The 1860s were a period of transition. Furniture designers of the Georgian tradition were being replaced by compilers of trade catalogues and by writers, mainly architects, who published analytical studies of interior decoration and furnishings. But every period of transition has its element of uncertainty of which a good example is Lorenzo Booth's *Exhibition Book of Original Designs for Furniture*, with the sub-title of *The Original Design Book for Decorative Furniture*, dated 1864 and containing nearly 300 designs. Booth, a lithographic draughtsman and designer, of 15 Coleman Street, London, includes in his book an essay on decorative furniture in which he is strongly critical of the furniture exhibited in 1851 and 1862 and of almost every fashionable style, including particularly the Renaissance and the various versions of French taste. He also refers to the Ionic volute as "a painful imbecility". No future historian, he writes, will be able to identify mid-nineteenth century styles with anything "except what we have borrowed or imitated, or positively copied from our predecessors. At present we have no style". His sweeping condemnations lack detailed analysis and by no means prevent him from designing in these fashionable styles, but in two respects his designs are worth noting. First, he presents belated examples of the 'Naturalistic Style' in which indisciplined forms and ornament are coupled with a certain novelty of inventiveness which add interest to this interpretation and make it, again, worth more detailed study. His upholstered couches are two good examples of this style.

Second, Booth points to the future area of reform when he comes out firmly in favour of the Gothic as "a living style, applicable to any purpose and as perfectly English now in its present form and under conditions in harmony with existing

Booth 1864

associations, as it was medievally English". This may be taken as confirming, at long last, that Pugin's ideas were beginning to point the way to reform, but this required far more skilled designers than Booth proved to be.

Examples: Gothic, 58; prie-dieu chairs, 262-3; 'Naturalistic Style', 308 (no.29), 322 (no.28).

MORRIS AND COMPANY

By the late 1860s the critics of the Exhibitions of 1851, 1855 and 1862 were beginning to achieve results. A landmark was reached in 1861 with the foundation of Morris, Marshall, Faulkner and Company, later to be known as Morris and Company, whose exhibits in 1862, mentioned above, included decorative furniture, painted in medieval fashion, and stained glass. The *Dictionary* includes selections from a later catalogue of the firm.

Morris's proclaimed mission was to combat the ugliness of commercial production which he later summed up in his famous exhortation: "Have nothing in your house that you do not know to be useful or believe to be beautiful". He was not himself particularly interested in furniture design, but from its earliest years his firm produced simple oak furniture designed by a number of designers, principally Philip Webb, in which revealed construction of medieval inspiration (as first shown by Pugin) often formed an integral part of the design. From about 1865 the firm produced its famous 'Sussex' chair based on a traditional cottage type, of simple form and with rush seat, which was to become very popular. In addition to this plain rugged furniture, which Morris described as "the necessary workaday furniture ... simple to the last degree", the firm also made grander pieces — "state-furniture ... sideboards, cabinets and the like" — with panels painted by Morris himself and by his friend Burne-Jones and other artists.

Morris was to prove one of the most potent influences of the Victorian era. His ideals were disseminated through his many writings and lectures. He was his own best propagandist, especially when he later turned socialist and linked his ideals in craft work and design with social reform. The repercussions of this will be dealt with when the developments of the later part of the century are considered.

See page xliii for references to the Company's furniture, c.1900.

Above: Upholstered adjustable chair designed by Philip Webb and made from c.1866 by Morris and Company. Courtesy Victoria and Albert Museum.

Right: Wardrobe designed by Philip Webb, painted by Sir Edward Burne-Jones and given to William Morris, c.1858. Courtesy Ashmolean Museum.

Below left: Cabinet, 1861, painted by Rossetti, Ford Madox Brown, Burne-Jones and William Morris. Courtesy Victoria and Albert Museum.

Below right: Carved oak table, designed by Philip Webb c.1865. Courtesy Victoria and Albert Museum.

ART FURNITURE

'Art Furniture' is the name given to that produced from the late 1860s until the 1880s by firms who were known at the time as 'art furniture manufacturers' and who considered themselves quite distinct from ordinary furniture-makers. This distinction is by no means clear to us today, aware as we are of the results of the cherished Victorian conviction that beauty could be achieved by adding 'art' in the form of ornament to household possessions. But if trade debasement was in time to be all too apparent, it is also true that some Art Furniture designers showed a refreshingly progressive approach and attractive and well-made furniture was the result. Two quite separate trends are distinguishable.

Ebonised furniture became an accepted part of the Victorian interior. The fundamental influence was undoubtedly France whose *ébénistes* had displayed their traditional skills at all the international exhibitions. English exhibitors were quick to emulate their French rivals. Holland and Sons had shown a much-praised ebony cabinet at the Paris Exhibition in 1855, and later, at the London Exhibition of 1871, T.E. Colcutt designed a cabinet of ebonised wood with painted panels which created great interest and had many imitators. Reputable firms turned their attention to ebonised furniture, among them Collinson and Lock, who made Collcutt's exhibit, Gillow and Shoolbred. Morris's rural-type chairs were also ebonised or stained dark green.

Ebonised beech 'Sussex' chair, Morris and Company from c.1865. Courtesy Victoria and Albert Museum.

Where strength in construction was necessary, this kind of furniture employed ebonised oak or mahogany, but dark woods of all kinds, including black walnut, or woods stained green, were also found. Straight lines, slender turned supports (legs, uprights and balusters), often with incised rings and lines picked out in gold, and, in larger pieces such as cabinets, a surmounting gallery of turned spindles, or a coved top, were all characteristic features. For decoration, painted panels were universally accepted in place of carving, and floral sprays or human figures were the most fashionable themes. Divisions and numerous small shelves were often added for display of knick-knacks.

Quite distinct from ebonised pieces, but still under the umbrella of the art movement, was reformist Gothic furniture for which some designers of the 1860s, Charles L. Eastlake, William Burges and Bruce Talbert, have gained special fame. Eastlake, who was Keeper and Secretary of the National Gallery (and not to be confused, though confusion is readily excusable, with his namesake and uncle, Sir Charles L. Eastlake, Director of the same Gallery), ranks as the chief theorist and propagandist of this new phase with his *Hints on Household Taste*, published in book form, based on earlier articles, in 1868, the year in which the term 'Art Furniture' seems to have been first used. Eastlake detested "the tendency of the last age of upholstery . . . to run into curves" and took his stand on simple, cheap, rectangular Gothic furniture, panelled and boarded, practically without decoration. His designs were perhaps plain at times to the point of crudity; he favoured joined construction fully revealed, without glue, and avoided staining and French polishing. Too severe for some tastes ("in construction too much like a packing case", wrote J. Moyr Smith), this 'Eastlake Style' nevertheless stimulated interest generally in Art Furniture and had a considerable following in the United States.

RICHARD CHARLES

Attention must be directed to the work of a much underrated designer of the time who certainly needs to be rescued from the near oblivion into which his name has fallen and who may be considered perhaps the last of the old traditional type of designer. This is Richard Charles whose designs anticipate in many ways the 'Early English' revival of Eastlake and Talbert. Unlike practically all the designers whose work is shown in the *Dictionary*, his centre was not London but Manchester. At the Manchester Art Treasures Exhibition in 1857 he is referred to as the designer and

Ebonised wood cabinet with painted panels designed by T.E. Collcutt and exhibited at the 1871 London International Exhibition. Courtesy Victoria and Albert Museum.

maker of the Warrington State Bedstead. His work appears in 1860 in the *Cabinet-Makers' Monthly Journal of Design*, in the foreword to which he writes that the few pieces of furniture of merit to be found in England "emanated principally from foreigners in this country" and that furniture design was vitiated by "a kind of disorder which is better understood than described". The *Cabinet Makers' Book of Designs* which appeared later (one of its plates is dated 1867) has sixty one lithograph colour plates which seem to have been originally intended for the *Monthly Journal of Design*, and it is these which apply the Early English style to all types of furniture. A study of Charles's designs show how closely they are related to, even if they do not actually precede, those of Eastlake and Talbert and how markedly they contrast with the work of contemporaries like Booth and Lawford. Their chief features are panelled construction filled with boards, chamfered and marked edges to the framework, battlemented tops to bed testers and sideboards and frequent use of roundels as decoration. But though Charles must be given much of the credit for his pioneer work in the Early English style, and for originality of construction and decoration, he nevertheless clung in general to accepted forms, with only occasional innovations. For instance, his beds, with one exception of a four poster, are all half testers; he perseveres with rounded ends to his chiffoniers; couches and ottomans are also contemporary models, and pedestal forms are retained in sideboards and dressing tables.

Charles may well have used current forms from motives of cheapness and speedy production, as a means, that is, for making an immediate impact. He is surely a designer who is worth a great deal more research.

Designs closely related to those of Eastlake, Talbert and Burges can be seen in: beds, 11, 28; dressing tables and wash-stands, 35, 76; chairs, 170, 199; sideboards, 438-9. A very comprehensive selection of decoration can be found in sideboards, 457-62.

BRUCE J. TALBERT (1838-1881)

The outstanding figure of the whole Art Furniture period was probably Bruce J. Talbert. Originally trained as a wood carver and then as an architect, he soon turned to furniture design and was employed by a number of leading firms, first by Doveston, Bird and Hull of Manchester and later, from 1865, by Holland and Sons and others in London. He is one of the earliest professional designers to achieve a national reputation. In 1867 he designed a large 'dressoir' or sideboard for Holland which gained a medal at the Paris Exhibition. Its smaller companion piece, the 'Sleeping Beauty' cabinet, now in the Victoria and Albert Museum, is one of the best known examples of High Victorian design.

Talbert's principles became widely known through his *Gothic Forms Applied to Furniture, Metal Work and Decoration for Domestic Purposes*, published in 1867 with thirty pages of sketches. He is clearly influenced more by the work of Burges, Webb and Shaw than that of Pugin, for he recommends, in his introduction, the Early English style of the twelfth and thirteenth centuries for its "great breadth and simplicity", maintaining that the "lavish display of ornament" which was characteristic of later Gothic was "quite undesirable for cabinet work". He is, however, a wholehearted supporter of Pugin's approach to the basic principles of good design through construction, for he writes: "In these old works the wood is solid, the construction honestly shown and fastened by tenons, pegs, iron clamps, nails, etc., it is to the use of glue that we are indebted for the false construction modern work indulges in; the glue leads to veneering and veneering to polish". Talbert is here criticising the makers of cheap furniture, particularly in the East End of London who covered shoddy furniture with glossy veneers — a custom which now gave veneering its secondary pejorative meaning and led Dickens, in *Our Mutual Friend*, 1864-5, to give his family of social upstarts in the novel the readily understood and appropriate name of the Veneerings.

Carved and painted wash-stand designed by Burges, c.1880. Courtesy Victoria and Albert Museum.

Talbert's practical interpretation of Gothic avoided rounded forms and elaborate carving and relied mainly on framed construction and decoration of low-relief carving, inlay and piercing. Inlaid geometrical patterns and low relief metal panels were other special features. Bold Gothic metal hinges were also used. Perhaps Talbert's most celebrated piece is the 'Pet Sideboard' (also in the Victoria and Albert Museum) which was made by Gillows to his design for the International Exhibition, London, 1873. Its inset panels of carved boxwood set a fashion and led Gillows to call this fresh treatment of the Gothic 'Medieval' to distinguish it from the 'New Palace Westminster' of Pugin's version. Talbert's impact was immediate, for J. Moyr Smith in his *Ornamental Interiors*, 1867, writes that the drawing-room furniture designs in *Gothic Forms* "were without doubt the cause of the new style of decoration taking hold of the public," adding that the book "soon found its way to the chief designers and cabinet-makers in the kingdom and imitations, which were sometimes improvements, were produced on all sides."

Talbert's later book, *Examples of Ancient and Modern Furniture, Metal Work, Tapestries, Decoration*, 1876, proved something of a disappointment. The originality which distinguished *Gothic Forms* largely disappeared in favour of late Tudor and early Stuart designs, with emphasis on the Jacobean period, which were already in circulation. Imitators could now easily adapt his designs into their own often whimsical versions ranging from the Flemish Renaissance to Charles II.

The Gothic furniture designed by the architect William Burges (1827-1881) differed from Talbert's in its massiveness and its preference for painted decoration and insets in various materials, with little carving. He was influenced by thirteenth and fourteenth century furniture, both French and English, and his study of the subject convinced him that this furniture was of sturdy simple construction and covered with paintings. He attracted attention at the 1862 Exhibition with a cabinet with painting representing 'The Contest between the Wines and Beers'. This is in the Victoria and Albert Museum as is also Burges' gilded bed, designed for his own house in 1879, which has inset decoration of mirrors and a painting of a medieval version of the 'Judgement of Paris'. Unlike Talbert too, Burges was not a commercial designer but worked for rich patrons and made his views known through exhibitions, lectures and writings. He built and furnished the romantic fairy-tale Castell Coch, Glamorgan, for the Marquess of Bute.

Castellated wash-stand in the Lady's Bedroom, Castell Coch (Red Castle) Glamorgan. Courtesy National Monuments Record.

Burges was also one of the very first English designers to become interested in Japanese art. Japan was henceforth to exert increasing influence on English designers, particularly, strangely enough, among those whose chief inspiration was the medieval period.

We must note in passing that Richard Charles' designs contained elements closely resembling Burges.

Examples: See interiors for differences between Talbert's 1867 reformist Gothic and his 1876 retardatory 'Jacobean'; also reformist cabinet, 116. Burges' 1862 cabinet: see under J.B. Waring.

Lady's Bedroom, Castell Coch (Red Castle) Glamorgan. Designed by William Burges, c.1875. Courtesy National Monuments Record.

J. SHOOLBRED AND COMPANY

After 1860 Tottenham Court Road and the surrounding area became the centre of large furniture shops which specialised in high-class, ready-made furniture. John Maple, one of the early pioneers of the fashionable shops, set up in Tottenham Court Road in 1841 and built up a flourishing business (and fortune) largely by buying furniture from a multitude of outworkers who worked in their own small workshops in the neighbourhood. In the 1880s it was said that Maples bought from something like a thousand different shops and made less than ten per cent of what they sold on their own premises.

Tottenham Court Road, however, had two large shops, Shoolbreds and Heals, which were distinguished for the high quality of their furniture, making much of it themselves and employing professional designers. Extracts from the catalogues of both firms in the *Dictionary* illustrate the range and quality of their products.

James Shoolbred and Company (now defunct) began business in Tottenham Court Road in a small way as linen drapers and gradually expanded their business to become one of London's first great departmental stores. Their trade extended until about 1860 both in scope — they called themselves then silk mercers, hosiers, haberdashers and carpet warehousemen as well as linen and woollen drapers — and in premises, for they enlarged their original shop and acquired three additional workshops and warehouses in the neighbourhood, but it was not until about 1870 that they branched out into the furniture trade as cabinet manufacturers. Thereafter expansion was very rapid; by 1879 they had enlarged or added premises to include a cabinet factory and specialist centres for upholstery and bedding, venetian and sun blinds, carpets, carpentry, decorating and ironmongery. By 1900 their general stores had launched into groceries, provisions and drink, and china and glass.

Shoolbreds were among the royal appointees in the mid-1880s. They made good furniture in all the prevailing styles with special emphasis on 'Old English' and 'Japanese'. Among their designers was W.H. Batley who in 1878 designed an outstanding example of Art Furniture, a piano with carved Japanese ornament in boxwood panels set in a light-coloured mahogany ground on turned legs connected to the framework by small spindle galleries. Talbert's influence here is paramount, inevitably so as Batley had been a pupil of Talbert. Batley's other designs show references to Gothic, Jacobean and Egyptian sources.

A certain conservatism in taste can be detected in Shoolbreds' designs, no doubt owing to their success. Plates of the furnished interiors of some rooms were repeated in the firm's catalogues for over twenty years. They made some fine examples of ebonised furniture with painted panels. They also made furniture in Louis Seize style which reveals a competent understanding of the style while still applying it to standard fashionable forms.

Examples: The designs and interiors show good examples of middle class furniture c.1875. Among chairs note the abiding emphasis on comfort, 151-2; prevalence of square backs, 200-1; Elizabethan survivals, 201 (no.128), 263 (no.129 prie-dieu). Art Furniture (Collcutt) influence in sideboards, 446 (bottom right).

WILLIAM WATT: ART FURNITURE AND E.W. GODWIN (1833-1886)

The designs of E.W. Godwin gave further impetus to the fashion for ebonised furniture of the art movement. In 1877 appeared *Art Furniture, from Designs by E.W. Godwin, with Hints and Suggestions of Domestic Furniture by William Watt, London*. This was a catalogue of the furniture made at William Watt's Art Furniture Warehouse in Grafton Street, containing a comprehensive survey of Godwin's Anglo-Japanese designs. In the preface, which takes the form of a letter from Godwin to Watt, it becomes clear that not only had most of the furniture been already in production for some time, but it had also been widely imitated. This illustrates the vogue for Anglo-Japanese furniture which was to reach its height in the 1880s.

Shoolbred 1876

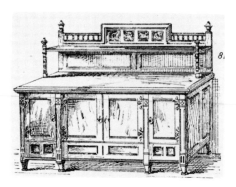

Shoolbred 1876

W. Watt 1877

Godwin, one of the most original designers of the nineteenth century, was trained as an architect. In 1867 he transferred his architectural practice from his native Bristol to London and designed furniture for both private commissions and for leading firms, including, in addition to Watt, Gillows, Collinson and Lock, and Smee. He was a friend and admirer of Burges but was not influenced by the latter's massive medieval designs. He was a tireless note-taker and sketcher and his numerous notebooks, preserved in the Victoria and Albert Museum, reveal that he found inspiration in many sources, ancient, medieval, Renaissance and oriental. Unlike so many of his contemporaries, he steered clear of eclecticism and refused to imitate exactly historical styles. His aim, announced in *Watt's Catalogue,* was "a modern treatment of certain well-known and admired styles". The keynote was functional simplicity, the achievement of which was the secret of the success of English furniture design in the Georgian period, as is universally recognised today. Hence the appeal to Godwin of the simplicity of Japanese furniture.

Watt 1877

Godwin favoured ebonised wood, but not exclusively. Attenuated supports, rectilinear forms and what he called the "grouping of solid and void" were features inspired by, but never copied from, Japanese sources. These features are perhaps most typically seen in his famous sideboard, designed for his own use in 1867 and now in the Victoria and Albert Museum. The Japanese influence is confirmed by the inset panels of embossed Japanese leather in the cupboard doors. The only other touch of decoration is startling in its simplicity — silver-plated fittings with a pierced keyhole motif. The considerations of economy and utility which underlay this kind of furniture produced simple and elegant pieces which differed radically from the painted and gilded kind of his contemporaries. Another cabinet, this time in walnut, designed about 1876, has carved Japanese boxwood panels and carved ivory handles in the form of minute monkeys.

Watt's Catalogue illustrates a so-called 'Jacobean' chair which again betrays Japanese influence. It has rectilinear supports and a round cane seat and was imitated extensively. Another type of chair ('Greek' in the *Catalogue*) has elongated uprights and is made of ebonised oak. All this furniture has an exciting novelty about it. It is well worth the collector's attention, and too widespread plagiarism must mean that much more of its kind is due to be discovered. No doubt some imitations were of good standard, but it will be left to the collector's judgement to distinguish the Godwin pieces from inferior substitutes.

Analysis of Godwin's designs proves that economy and utility were problems that he set out to solve, that unnecessary ornament and hence display were to be eliminated, and that line and form were the principal elements in making a satisfactory piece. He has been called the first Victorian designer whose prime concern was not style but function and as such his work created much interest abroad, especially in Germany and Austria, where he was considered by many competent observers to be the earliest pioneer of modern design.

Examples: In addition to the interiors, examples of Anglo-Japanese designs are seen in 37, 59, 77, 102, 116; sideboards, 439. The celebrated Victoria and Albert Museum sideboard, 474 (bottom right). Jacobean chair, 259 (top right).

The famous ebonised wood sideboard designed by E.W. Godwin, c.1867. Courtesy Victoria and Albert Museum.

GEORGIAN REVIVALS: ART AT HOME: A. JONQUET

At the Paris Exhibition, 1867, Wright and Mansfield of London created great interest by winning the supreme award for furniture, outstripping their French competitors. Their exhibit was a satinwood cabinet decorated with Wedgwood plaques in full Adam taste, remarkably restrained for an exhibition piece. At long last the neglected eighteenth century had returned to full favour. One result was to encourage many firms to reproduce examples of that period, sometimes so closely that after a century or so of use it can be virtually impossible today to distinguish the copy from the original. Some firms became well-known for the high standard of their reproductions, notably Edwards and Roberts of London, who like other leading firms stamped or labelled their furniture, for it was not their intention to deceive buyers.

By the 1870s the Georgian revival had extended back into the Queen Anne period. By this time too, the beneficial reforms of Godwin had reached many of the middle classes. There was now interest in clearing out much of the ponderous furniture of the mid-century to make way for simpler ebonised pieces or for eighteenth century models. This was the age of the sanitary engineer and of preoccupation with health matters, and this simpler furniture could be easily moved for dusting and cleaning. A series of small books of the late 1870s, published under the title of *Art at Home*, directed at the middle class market, confirm the increased interest in both ebonised furniture and in pieces based on prototypes from Queen Anne to Sheraton.

It is naturally too much to expect universal understanding, let alone acceptance, of these trends. Revivals were particularly subject to misinterpretation by inferior designers. Among these may be mentioned A. Jonquet's *Original Sketches for Art Furniture in the Jacobean, Queen Anne, Adams and Other Styles*, 1877-79. 'Adams', it should be noted, was often used at the time for the Adam style. Some of Jonquet's designs were published in 1880 by the *Cabinet Maker* in a collection with the title of *Fashionable Furniture* and in 1890 he published *Present Day Furniture* which included some strange 'Renaissance' pieces. Jonquet's designs are of mediocre quality; they can serve perhaps the useful purpose of a basis of comparison with the work of progressive firms.

Examples: Jonquet's revived Hepplewhite, 39 (shield back), Adam, 62, 137; compare with his current Art Furniture designs, 464.

Adam-style marquetry satinwood cabinet made by Wright and Mansfield for the Paris Exhibition, 1867. Courtesy Victoria and Albert Museum.

G.W. YAPP

The impact of exhibitions persisted. A nostalgic view of the past is given in *Art Industry. Furniture, Upholstery and House Decoration. Illustrative of the Carpenter, Joiner, Cabinet-Maker, Painter, Decorator and Upholsterer. Edited by G.W. Yapp*, c.1879. Like J.B. Waring, Yapp had been actively associated with the organisation of exhibitions. He was Assistant Commissioner at the 1851 Exhibition and compiler of the Official Catalogue. His *Art Industry* has some 1,200 illustrations. An important introductory section on woodworking has sketches of joints and of machinery, with technical descriptions. There are also descriptions of papier mâché, carton pierre and other materials connected with furniture making. For illustrations of furniture Yapp selects some of the more elaborate exhibits from the International Exhibitions of 1851, 1855 and 1862, as well as examples from a collection of antiques shown at Gore House, London, in 1853. He expresses approval of the Gothic designs of Pugin, "a learned and skilful revivalist", but is strongly critical of the "modern medieval" pieces of contemporary designers. *Art Industry* is indeed backward-looking; it ignores the changes of the 1870s and stamps its approval of mid-Victorian taste.

Examples: Collcutt's 1871 cabinet, 117 (centre right). A.W.N. Pugin's cabinet for Abney Hall, c.1847, is basis for design, 110 (top centre). Sideboards, 439.

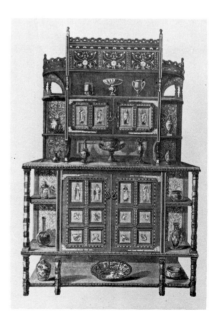

Yapp 1879

ARTS AND CRAFTS MOVEMENT

The influence of William Morris is clearly seen in the last twenty years of Victoria's reign in the Arts and Crafts Movement, which combined his ideals of good design and craftsmanship with his gospel of social reform. Whereas previously the practice had been for professional designers to supply their designs to leading firms, with the result that other firms, who controlled so much of the total output of furniture, could imitate them, usually with depressing effect, now the members of this new movement aimed at promulgating their ideals and maintaining their high standards, by producing their furniture themselves. This was achieved by the formation of various guilds and societies, strongly influenced by the medieval guilds, of artists and craftsmen, usually under the direction of an architect. The pioneer group was the Century Guild founded by the architect, A.H. Mackmurdo, in 1882. Then followed the Art Workers' Guild in 1884 (this is still very active), the Arts and Crafts Exhibition Society, which gave its name to the whole movement, in 1888, and C.R. Ashbee's Guild and School of Handicraft, also in 1888. The members of these and other groups in the movement presented their furniture as a cooperative effort without attribution to individuals and spread their ideals through frequent exhibitions of their work, a number of which were held between 1888 and 1899. Though the term 'arty-crafty' was coined by its critics, the movement produced some of the most attractive and interesting furniture of the whole Victorian period, well-designed and superbly made, and much sought after today. There was an impressive range of design, by no means confined to the austere cottage joinery of the early Morris phase, but inspired also by eighteenth century furniture. The exhibitions could reach only a limited public, but three very beneficial results are discernible by 1914: the movement merged partly into art nouveau, providing this *fin-de-siecle* style with many fine craftsmen and designers; it influenced a number of progressive manufacturers; and it inspired a remarkable off-shoot in the Cotswold School, directly faithful to Morris's ideals.

In 1893 Ernest Gimson, an architect and prominent figure in the short-lived Kenton and Company, part of the Arts and Crafts Movement, left London with the two brothers, Sidney and Ernest Barnsley, to establish a workshop near Cirencester in the Cotswolds and make plain but elegant and beautifully finished furniture in the best tradition of English rural craftsmanship. Gimson's influence was to prove beneficial and lasting.

One easily recognisable feature of many pieces of Arts and Crafts furniture is the tiny edging of chequered dark and light veneers run round the edges of drawers and the tops of bureaux and tables. This added the final touches of the skilled craftsmen to their work, almost as a kind of signature.

Above: Rush-seated ladder-back armchair designed by E.W. Gimson. Courtesy Victoria and Albert Museum.

Right: Mahogany writing cabinet with inlay, designed by E.W. Gimson and exhibited at the Arts and Crafts Exhibition, 1890. Courtesy Victoria and Albert Museum.

ART NOUVEAU: LIBERTY

Art nouveau is the name of the new style which became fashionable shortly before 1900. It was a style which had the new century in mind, reflecting the ambition of designers and artists to create a style which could make a complete break with the past and free itself from historical origins. The inspiration came from nature, in the waving forms and sinuous curves of plants and in the flowing shapes of waves and flames. The new style spread throughout Europe and America after about 1890 and was known by various names which merged into the generally accepted art nouveau after the opening of Samuel Bing's famous shop of that name in Paris in 1895. In spite of the foreign name, however, England played a leading part in the movement and was indeed regarded by many abroad as its main source. About 1882 Mackmurdo of the Arts and Crafts Movement had already designed for the Century Guild a remarkable chair with a back of undulating flame-like curves which now ranks as one of the very first examples of art nouveau in applied art.

Among the chief characteristics of the new furniture was a distinct structural mannerism. The legs of tables, sideboards, cabinets, desks and similar pieces were carried up clear of the top and ended under a cornice or, more often, as flat-capped square uprights. In some cases these uprights functioned as candle-holders. Verticality was stressed. Chairs had tall narrow backs, their uprights carried also above the cresting. Stretchers on both chairs and tables tended to be nearer the floor than usual, and legs ended on a flattened base. Curved floral motifs and pierced hearts were common decorations. In place of carving, inlay was universal, in stained woods or in a variety of materials, including mother-of-pearl, stained glass and pewter. Copper was a favourite for panels and large hinges. Another feature was the fondness for mottoes inscribed on the furniture.

The best art nouveau furniture is witness to the impressive liveliness of English design and craftsmanship at the end of Victoria's reign. C.F.A. Voysey, the architect-designer, was the most widely admired English designer of art nouveau furniture abroad. He understood intimately the native genius for simple elegance when he condemned the "lazy and contemptible practice of relying upon precedent for justification" and he reminded designers that "simplicity required perfection in all details, while elaboration is easy in comparison with it." He takes his place as one of the first industrial designers.

In contrast, the most spectacular art nouveau designer, also much admired abroad, was C.R. Mackintosh, the Scottish architect. He is remembered in particular for his tall chairs, some of them five feet high. He made much more impact in Scotland than in England and did not have close links with the Arts and Crafts Movement.

Libertys were distinguished for the high quality of their art nouveau furniture. This firm were comparative newcomers to the Victorian scene, for they were founded in Regent Street in 1875 by Arthur L. Liberty who had had long experience in the drapery trade. They made a rapid impact for they were a household name within ten years. They began as an 'Oriental Warehouse', importing goods from Japan, India and Egypt and also sponsored the fashion for Moorish furniture for smoking rooms in oriental style. Many of their best art nouveau pieces of furniture were made to the designs of George Walton, the Glasgow architect, whose elegant work, marked by graceful attenuated supports, owed much to the eighteenth century. Liberty furniture and other products in art nouveau attracted so much interest abroad that the style itself was known in Italy as the 'Liberty Style'.

Above: Mahogany fretwork chair designed by A.H. Mackmurdo, c.1882, for the Century Guild. Courtesy William Morris Gallery, London.

Centre: Oak sideboard designed by C.F.A. Voysey and made c.1900. Courtesy Victoria and Albert Museum.

Right: Oak writing desk, designed by C.F.A. Voysey and made 1896. Courtesy Victoria and Albert Museum.

Liberty also specialised in simple cottage style furniture made by High Wycombe workshops, the home of the Windsor chair, particularly by William Birch. They had a flair, too, for producing unusual pieces, some of them from patented designs. One such piece was the 'Thebes' stool, made in mahogany from about 1896, with three outward-curving legs and round concave seat. Another 'Egyptian' stool had turned legs, stretchers and struts and a leather seat, the fashion being prompted by recent

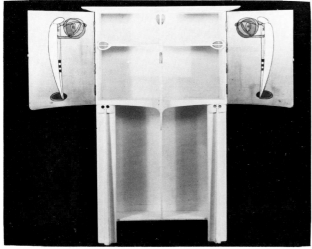

Oak chair designed c.1897 by C.R. Mackintosh. Courtesy Victoria and Albert Museum.

Above: White painted oak cabinet; designed by C.R. Mackintosh c.1902. The inside doors are inlaid with white and coloured glass. Courtesy Hunterian Art Gallery, University of Glasgow.

Right: Oak chair designed by C.R. Mackintosh, c.1900. Courtesy Glasgow School of Art.

Right: Beech armchair made c.1894 by Liberty & Co. Courtesy Nordenfjeldske Kunstindustrimuseum, Trondheim.

Below: 'Lochleven' Buffet, c.1890, made by Liberty & Co. Courtesy Österreichisches Museum für Angewandte Kunst, Vienna.

Art nouveau mahogany music cabinet, c.1897 by Liberty & Co. Courtesy The Bowes Museum, Co. Durham.

Right: Liberty 'Thebes' stool made c.1896. Courtesy Nordenfjeldske Kunstindustrimuseum, Trondheim.

archaeological discoveries in Egypt. A Windsor chair of beech stained green was produced about 1894. Stained oak was employed on a number of pieces such as sideboards which had boarded construction.

In the hands of ordinary commercial dealers, art nouveau often became what was known as the 'Quaint Style', a mixture of art nouveau, Anglo-Japanese and Arts and Crafts. The result was a great deal of spindly furniture which sometimes carried flimsiness to the point of insecurity (some pieces found four legs insufficient and had six or even eight). Quite extraordinary forms and inlaid decoration were found, using commonly polished rosewood or cheap stained woods.

Examples: Art nouveau: cabinets, 87 (bottom centre); Anglo-Japanese, cabinets 107, 120. Compare armchairs with fringed upholstery with Arts and Crafts chairs, 252-3, including ladder-backs. 'Syrian' coffee table, 499 (bottom right).

Egyptian stool made by Liberty & Co. c.1884. Courtesy Victoria and Albert Museum.

GEORGE MADDOX: WYMAN AND SONS: C. AND R. LIGHT

The publications of these three firms can be taken to represent stock commercial production of furniture in the 1880s. George Maddox is in London directories for some twenty five years after about 1860 as upholsterer and store warehouse keeper, his business address in Baker Street and his warehouse in Great Barlow Street, Marylebone. The firm were previously Maddox and Son in the 1850s at the same Baker Street address. The catalogues specialised in bedroom furniture. An early issue, about 1865, the *Illustrated Catalogue of Bedroom Furniture and the New Exhibition Chamber Furniture*, was based on the furniture exhibited at the International Exhibition, 1862. The extracts in the *Dictionary* are taken from the firm's 1882 catalogue, in which bedroom furniture is again prominent.

Wyman and Sons differed from commercial producers in that they were printers, of Great Queen Street, London. From this address they published a number of periodicals including the *Furniture Gazette*, hence their connection with furniture catalogues. They published a series of *Cabinet Makers' Pattern Books* in 1877, with a third edition in 1882 and subsequent editions at intervals. Price lists were issued with the *Pattern Books* so that retailers could take orders and quote prices with the knowledge that they could obtain the items from the big wholesalers such as C. and R. Light.

Charles and Richard Light, previously known as Charles Light in the 1860s and 1870s, were cabinet-makers and looking-glass manufacturers of Curtain Road, Shoreditch, the area particularly well-known for its large-scale firms producing immense quantities of cheaper lines of furniture. C. and R. Light were one of the largest wholesale businesses in the trade. They opened a new factory in Great Eastern Street in 1898 and had their own timber yards in Rivington Street. In 1880 they issued their catalogue: *Cabinet Furniture: Designs and Catalogue of Cabinet and Upholstery Furniture, Looking-Glasses, etc.* This was typical of the trade publications now available for shops in any part of the country that wished to make up their stocks. It is evident that machinery played an important part in the Lights' output. Their bedroom suite factory of 1898 was described as having an "almost unique plant of the most modern English and foreign woodworking machinery available, driven by electric motors".

Oak arm chair with inlay and rush panels made by William Birch in 1901. Courtesy Victoria and Albert Museum.

Examples: Maddox bedroom furniture: beds, 2, 28; dressing tables, 42; wardrobes, 67-9; wash-stands, 83. Compare with Wyman's dressing tables, 37-8, and his Art Furniture pieces: cabinets, 116, sideboards, 450, 452, 469-70. Extensive extracts from Light's publication show general standard of current commercial production.

HEAL AND SON

Like Shoolbred, the firm of Heal built up their reputation in Tottenham Court Road to reach a position of eminence by the end of the century; but unlike Shoolbred, Heals are still very active and today rank as one of the most progressive furniture designers of the twentieth century.

The illustrations in the *Dictionary* are taken from a catalogue issued in the early 1880s, prior to the advent of the firm's most distinguished figure, Ambrose Heal. This catalogue gives us a summary of the last phase of Art Furniture at its best, before the impact of the Arts and Crafts Movement. It already has the stamp of the firm's quality, marked by good craftsmanship and firm control of style and form. It will be seen that many pieces have absorbed the changes introduced in the 1860s, in the Collcutt tradition of panel and frame, turned supports, spindle galleries and, where suitable, small shelves. Sideboards are good examples of this treatment; they stress straight lines with their preference for pedestal forms and bevelled glass backs. Dining and library chairs have in general square backs and straight turned legs. Upholstered chairs and couches make controlled use of their buttoned upholstery.

The most significant changes were to occur after 1893, the date when Ambrose Heal, who was trained as a cabinet-maker, entered the family firm and became in 1896 responsible for designing the furniture. Heals had the distinction of being the only commercial firm to have close connections with the Arts and Crafts Movement. Ambrose Heal was one of the very few English exhibitors at the Paris Exhibition of 1900 — there had been growing disenchantment with international exhibitions among English designers by the end of the century — and he gained a Silver Medal for a bedroom suite in oak inlaid with pewter and ebony in full Arts and Crafts style. In 1898 he issued the first catalogue of his designs and among his outstanding achievements was the reintroduction of wooden bedsteads which ultimately were to oust the universal Victorian metal bedsteads. It was fitting that the last years of the Queen's reign should produce a designer able to carry the most progressive features of late Victorian furniture into the next half century.

Examples: General Art Furniture influence: cabinets, 106, 119, 140; sideboards, 440 (with traditional touches, e.g. Adam); mantelpieces, 369-70. Anglo-Japanese, 143. Compare controlled comfort of armchairs, 154, with simple chair forms, 234 (including shield-backs).

Oak wardrobe, inlaid with ebony and pewter. Designed by Ambrose Heal and made by Heal and Son, c.1900. Courtesy Heal and Son.

Right: Chest of drawers painted red and green, designed by Ambrose Heal and made by Heal and Son, 1899. Courtesy Heal and Son.

MORRIS AND COMPANY

The *Dictionary* illustrates selections from a Morris and Company catalogue issued at the end of the century. William Morris died in 1896 after having influenced so strongly the revival of handicraft of the Arts and Crafts Movement. His firm continued after him and did not wind up until 1940. About 1890 Philip Webb, whose furniture in the firm's early years had done so much to revive interest in plain oak furniture of traditional stamp, retired, and was succeeded by George Jack who had been trained in Webb's office. Jack exhibited work at the Arts and Crafts exhibitions and the fine quality of his furniture maintained the firm's high reputation. There was, however, a distinct difference between the firm's furniture of the 1890s and later, and the earlier Morris pieces. Much of the furniture now employed mahogany and rosewood, with marquetry decoration. A typical example of this kind, made in 1893 and repeated later, is an escritoire on stand in mahogany with marquetry of tendrils, oak leaves and acorns in sycamore and other woods. This is in full Arts and Crafts tradition, but a cabinet of mahogany made for Lady Shand about 1900, with marquetry and cast brass handles, is much more elaborate. Morris's successor as chairman of the company, W.A.S. Benson, designed furniture with emphasis on metal mounts. A well-known piece made by the firm to his design is a rosewood cabinet inlaid with ebony, tulipwood and purplewood with large hinges and circular metal decoration. After 1890 the firm's name began to be stamped on this kind of furniture. There is no such means of identification on the earlier pieces which are now considered to be more typical of the firm's work as embodiment of Morris's message.

Examples: George Jack's cabinet (escritoire), 88 (centre); satinwood and amboyna cabinet in Hepplewhite taste, 141 (bottom left). 'Royal' chair, 175. Plain wooden beds, 17; dressing tables, 42. Compare panelled cabinet with decorated example, 99.

Marquetry escritoire, designed by George Jack and made by Morris and Company in 1893. Courtesy Victoria and Albert Museum.

Inlaid rosewood cabinet designed by W. Benson and made c.1899 by Morris and Company. Courtesy Victoria and Albert Museum.

NORMAN AND STACEY

The *Dictionary* concludes chronologically with extracts from the catalogue of Norman and Stacey who were prominent shortly before and after the Queen's death in 1901. Their catalogue can be taken as representing fashionable furniture of good standard towards the end of the short reign of Edward VII (d.1910). The firm, listed in directories as "art furnishers and decorators", were in 1890 in Queen Victoria Street, the address which they retained as their City offices when they moved into Tottenham Court Road after 1902. They later moved back to Queen Victoria Street and their Tottenham Court Road premises were occupied by the well-known firm of Wolfe and Hollander, upholsterers, decorators, estate agents and electricians, who were already established in their shop close by.

Norman and Stacey's *Catalogue of Artistic Furniture, Decorations, Carpets and Antiques* is illustrated by photographs in which historical styles are shown side by side with current versions of art nouveau and with antiques. The English historical styles include Jacobean, Queen Anne, Chippendale, Hepplewhite and Sheraton. These are favoured for dining-rooms. For drawing-rooms the best suites are in Louis Quinze and Louis Seize taste, with some pieces decorated with buhl work. Both French styles are offered in some instances as gilt suites. Other furniture is inspired by art nouveau, as can be seen in cabinets and bedroom suites. There is also evidence of Liberty's influence. Much of the furniture is in dark mahogany, but fumed oak and rush-seated settees and chairs are tributes to Arts and Crafts.

The antiques advertised make up the most curious section, for although some pieces appear to be genuinely antique ("Good examples of Old Italian and Portuguese work, and all the well-known English and French Periods always on view") it is clear from the photographs (and the prices) that a great deal of it is reproduction. A glance at the so-called 'Chippendale' and 'Hepplewhite' chairs, for example, makes this obvious. Even among what seems to be genuine old furniture confusion prevails. A "medieval oak chest, a genuine piece in perfect condition", turns out to be a chest of drawers with Jacobean mouldings on the front and bracket feet of c.1700.

Norman & Stacey 1910

Examples: Photographs in catalogue show general commercial production at end of Edward VII's reign. Art nouveau influence: cabinets, 120 (bottom left), 112 (this page shows art nouveau, Georgian revivals and buhl work); chairs, 183 and 234-5 illustrate varieties of Georgian and Queen Anne influences.

Contents to Pictorial Dictionary

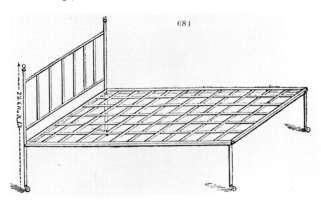

J.C.Loudon — 1833

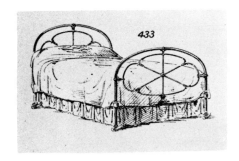

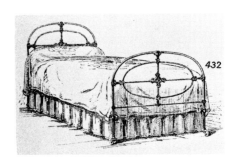

J.Shoolbred — 1876

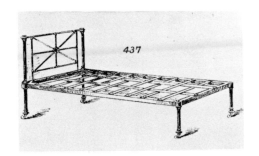

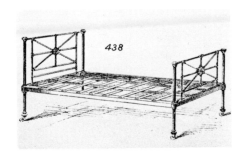

J.Shoolbred — 1876

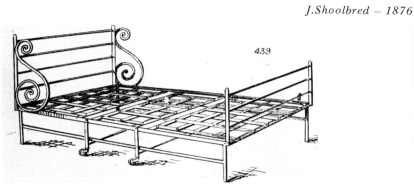

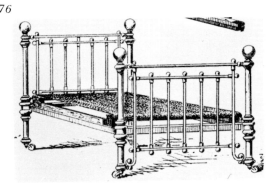

1

C. & R. Light — 1881

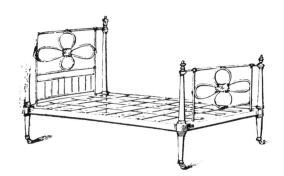

Maddox — 1882

J.C. Loudon – 1833

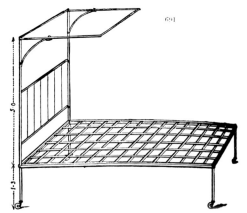

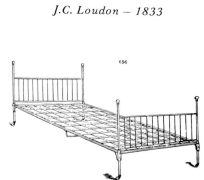

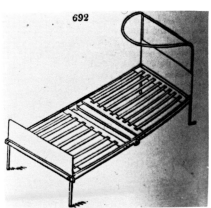

Shoolbred – 1876

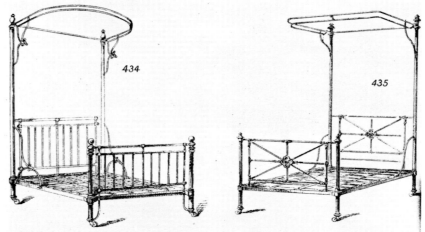

Shoolbred — 1876

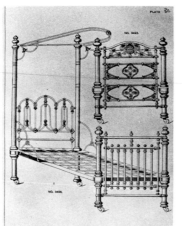

Wyman — 1877

C. & R. Light — 1881

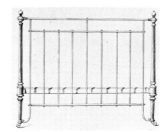

C. & R. Light — 1881

Maddox — 1882

Maddox — 1882

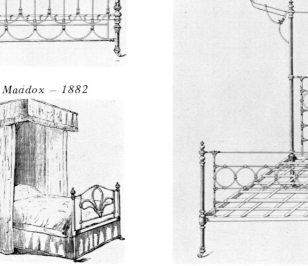

J.Shoolbred — 1876

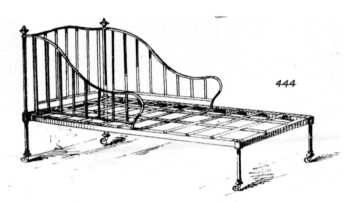

444

Maddox — 1882

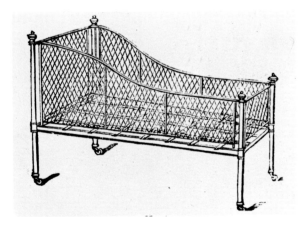

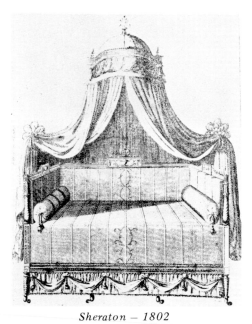

Sheraton – 1802

Sheraton – 1804

G. Smith – 1808

P. & M.A. Nicholson – 1826

P. & M.A. Nicholson – 1826

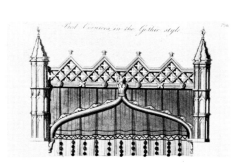

G. Smith – 1808

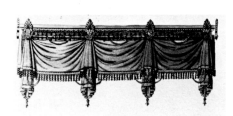

P. & M.A. Nicholson – 1826

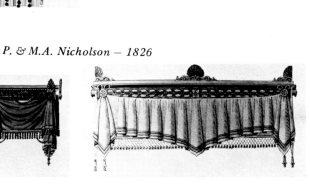

G. Smith – 1826

H. Whitaker – 1825

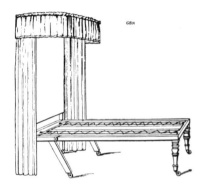

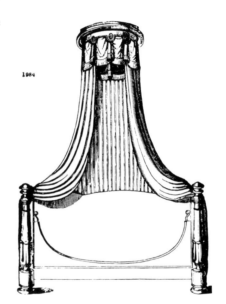

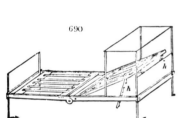

J.C. Loudon – 1833

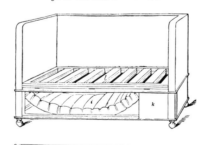

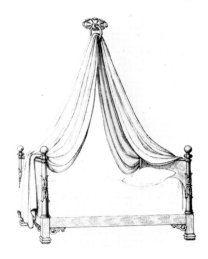

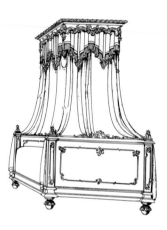

T. King — 1839

W. Smee & Sons — 1850

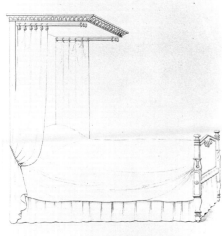

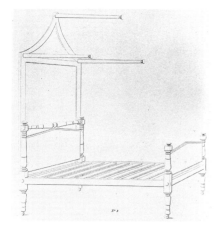
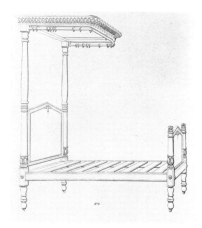

W. Smee & Sons — 1850

Braund — 1858

Blackie — 1853

Blackie — 1853

Booth – 1864

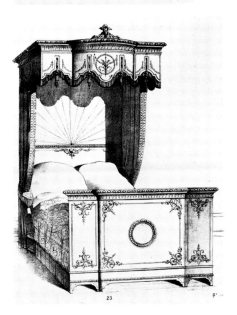

Richard Charles – 1866

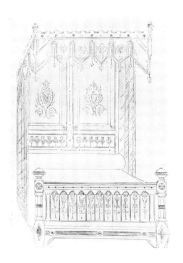

Yapp — 1876

Yapp — 1876

C & R Light — 1881

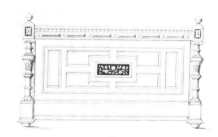

C & R Light – 1881

G. Maddox
– 1882

Norman & Stacey – 1910

No. 339. INLAID
MAHOGANY ITALIAN

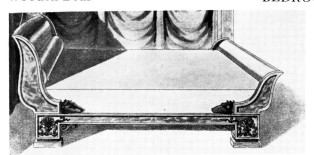

G.Smith — 1808

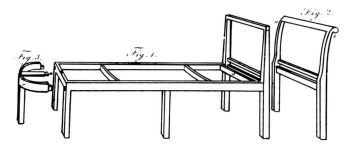

London Chairmakers' — 1823

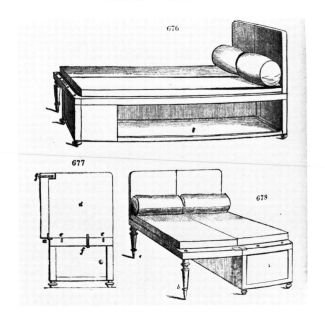

J.C.Loudon — 1833

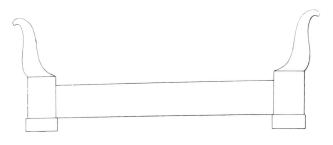

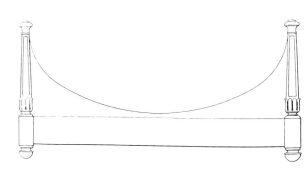

T. King — Supplementary Plates

Pugin — 1835

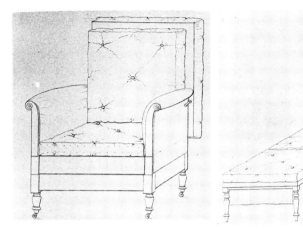

W.Smee & Sons — 1850

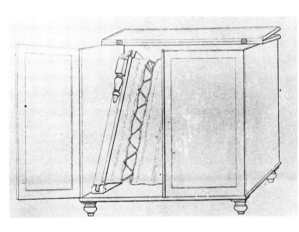

W.Smee & Sons — 1850

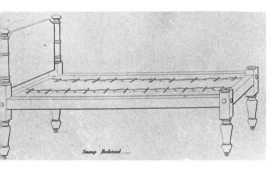

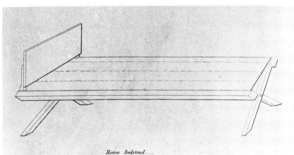

Blackie — 1853

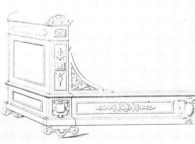

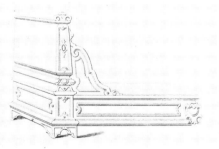

Blackie — 1853

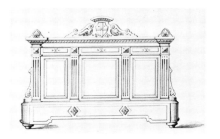

Wyman — 1877   *C. & R. Light — 1881*

C. & R. Light — 1881   *C. & R. Light — 1881*

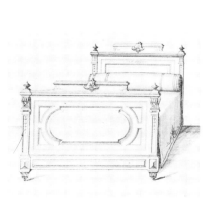

C.& R. Light — 1881

Morris — 1900

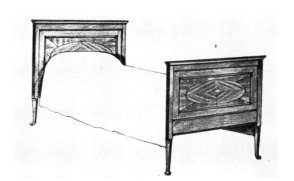

Norman & Stacey — 1910

Norman & Stacey — 1910

Sheraton — 1802

Sheraton — 1804

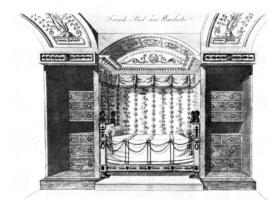

G. Smith — 1808

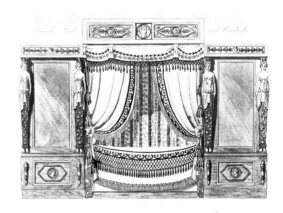

G. Smith – 1808

19

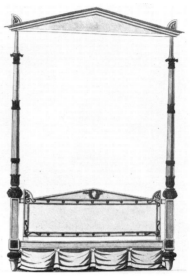

G. Smith — 1808

G. Smith — 1808

R. Brown — 1822

P. & M.A. Nicholson — 1826

G. Smith – 1826

P. & M.A. Nicholson – 1826
–1826

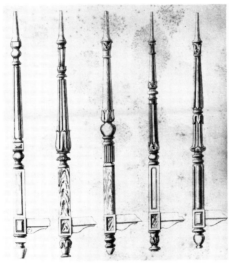

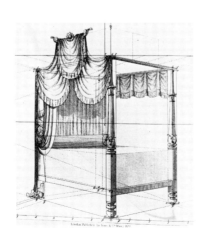

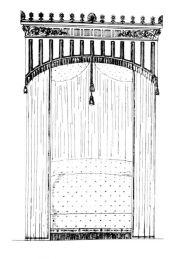

Whitaker — 1825

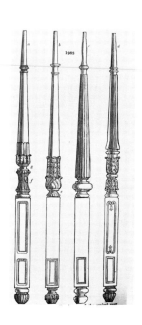

J. C. Loudon — 1833

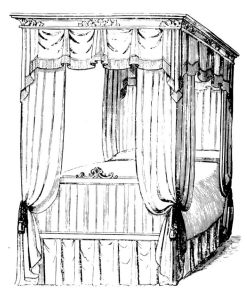

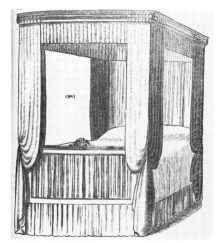

A. W. N. Pugin — 1835

T. King — 1839

T. King — 1839

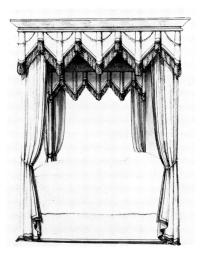

T. King — 1839

Whitaker — 1847

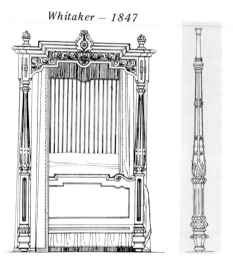

R. Bridgens — 1838

J. Taylor — 1850

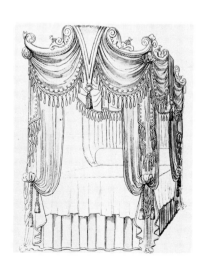

J. Taylor — 1850

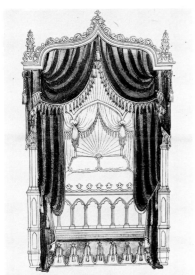

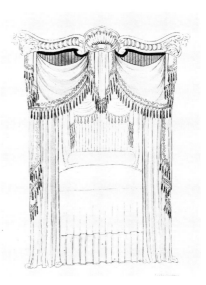

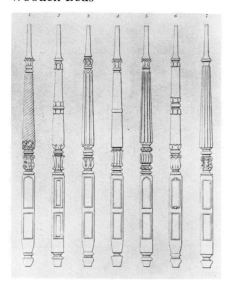

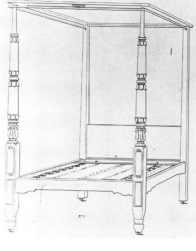

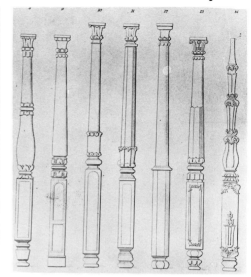

W. Smee & Sons – 1850

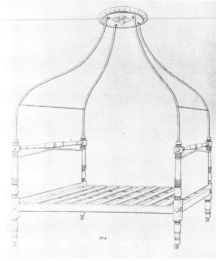

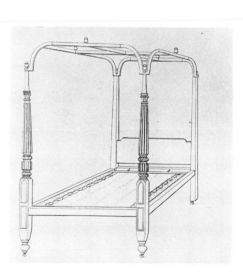

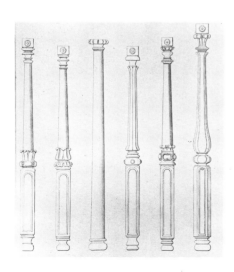

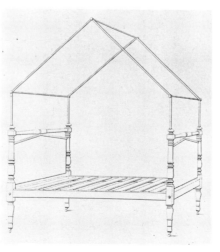

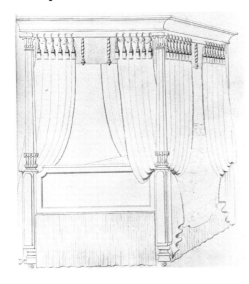

W. Smee & Sons – 1850

W. Smee & Sons – 1850

W. Smee & Sons – 1850

J. Braund –1858

J. Braund – 1858

Blackie – 1853

Blackie – 1853

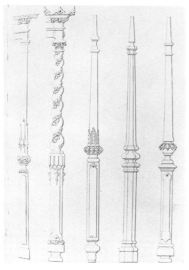

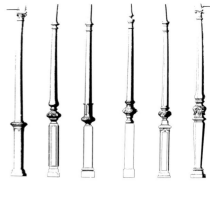

Blackie — 1853

Blackie — 1853

Yapp — 1879

R. Charles — 1866

Booth — 1864

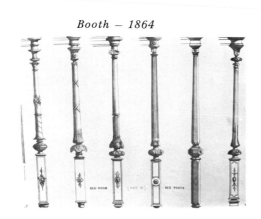

Yapp — 1879

Yapp —1879

G. Maddox — 1882

G. Smith – 1808

R. Brown – 1822

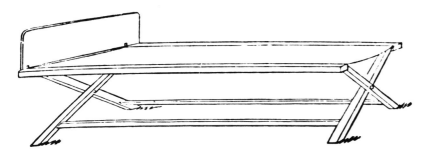

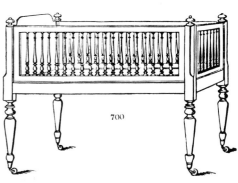

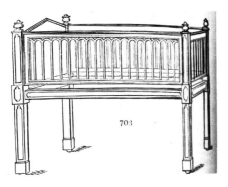

J.C.Loudon – 1833

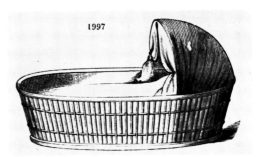

W. Smee & Sons – 1850

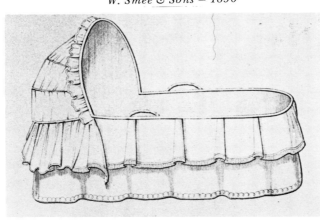

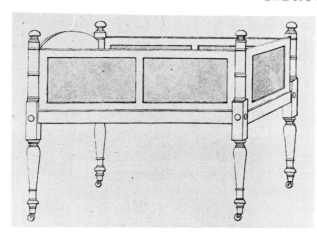
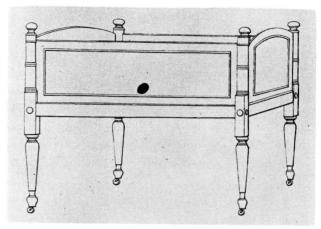

W. Smee & Sons — 1850

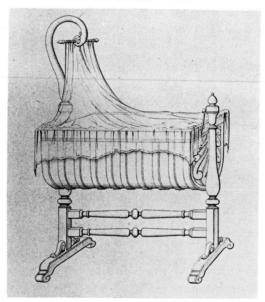

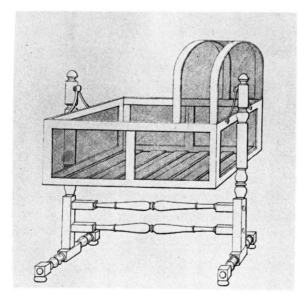
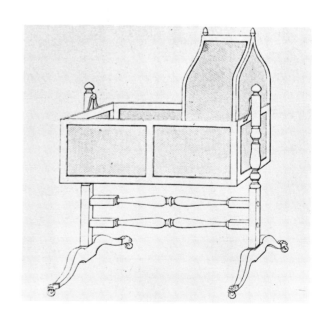

Braund — 1858

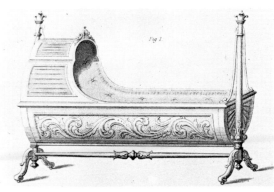
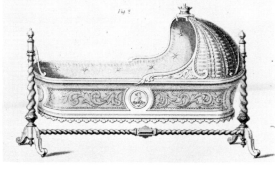

Blackie — 1853

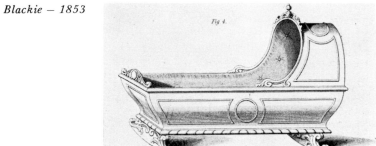

Yapp — 1879

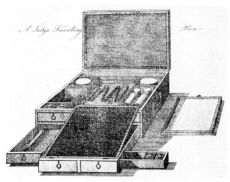

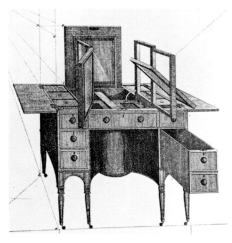

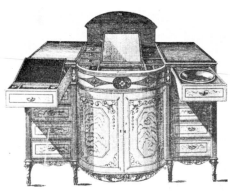

Sheraton — *1802*

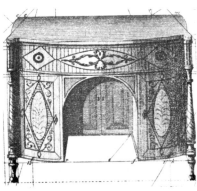

G.Smith — *1808*

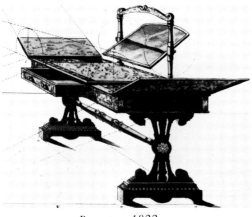

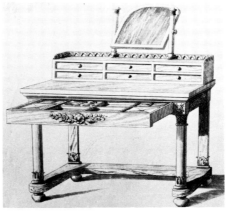

Brown — 1822

G.Smith — 1826

G.Smith — 1826

P. & M.A. Nicholson — 1826

Modern Style Exemplified — 1829

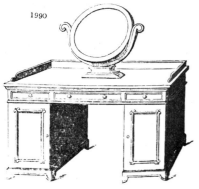

T.King — 1835

Loudon — 1833

Whitaker — 1847

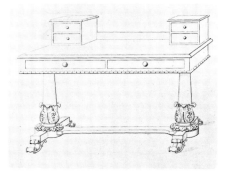

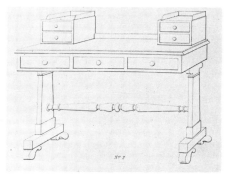

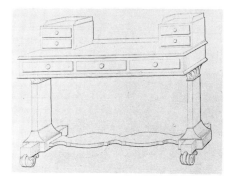

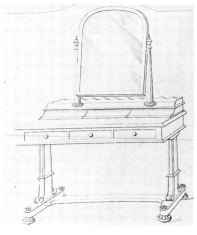

W. Smee & Sons – 1850

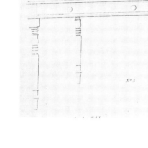

Blackie – 1853   *Blackie – 1853*

53

Booth — 1864

Richard Charles — 1866

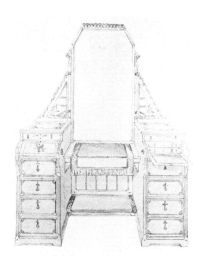

TOILET TABLES IN EVERY VARIETY OF WOOD & TREATMENT.

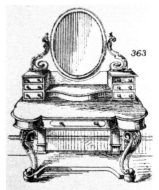

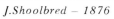

J.Shoolbred — 1876

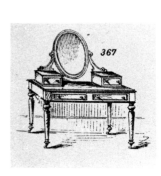

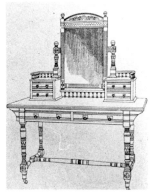

W.Watts — 1877   *Wyman — 1877*

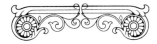

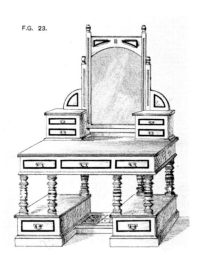
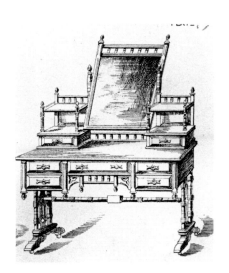

Wyman — 1877

Wyman — 1877

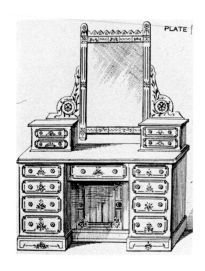

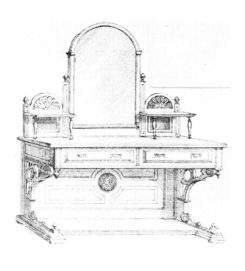

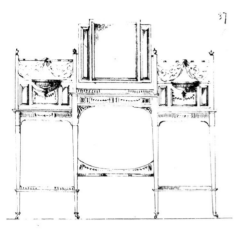

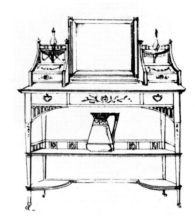

A.Jonquet — 1879

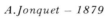

Yapp — 1879

Right: One other of similar design with fixed side mirrors and two drawers.

C. & R. Light – 1881

A dozen other similar designs differing in the arrangement of the drawers and shape of mirrors.

One other of similar design with arched mirror.

One other of similar design with arched mirror.

One other of similar design with rectangular mirror.

Two others of similar design with different shaped mirrors.

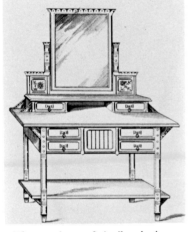

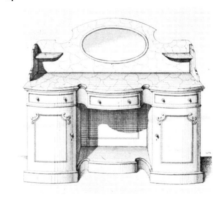

Three others of similar design.

Three others of similar design, all set on castors.

C. & R. Light – 1881

Left: Eleven others of similar design with different shape mirrors and drawer arrangement.

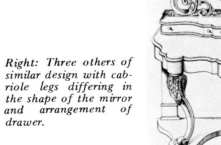

Right: Three others of similar design with cabriole legs differing in the shape of the mirror and arrangement of drawer.

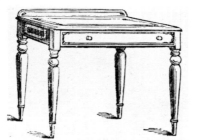

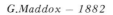

No. 26.

G.Maddox — 1882

Liberty — 1890

Morris — 1900

Norman & Stacey — 1910

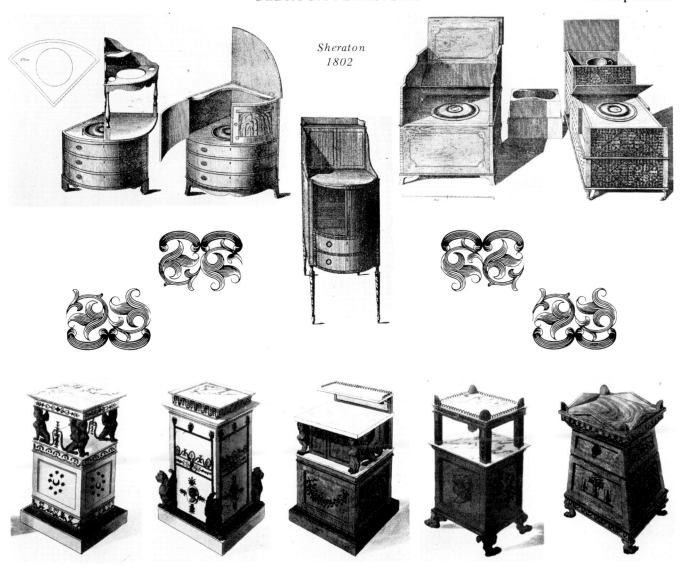

*Sheraton
1802*

G. Smith — 1808

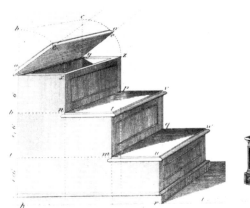

P. & M.A. Nicholson — 1826

1986

Loudon — 1833

1910

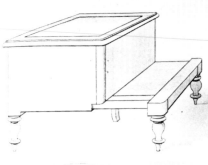

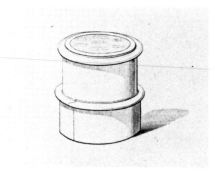

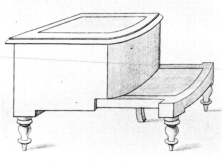

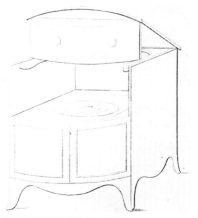

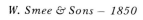

W. Smee & Sons — 1850

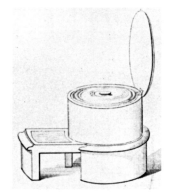

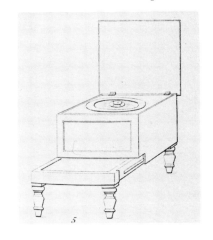

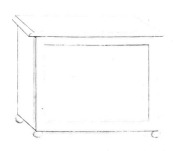

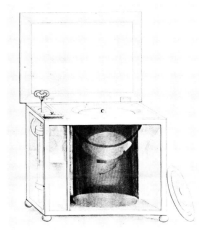

W. Smee & Sons – 1850

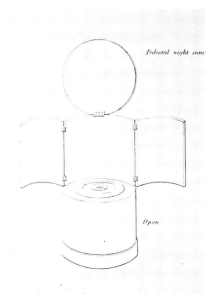

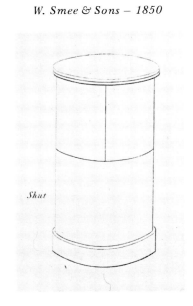

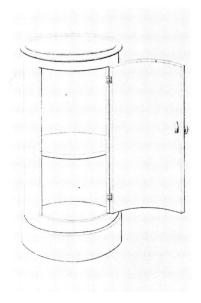

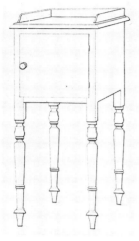

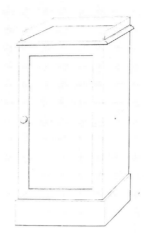

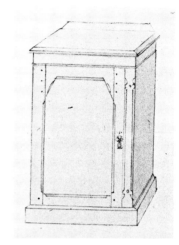

W. Smee & Sons – 1850   *Richard Charles – 1866*

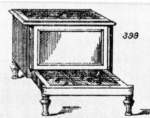

397   398   399   400

J. Shoolbred – 1876

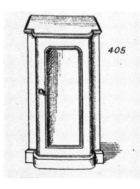
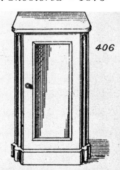
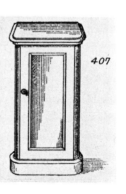

405   406   407

Wyman – 1877

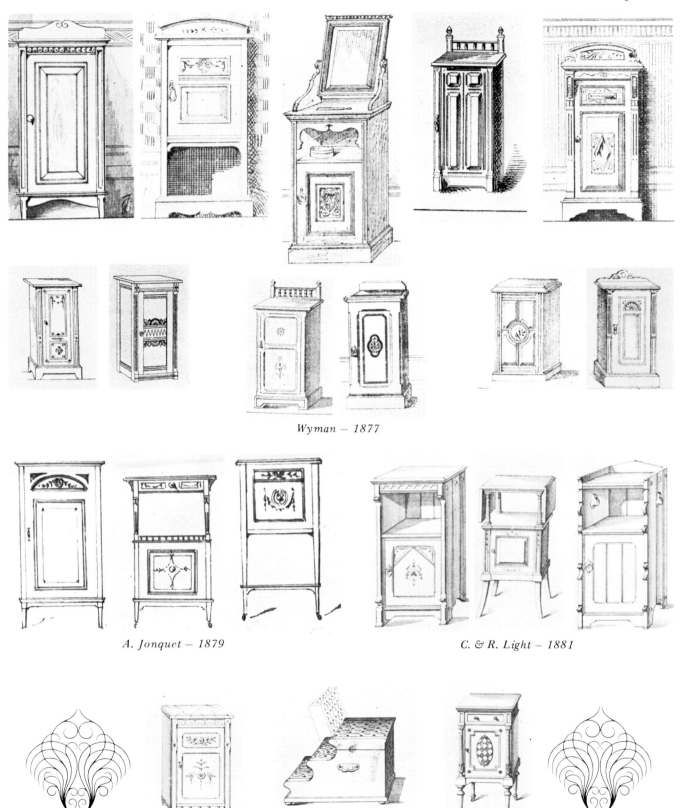

Wyman — 1877

A. Jonquet — 1879

C. & R. Light — 1881

C. & R. Light — 1881

C. & R. Light
—
1881

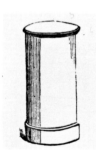

G. Maddox — 1882

Liberty — 1890

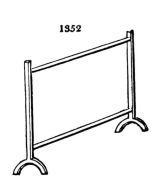

Loudon – 1833   *W. Smee & Sons – 1850*

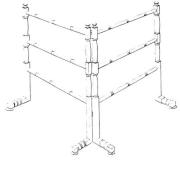

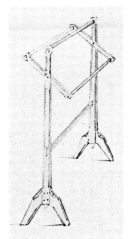

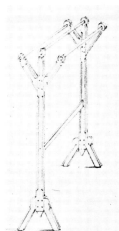

*R. Charles
– 1866*

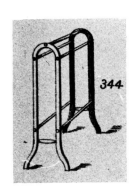

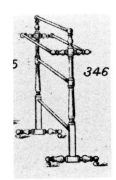

Shoolbred – 1876

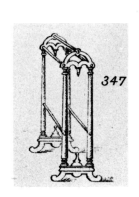

49

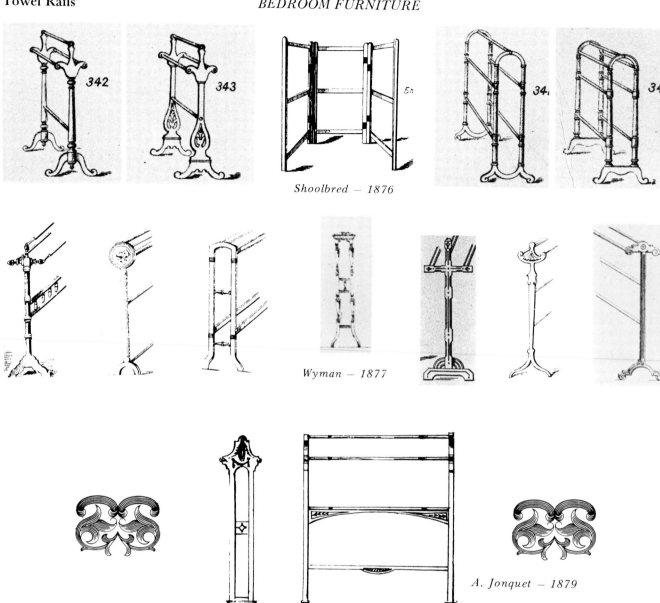

Shoolbred — 1876

Wyman — 1877

A. Jonquet — 1879

C . & R. Light — 1881

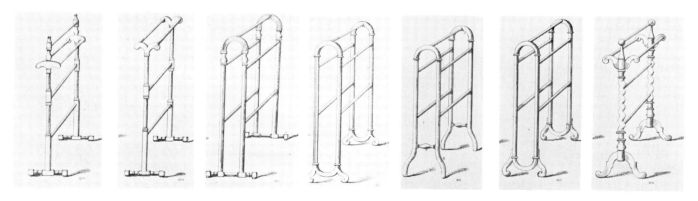

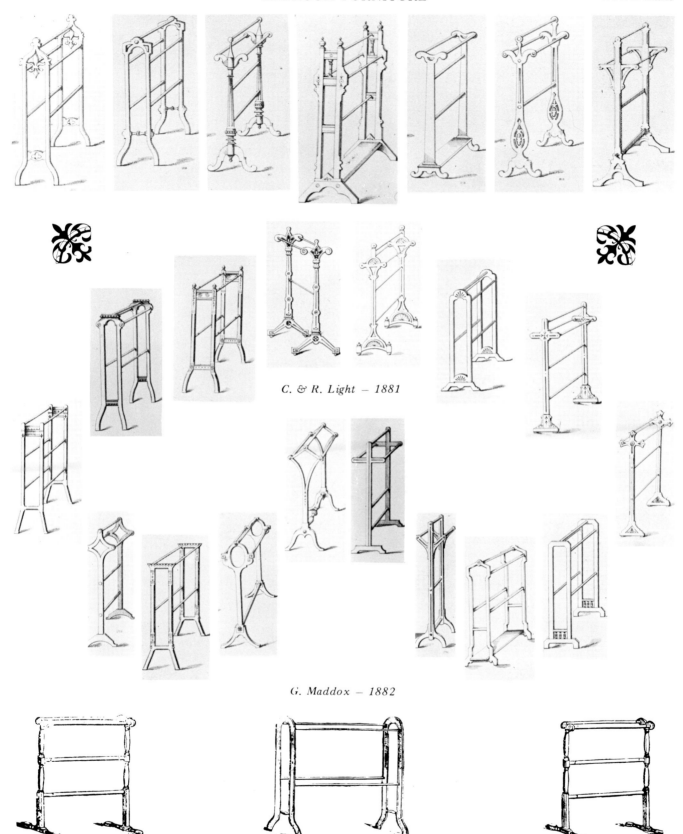

C. & R. Light — 1881

G. Maddox — 1882

Sheraton — 1802

*G. Smith —
1808*

G. Smith – 1808

G. Smith – 1826

*G. Smith –
1826*

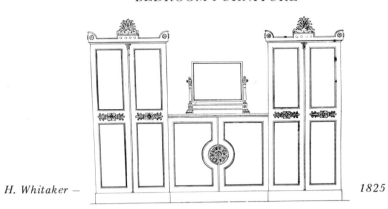

H. Whitaker —   *1825*

The Modern Style of Cabinet   *Work Exemplified — 1829*

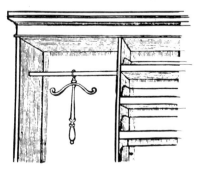

J.C. Loudon — 1833

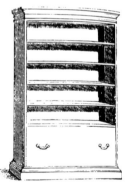

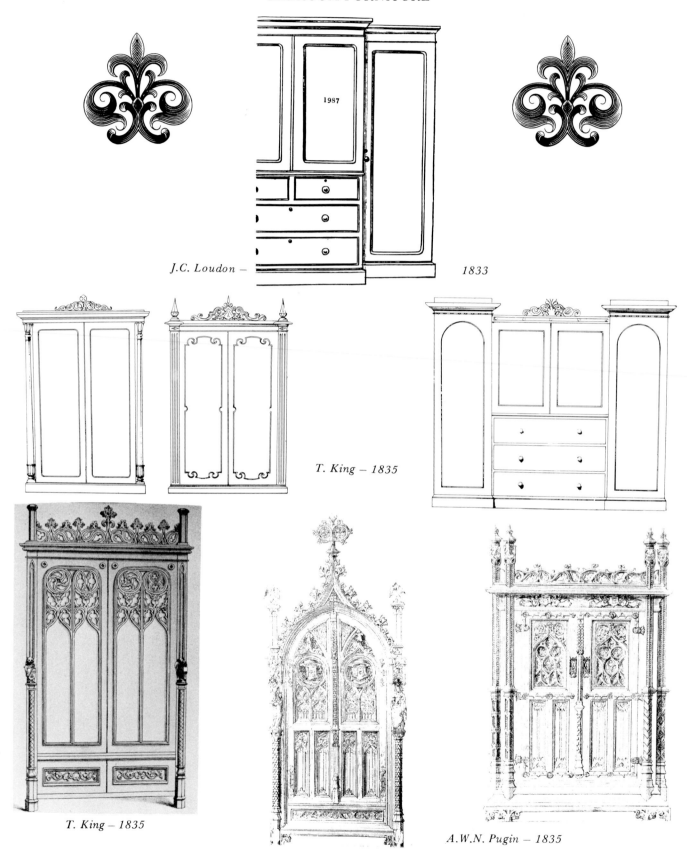

J.C. Loudon –   1833

T. King – 1835

T. King – 1835

A.W.N. Pugin – 1835

H. Whitaker — 1847

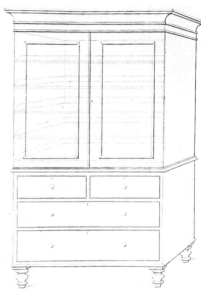

J. Taylor — 1850

W. Smee & Sons — 1850

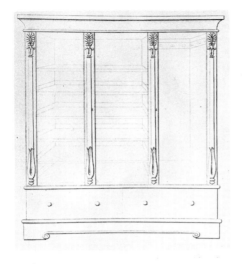

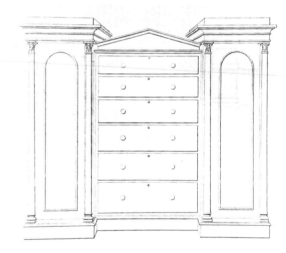

W. Smee & Sons – 1850

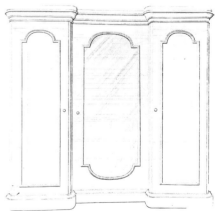

J. Braund — 1858

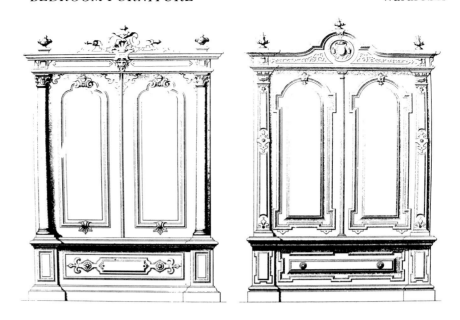

Blackie — 1853

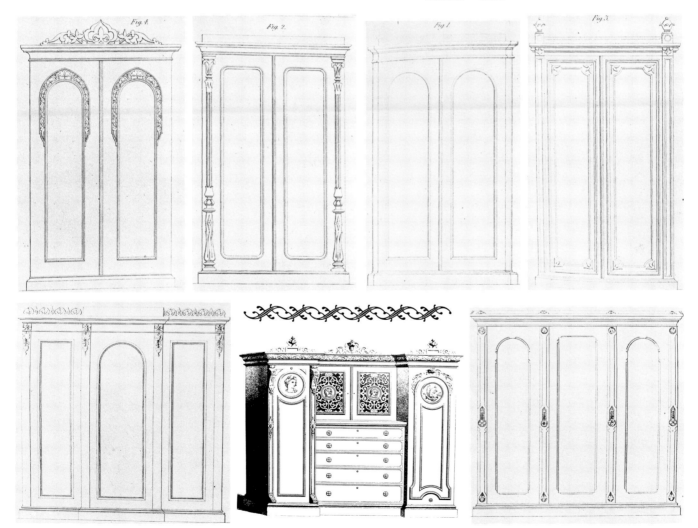

L . Booth – 1864

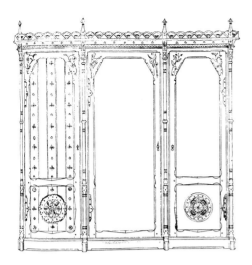

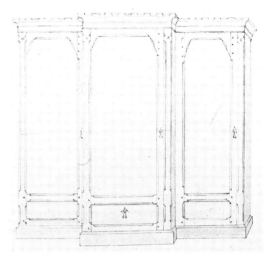

R. Charles — 1866

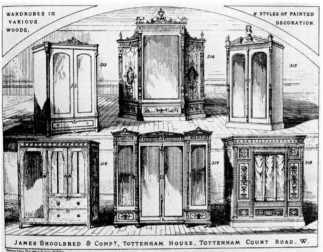

J. Shoolbred & Co. — 1876

W. Watt — 1877

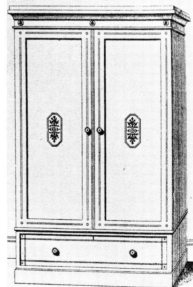

Wyman — 1877

Wyman — 1877

Wyman – 1877

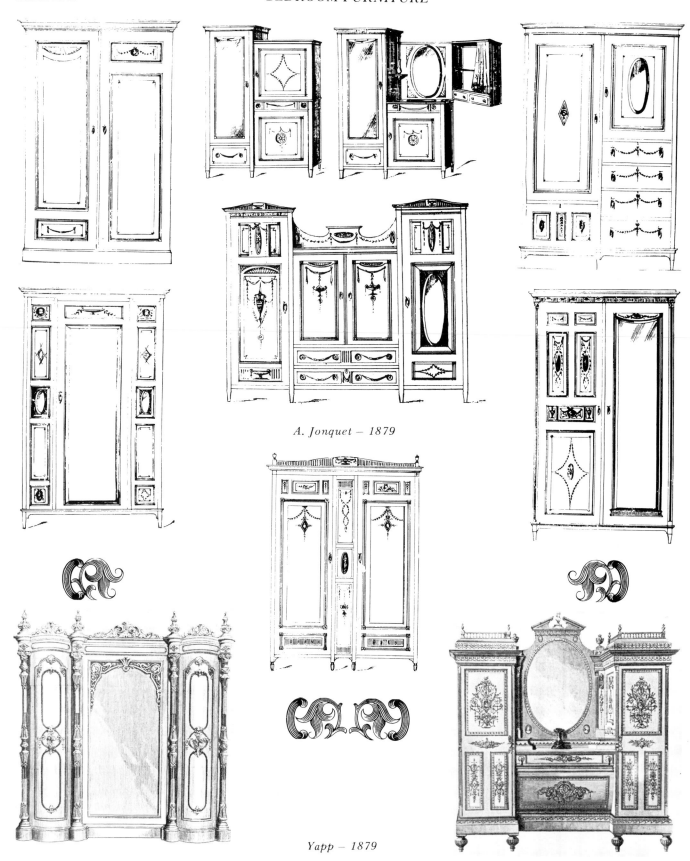

A. Jonquet – 1879

Yapp – 1879

Yapp – 1879

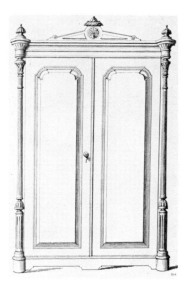

C. & R. Light – 1881

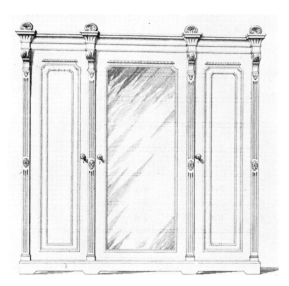

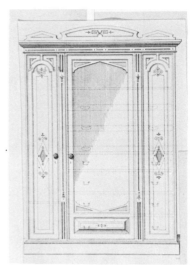

C. & R. Light — 1881

C. & R. Light – 1881

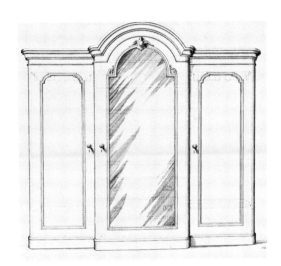

65

C. & R. Light – 1881

C. & R. Light – 1881

G. Maddox – 1882

G. Maddox – 1882

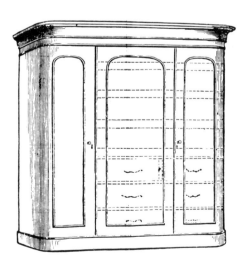

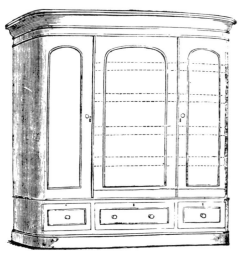
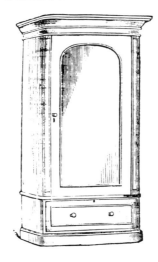

G. Maddox — 1882

Liberty — 1890

Morris — 1900   Norman & Stacey — 1910

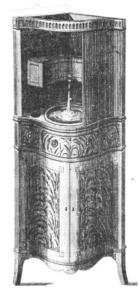

Sheraton — 1802

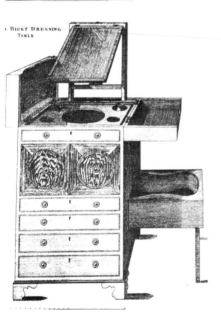
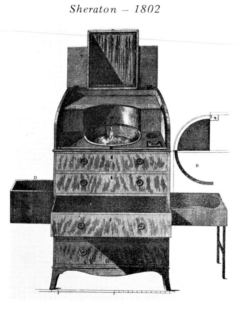
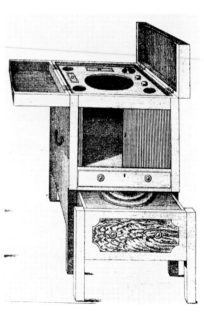

G. Smith   *1808*

G. Smith – 1826

P. & M.A. Nicholson – 1826

*The
Modern
Style
of
Cabinet
Work
Exemp-
lified
–
1829*

Loudon — 1833

1995

T. King

Supplementary Plates

W. Smee & Sons — 1850

W. Smee & Sons – 1850

Blackie — 1853

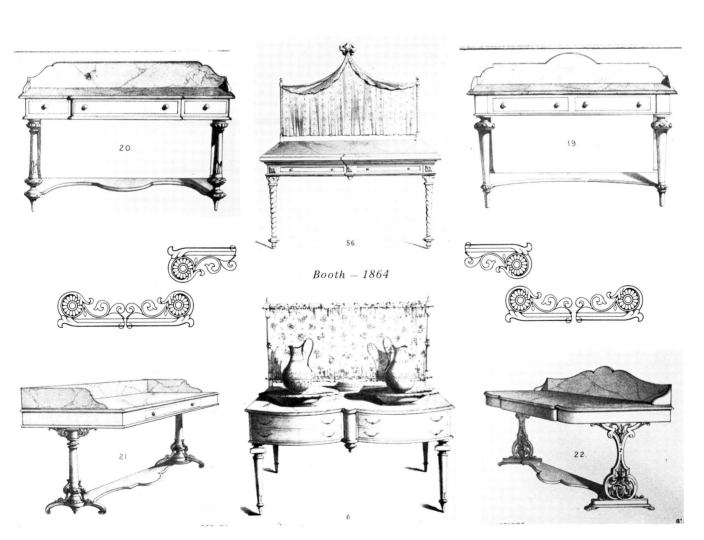

Booth — 1864

Richard Charles — 1866

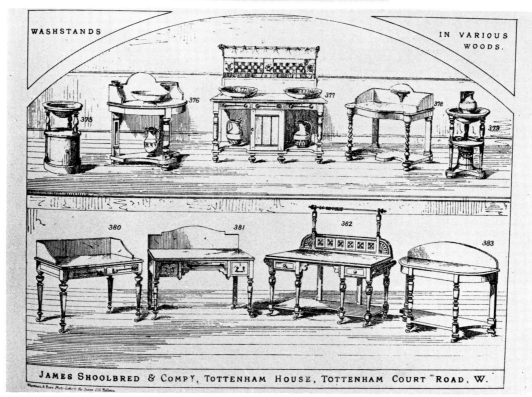

Shoolbred — 1876

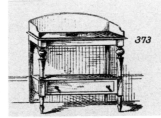

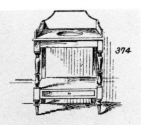

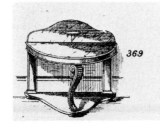

Shoolbred – 1876

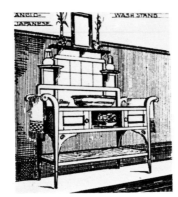

Watts – 1877

Wyman – 1877

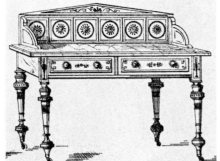

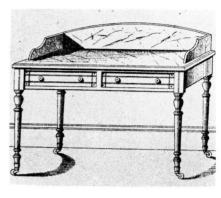

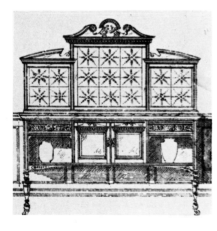

Wyman – 1877

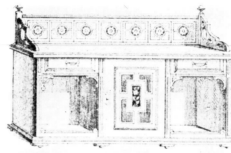

MARBLE TOP FOR WASH TABLE

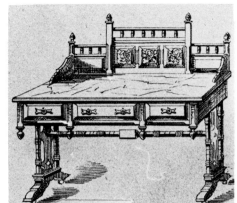

Wyman — 1877

Wyman — 1877

No. 20.

No. 22.

Yapp — 1879

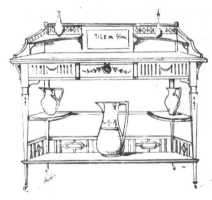

A. Jonquet — 1879

C. & R. Light — 1881

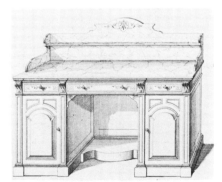

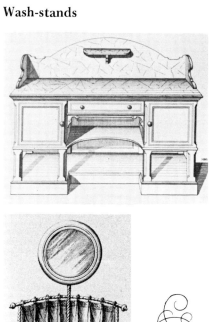

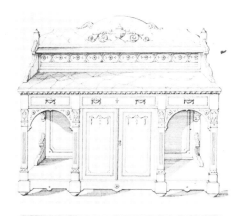

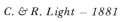

C. & R. Light – 1881

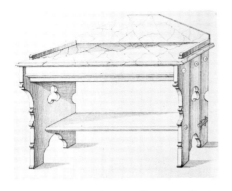

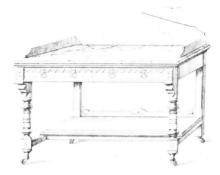

C. & R. Light – 1881

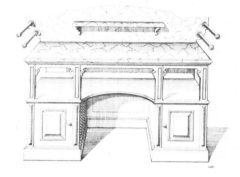

C. & R. Light — 1881

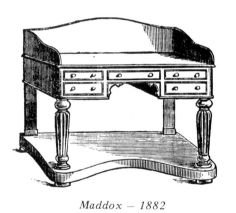

Maddox — 1882

Maddox — 1882

Liberty — 1890　　　　　　*Morris — 1900*

Norman and Stacey — 1910

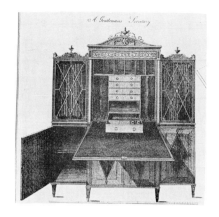

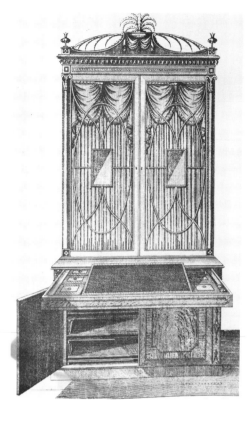

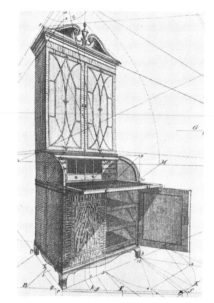

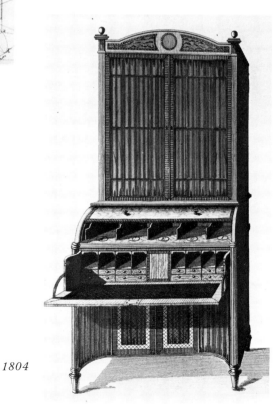

Sheraton   1804

G. Smith 1808

G. Smith 1808

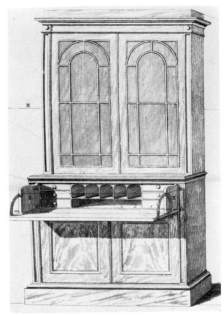

G. Smith   *1826*

Loudon 1833

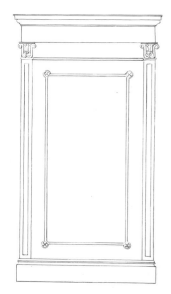

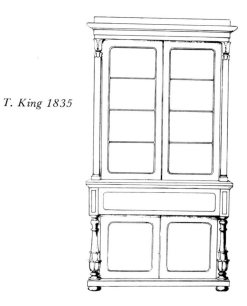

T. King 1835

T. King Supplementary Plates

Whitaker 1847

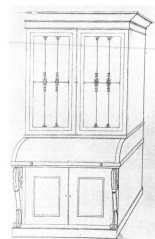

W. Smee & Sons 1850

Blackie 1853

W. Smee & Sons 1850   *Braund 1858*

Waring 1862

Yapp 1879

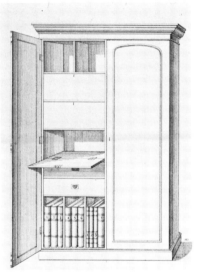

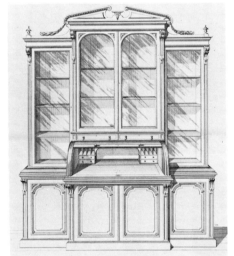

Heal 1884

C. & R. Light 1881

Liberty 1890

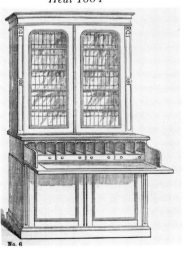

Morris 1900

Morris 1900

Norman & Stacey 1910

G. Smith 1808

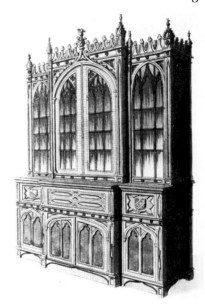

*Sheraton Appendix
1802*

Modern Style Exemplified 1829

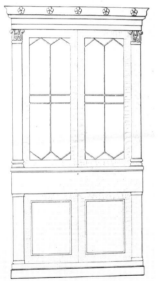

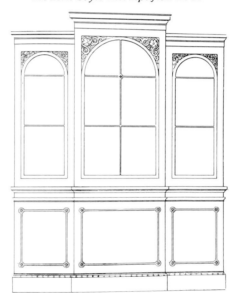

T. King Supplementary Plates

High   *CABINETS*   Doors top & bottom

Pugin 1835

Loudon 1833

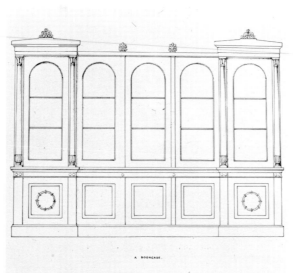

T. King 1835

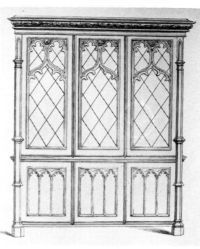

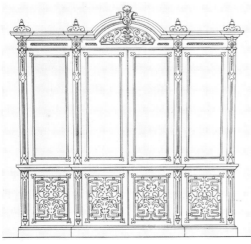

Whitaker 1847

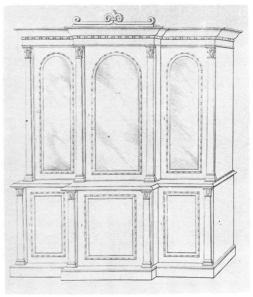

J. Taylor 1850

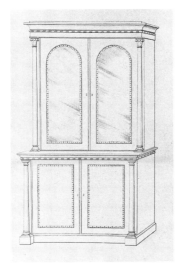

W. Smee & Sons 1850

Braund 1858

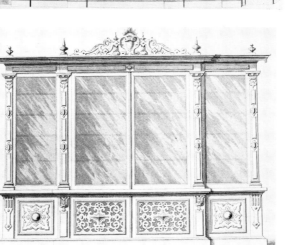

Blackie 1853

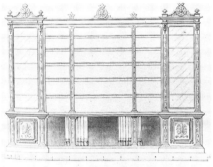

Blackie 1853

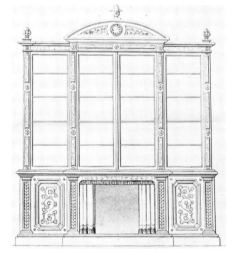

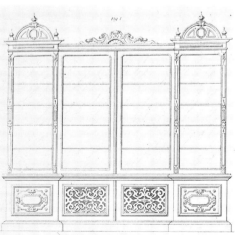

Waring 1862

Waring 1862

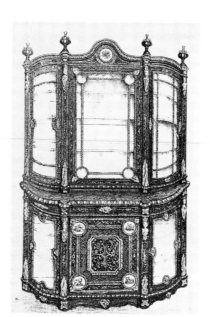

H.Lawford 1867

Booth 1864

Shoolbred 1876

Wyman 1877

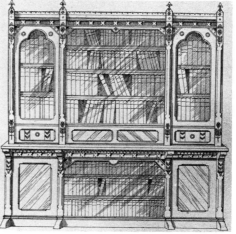

Yapp 1879

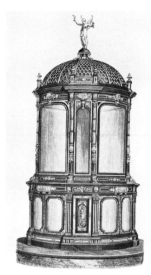

Yapp 1879

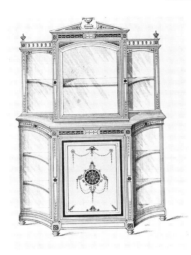

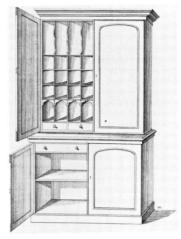

C. & R. Light 1881

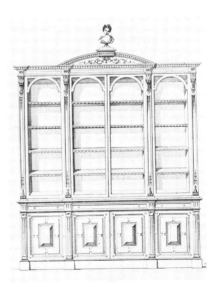

C. & R. Light 1881

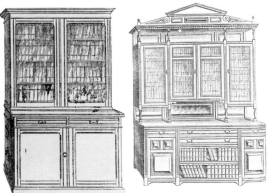
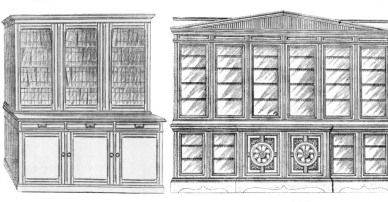

Heal 1884   *Wyman 1886*

Morris & Co. 1900

Norman   *& Stacey 1910*

Whitaker 1825

G. Smith 1826

P. & M.A. Nicholson 1826

P. & M.A. Nicholson 1826

T. King 1835

Pugin 1835

Whitaker 1847

J. Taylor 1850

Booth 1864

Booth 1864

Lawford 1867   *Lawford 1867*   *Lawford 1867*

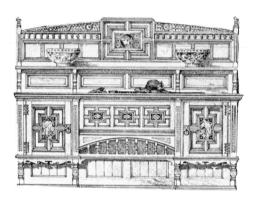

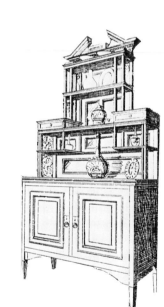

J. Talbert 1867   *W. Watt 1877*

Wyman 1877

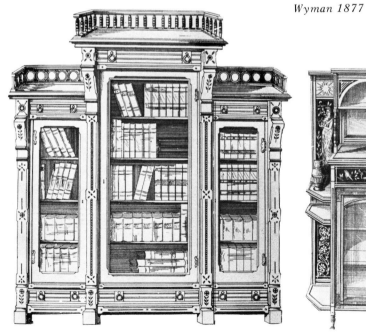

W. Watt 1877

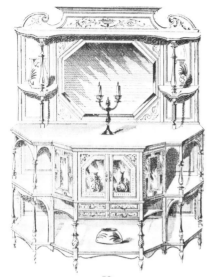

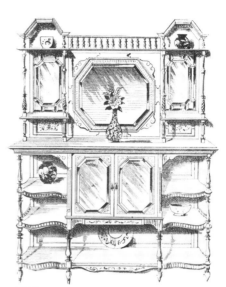

Wyman 1877   *Wyman 1877*

Jonquet 1879

Yapp 1879

Wyman 1877

Yapp 1879

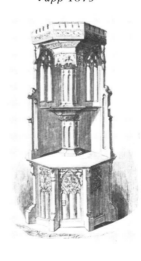

C. & R. Light 1881

C. & R. Light 1881

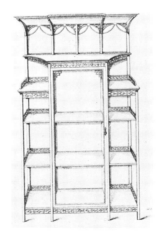

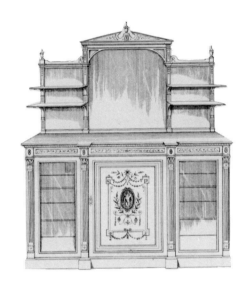

C. & R. Light 1881

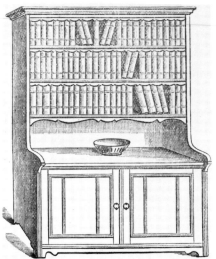

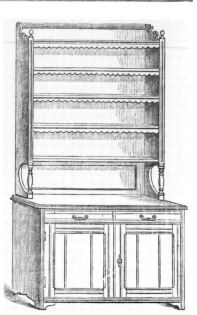

Heal 1884

C. & R. Light 1881

Heal 1884

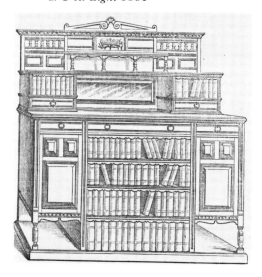

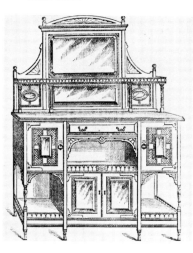

Heal 1884

Heal 1884

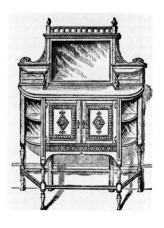

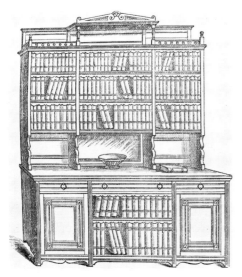

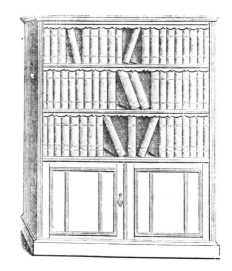

Heal 1884

Heal 1884

Wyman 1886   *Liberty 1890*   *Liberty 1890*

Norman &   *Stacey 1910*

Pugin 1835

Braund 1858

Waring 1862

Waring 1862

Yapp 1879

Yapp 1879

Yapp 1879

Yapp 1879

Yapp 1879

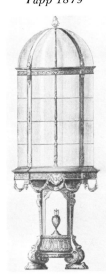

Yapp 1879

C. & R. Light 1881

C. & R. Light 1881

Heal 1884

Wyman

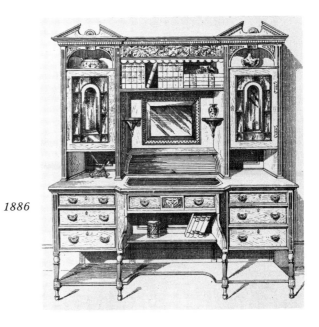

1886

Norman &

Stacey 1910

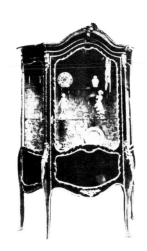

Norman & Stacey 1910

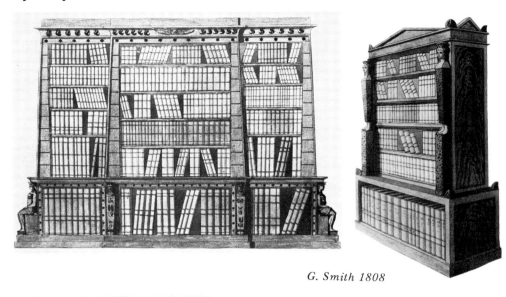

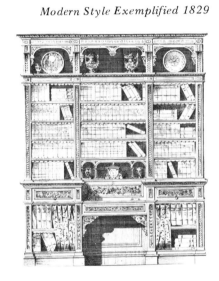

G. Smith 1808

Modern Style Exemplified 1829

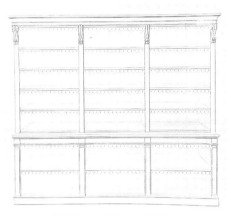

Modern Style Exemplified 1829

W. Smee & Sons 1850

Yapp 1879

Morris 1900

Sheraton 1802

G. Smith 1826

Loudon 1833

Pugin 1835

Loudon 1833

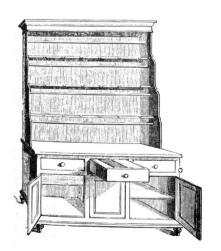

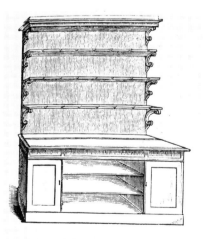

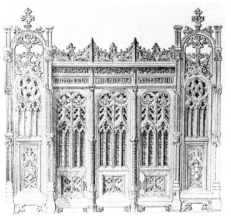

Pugin 1835

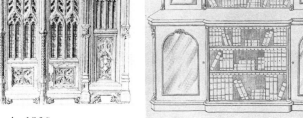

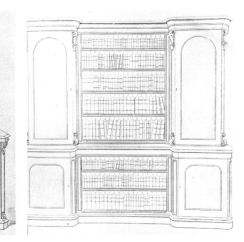

W. Smee & Sons 1850

J. Taylor 1850

Braund 1858

Braund 1858

Booth 1864

115

Shoolbred 1876

J. Talbert 1876
W. Watt 1877

Shoolbred 1876

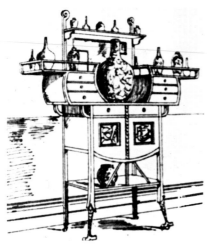

Wyman 1877

Wyman 1877

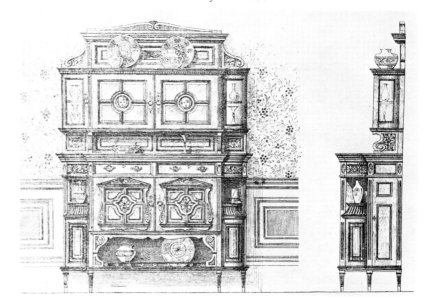

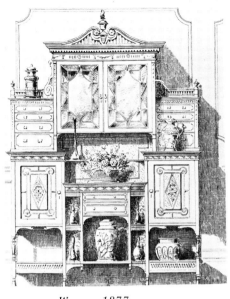

Wyman 1877   *Yapp 1879*

Yapp

1879

Yapp 1879

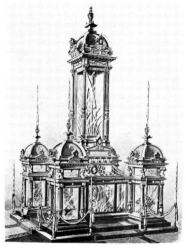

Yapp 1879

Yapp 1879

Yapp 1879

C. & R. Light 1881

C. & R. Light 1881

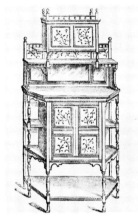

Heal 1884

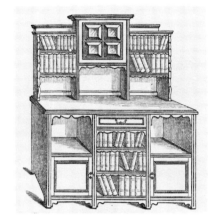

Heal 1884

Heal 1884

Wyman 1886

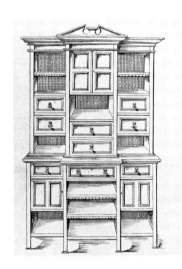

Wyman 1886

Wyman 1886

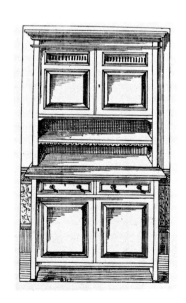

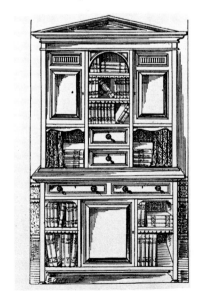

Wyman 1886

Morris & Co. 1900

Liberty & Co. 1890

Norman & Stacey 1910

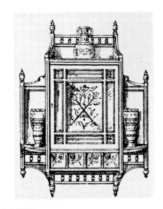

W. Watt 1877

Shoolbred 1876

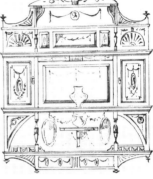

Jonquet 1879

W. Watt 1877

Yapp 1879

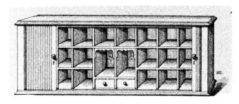

C. & R. Light 1881

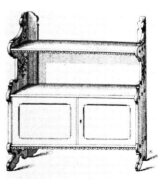

Heal

1884

No. 15

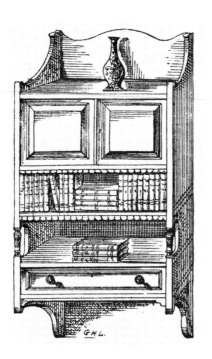

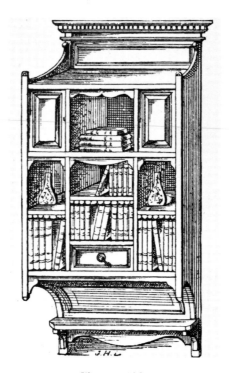

Wyman 1886

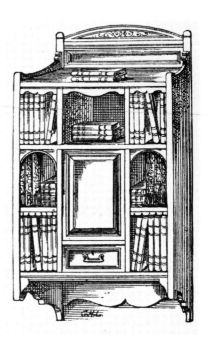

Wyman 1886

Morris & Co. 1900

Sheraton Appendix 1802

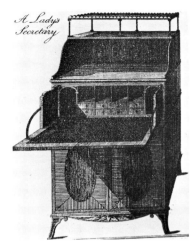

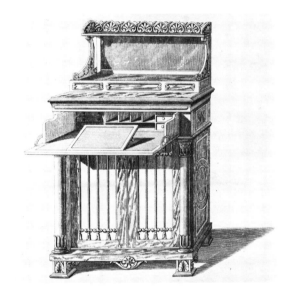

G. Smith 1826

G. Smith 1808

Yapp 1879

123

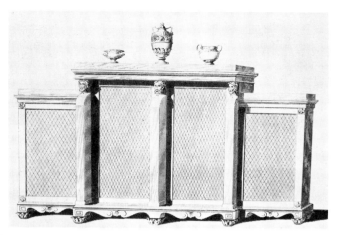

G. Smith 1826

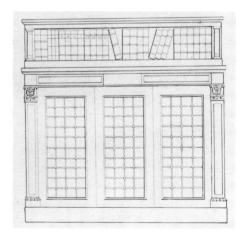

Modern Style Exemplified 1829

Bridgens 1838

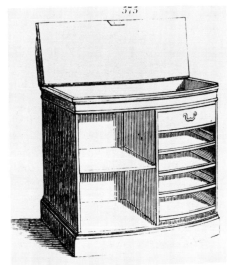

Loudon 1833

J. Taylor 1850

Loudon 1833

Braund 1858

125

Braund 1858

Waring 1862

Waring 1862

Booth 1864

Lawford 1867

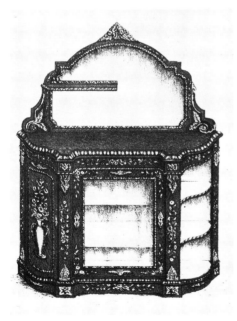

Lawford 1867

Lawford 1867

Lawford 1867

Lawford 1867

Shoolbred 1876

Lawford 1867

Shoolbred 1876

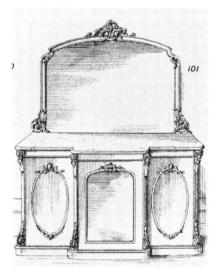

Shoolbred 1876

Yapp 1879

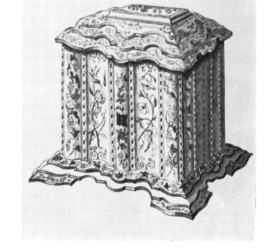

Yapp 1879

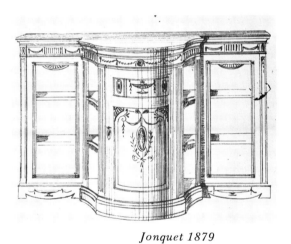

Yapp 1879

Yapp 1879

Jonquet 1879

C. & R. Light 1881

C. & R. Light 1881

C. & R. Light 1881

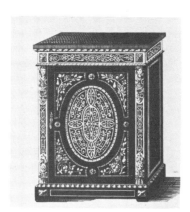

C. & R. Light 1881

C. & R. Light 1881

C. & R. Light 1881

C. & R. Light 1881

Norman & Stacey 1910

Sheraton Appendix 1802

G. Smith 1808

Whitaker 1825

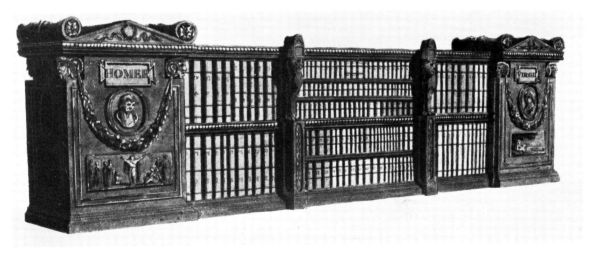

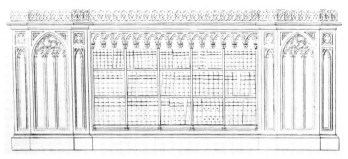

P. & M.A. Nicholson 1826

G. Smith 1826

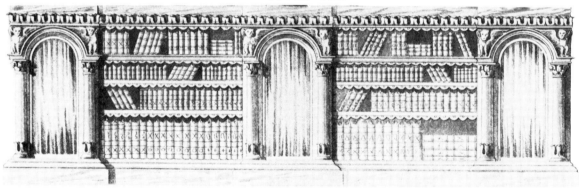

J. Taylor 1850

Waring 1862

Wyman 1877

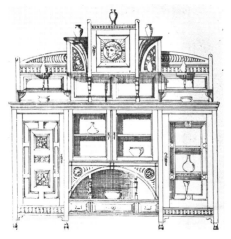

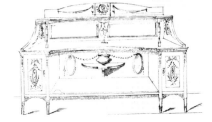

A. Jonquet 1879

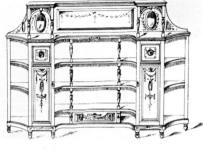

A. Jonquet 1879

Yapp 1879

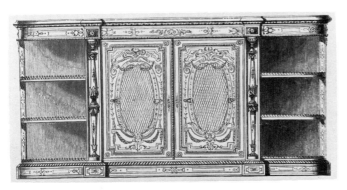

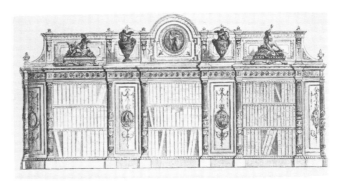

Yapp 1879

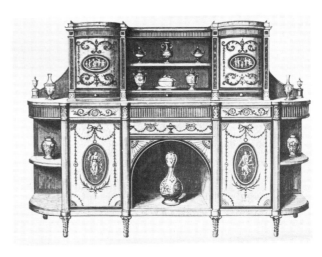

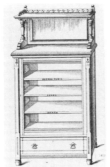

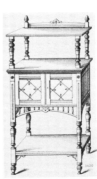

C. & R. Light 1881

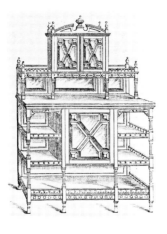

Heal 1884

Heal 1884

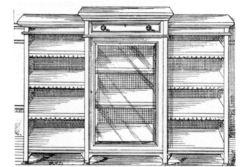

Wyman 1877

Wyman 1877

Morris 1900

Morris 1900

Norman & Stacey 1910

P. & M.A.
Nicholson
1826

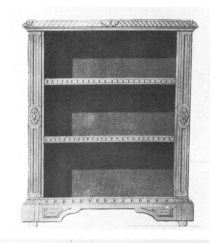

R. Bridgens
1838

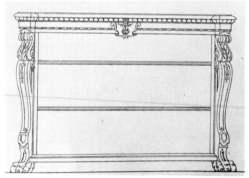

T. King Supplementary Plates   *Whitaker 1847*

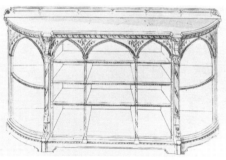

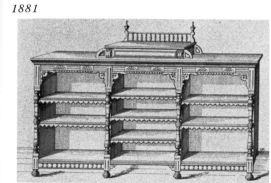

Richard Charles 1866

J. Taylor 1850

C. & R. Light   *1881*   *Yapp 1879*

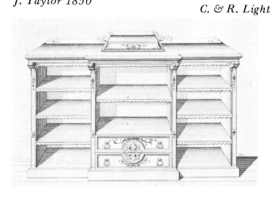

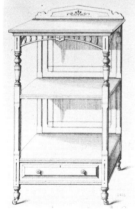

C. & R. Light   1881

Heal 1884

No. 5

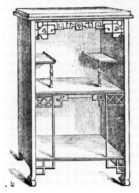

Wyman 1886

Morris 1900

Norman & Stacey 1910

Corner   *CABINETS*   **Floor standing**

Loudon 1833

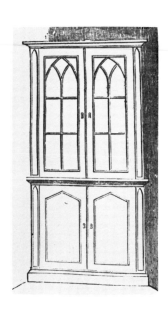

Loudon 1833   *Lawford 1867*

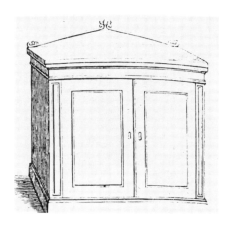

C. & R. Light 1881

Jonquet 1879

Heal 1884

Liberty 1890

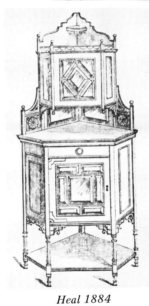

Heal 1884

Morris 1900

Angle Cabinet.

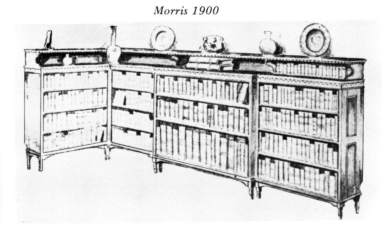

Norman & Stacey 1910

Corner CABINETS Hanging

Wyman 1886

C. & R. Light 1881

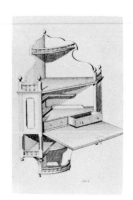

1881

Heal 1884

Heal 1884

G. Smith 1808

G. Smith 1808

Brown 1822

G. Smith 1826

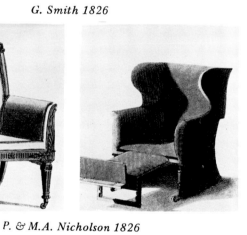

P. & M.A. Nicholson 1826

G. Smith 1826

T. King Modern Style Exemplified 1829

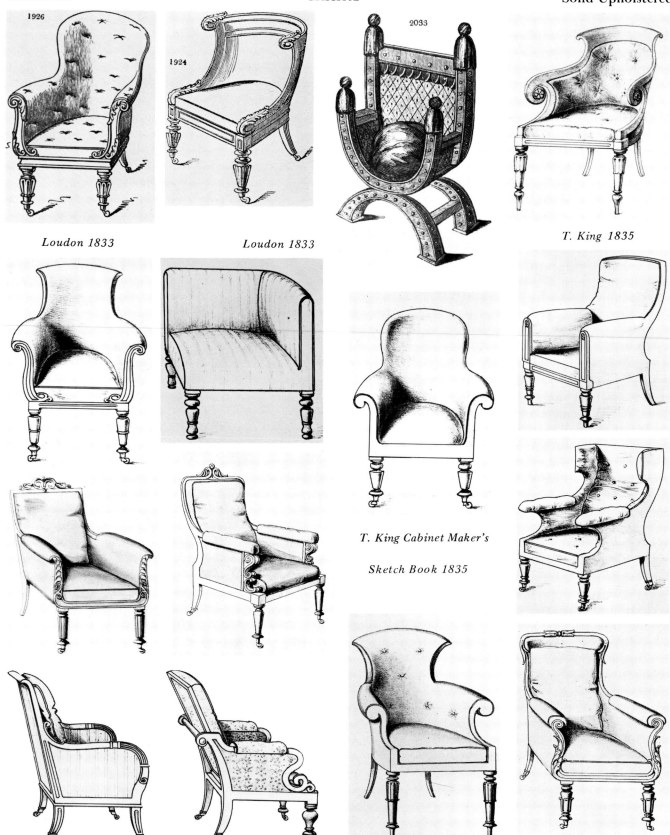

Loudon 1833

Loudon 1833

T. King 1835

T. King Cabinet Maker's

Sketch Book 1835

T. King 1840

T. King 1840

Whitaker 1847

Whitaker 1847

H. Wood 1848

W. Smee & Sons 1850

W. Smee & Sons 1850

W. Smee & Sons 1850

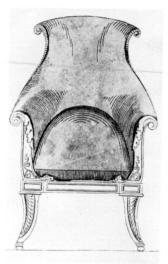

J. Taylor 1850   *J. Taylor 1850*

Lawford 1855

150

Lawford 1855

W. Blackie 1853

Booth 1864

Richard Charles 1866

Shoolbred 1876

151

Shoolbred 1876

W. Watt 1877

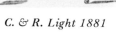

Yapp 1879

C. & R. Light 1881

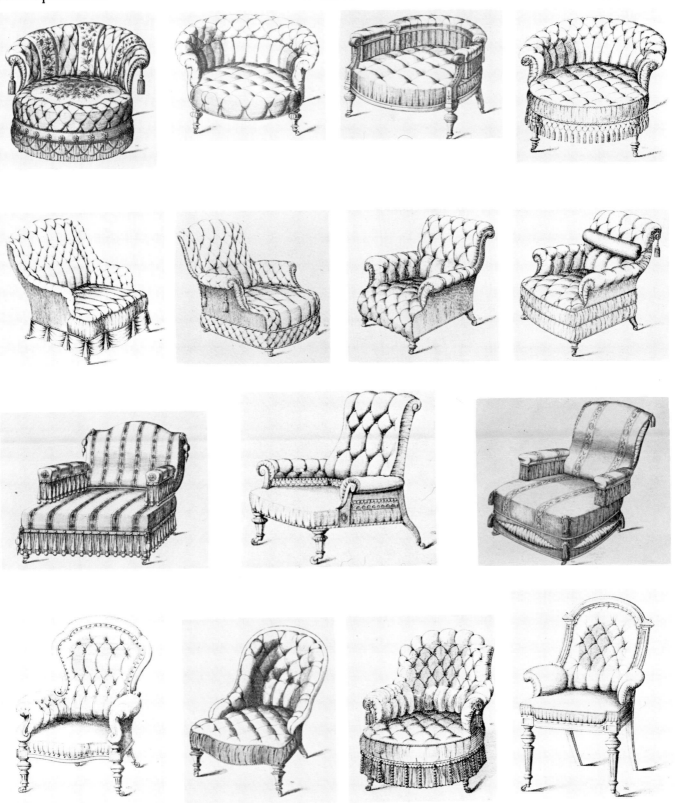

C. & R. Light 1881

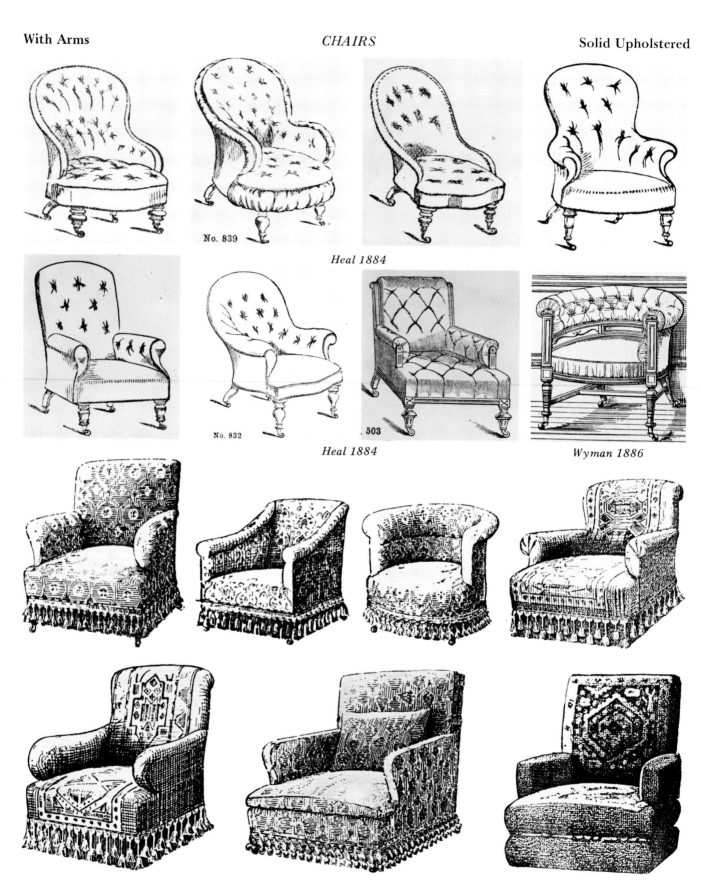

No. 839

Heal 1884

No. 832

503

Heal 1884

Wyman 1886

Liberty 1890

Norman & Stacey 1910

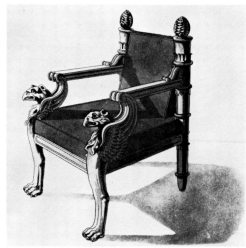

Sheraton Appendix 1802   *G. Smith 1808*

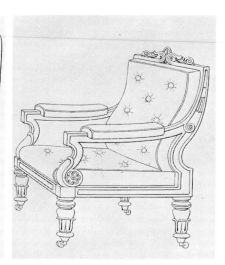

Whitaker 1825   *Modern Style Exemplified 1829*

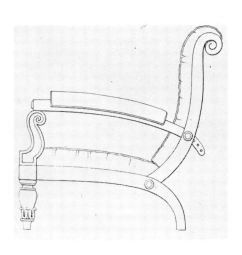

Modern Style

Exemplified 1829

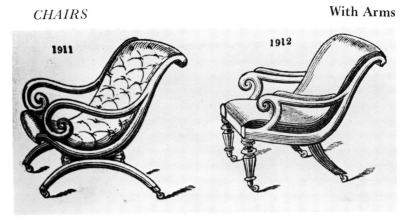

Loudon 1833

R. Bridgens 1838

T. King 1835

Pugin 1835

T. King 1840

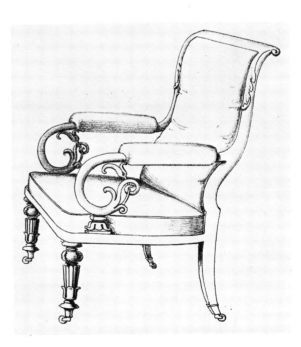

H. Wood 1848   *Whitaker 1847*

H. Wood 1848

J. Taylor 1850

W. Smee & Sons 1850

W. Smee & Sons 1850

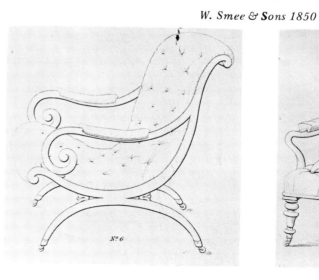

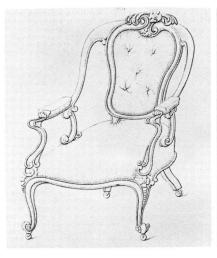

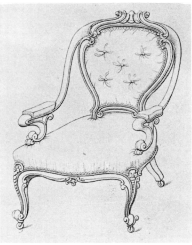

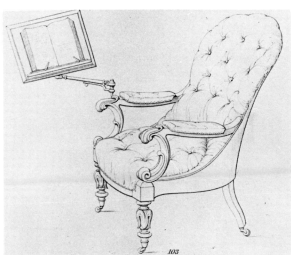

W. Smee & Sons 1850

Lawford 1855

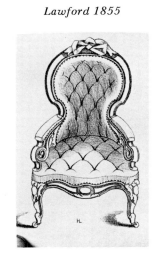

Lawford 1855

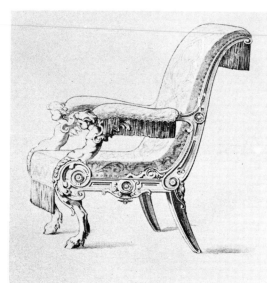

Braund 1858

Blackie 1853

Booth 1864

Richard Charles 1866

Shoolbred 1876

Shoolbred 1876

Shoolbred 1876

W. Watt 1877

Yapp 1879

Yapp 1879

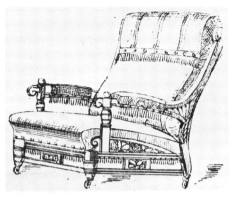

Jonquet 1879

C. & R. Light 1881

C. & R. Light 1881

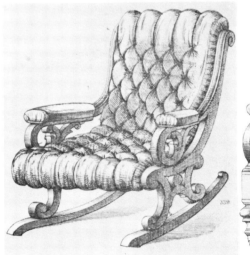

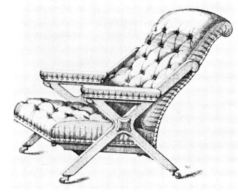

C. & R. Light 1881

C. & R. Light 1881

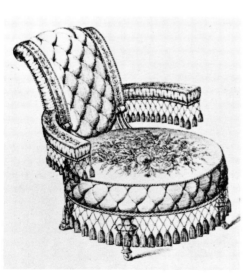

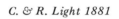

C. & R. Light 1881

506   501   500   No. 232

Heal 1884

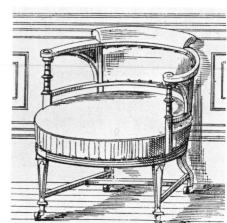

.507

Heal 1884   *Wyman 1886*

Liberty & Co. 1890   *Norman & Stacey 1910*

C. & R. Light 1881

C. & R. Light 1881

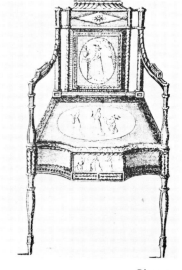

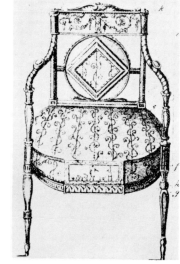

Sheraton Appendix 1802

G. Smith 1808

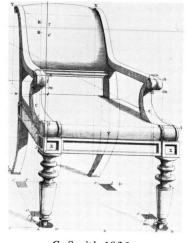

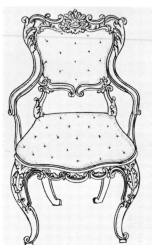

G. Smith 1826

T. King 1835

W. Toms 1840

H. Wood 1846

Whitaker 1847

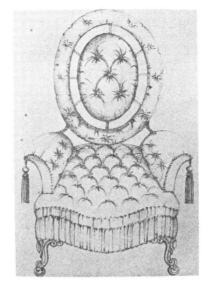

H. Wood 1848

H. Wood 1848

Lawford 1855

Lawford 1855

Braund 1858

Booth 1867

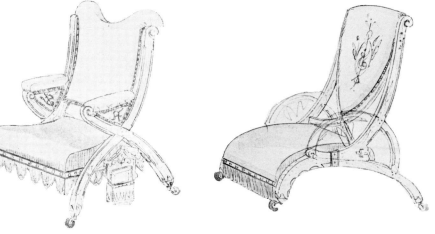

Booth 1864

Richard Charles 1866

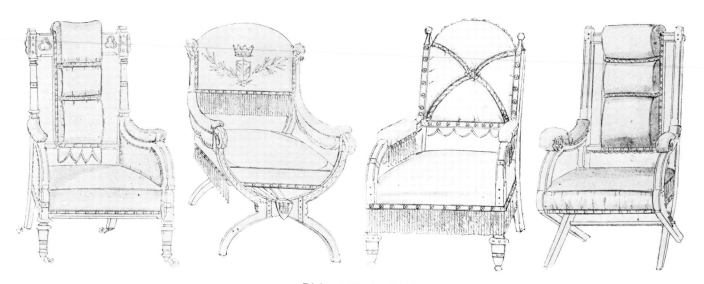

Richard Charles 1866

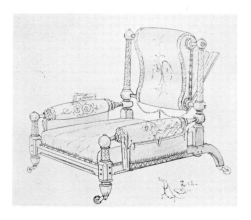

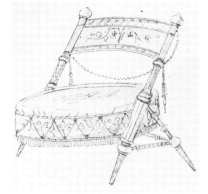

Richard Charles 1866

Wyman 1877

Wyman 1877

Jonquet 1879

Jonquet 1879

Yapp 1879

C. & R. Light 1881

C. & R. Light 1881

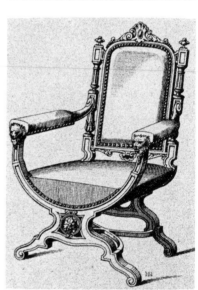

C. & R. Light 1881

C. & R. Light 1881

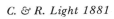

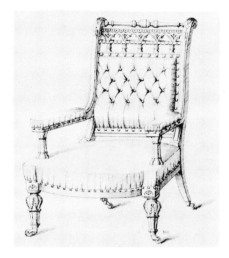

C. & R. Light 1881

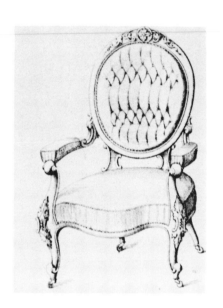

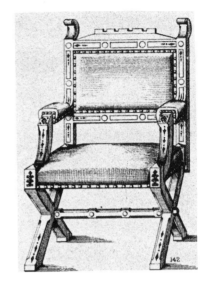

C. & R. Light 1881

C. & R. Light 1881

Heal 1884

Wyman 1886

Morris 1900

Norman & Stacey 1910

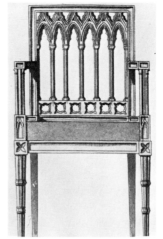

Sheraton Appendix 1802   *G. Smith 1808*

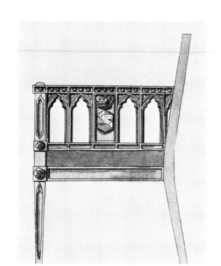
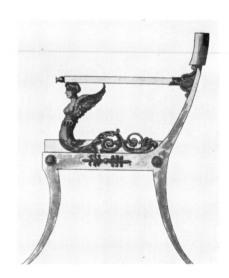

G. Smith 1808   *G. Smith 1808*

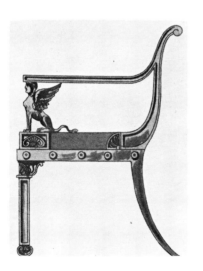
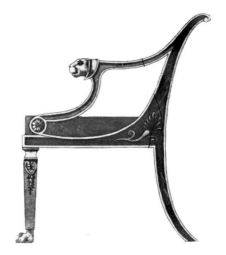

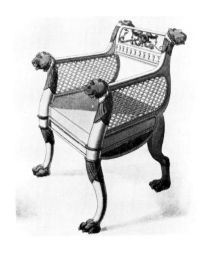

G. Smith 1808

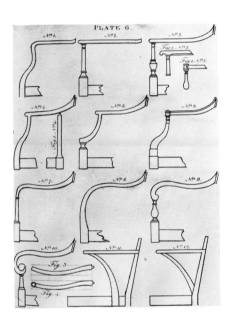

London Chairmakers 1823

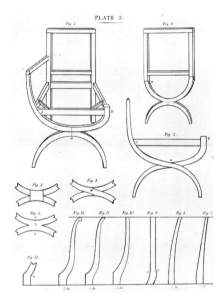

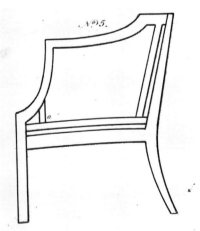

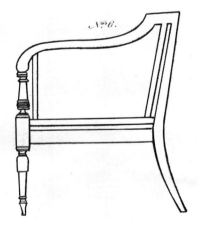

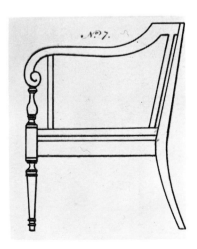

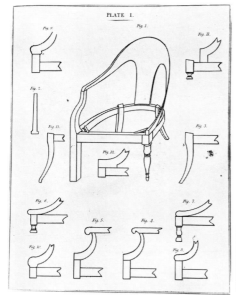

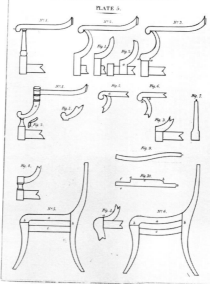

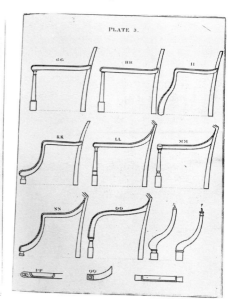

London Chairmakers 1823

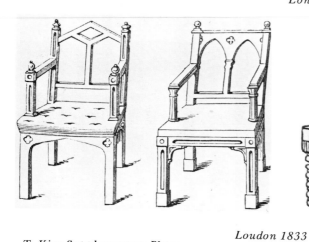

Modern Style Exemplified 1834

T. King Supplementary Plates

Loudon 1833

T. King 1840

T. King 1835

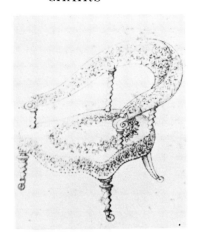

H. Wood 1848

H. Wood 1848

W. Smee & Sons 1850

J. Taylor 1850

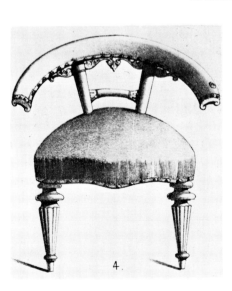

Booth 1864

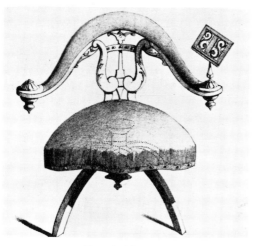

Booth 1864

Shoolbred 1876

W. Watt 1877

W. Watt 1877

Yapp 1879

C. & R. Light 1881

C. & R. Light 1881

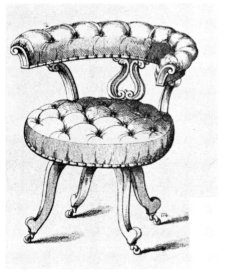

C. & R. Light 1881

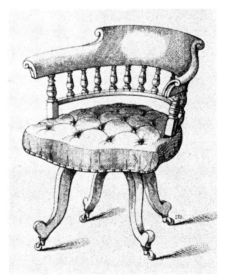

C. & R. Light 1881

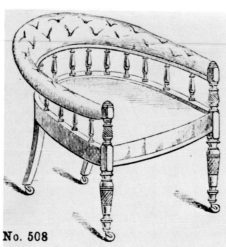

No. 508

Heal 1884

No. 233

No. 228

al 1884

Norman & Stacey 1910

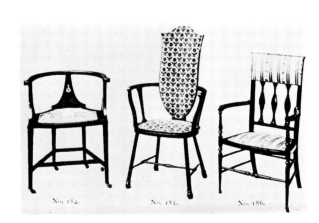

No. 184. No. 185. No. 186.

Norman & Stacey 1910

Norman & Stacey 1910

183

P. & M.A. Nicholson 1826   *Whitaker 1825*   *Loudon 1833*   *T. King 1835*

W. Smee & Sons 1850   *Lawford 1855*

Braund 1858   *W. Blackie 1853*

W. Blackie 1853

W. Blackie 1853

W. Blackie 1853

W. Blackie 1853

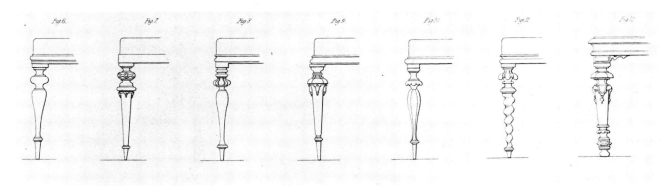

W. Blackie 1853

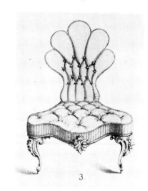

Booth 1864

Richard Charles 1866

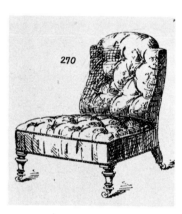

Shoolbred 1876

Shoolbred 1876

W. Watt 1877   *Wyman 1877*   *Jonquet 1879*

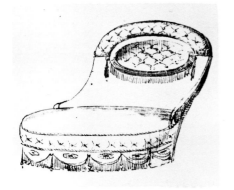

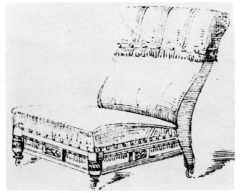

Jonquet 1879   *Yapp 1879*

C. & R. Light 1881

C. & R. Light 1881

C. & R. Light 1881

C. & R. Light 1881

C. & R. Light 1881

C. & R. Light 1881

C. & R. Light 1881

C. & R. Light 1881

No. 505   No. 221   502

Heal & Son 1884

Liberty 1890

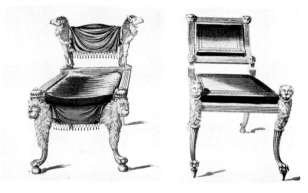

Sheraton Encyclopaedia 1804   *G. Smith 1808*

P. & M.A. Nicholson 1826

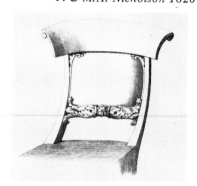

G. Smith 1826

G. Smith 1826

Bridgens 1838

Bridgens 1838

Loudon 1833   *T. King 1835*

T. King 1835

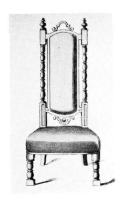
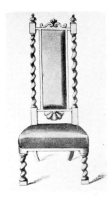

T. King 1835

T. King 1835

T. King 1835

T. K. 'g 1840

W. Toms 18·

Whitaker 1847

Whitaker 1847

H. Wood 1848

H. Wood 1848

 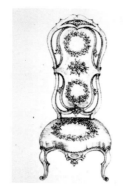  

H. Wood 1848

H. Wood 1848

   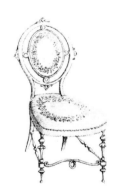

H. Wood 1848

J. Taylor 1850

194

W. Smee & Sons 1850

W. Smee & Sons 1850

W. Smee & Sons 1850

W. Smee & Sons 1850   *Lawford 1855*

195

Braund 1858

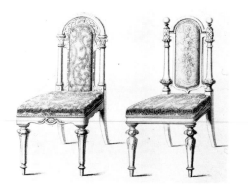

W. Blackie 1853

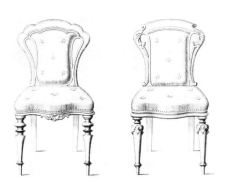

W. Blackie 1853

W. Blackie 1853

W. Blackie 1853

W. Blackie 1853

W. Blackie 1853

W. Blackie 1853

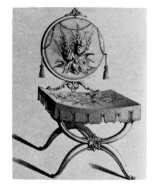

Booth 1864

Booth 1864

Booth 1864

Booth 1864

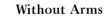

Richard Charles 1866

Richard Charles 1866

Richard Charles 1866

Richard Charles 1866

Shoolbred 1876

Shoolbred 1876

Shoolbred 1876

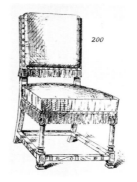

Shoolbred 1876

Shoolbred 1876

Shoolbred 1876

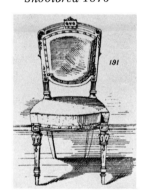

Shoolbred 1876

Shoolbred 1876

J. Talbert 1876   *W. Watt 1877*   *Wyman 1877*

Wyman 1877

Wyman 1877

Wyman 1877

Wyman 1877   *Wyman 1877*
Jonquet 1879

Yapp 1879

Yapp 1879

Yapp 1879

C. & R. Light 1881

C. & R. Light 1881

C. & R. Light 1881

C. & R. Light 1881

C. & R. Light 1881

C. & R. Light 1881

C. & R. Light 1881

C. & R. Light 1881

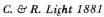

C. & R. Light 1881

C. & R. Light 1881

C. & R. Light 1881

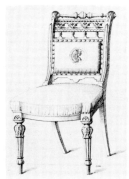

C. & R. Light 1881

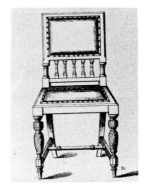

C. & R. Light 1881

C. & R. Light 1881

C. & R. Light 1881

C. & R. Light 1881

207

C. & R. Light 1881

C. & R. Light 1881

C. & R. Light 1881

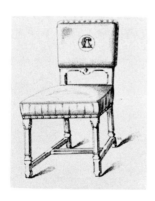

C.& R. Light 1881

C. & R. Light 1881

Heal 1884

Heal 1884   *Wyman 1886*

Wyman 1886

Liberty 1890

Norman & Stacey 1910

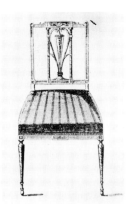
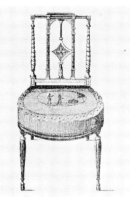
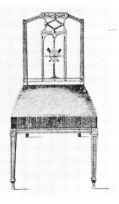

Sheraton Appendix 1802

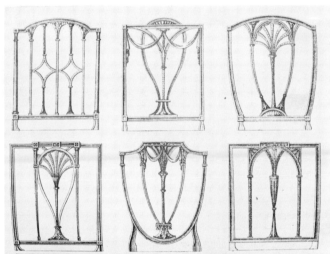

Sheraton Appendix 1802

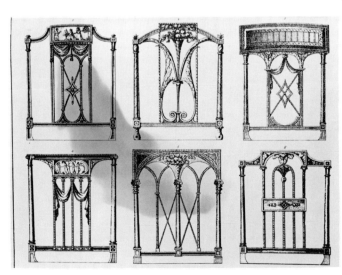
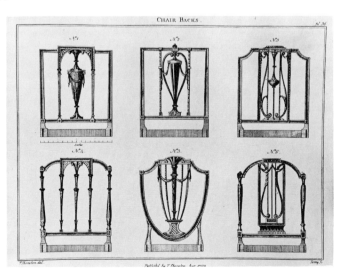

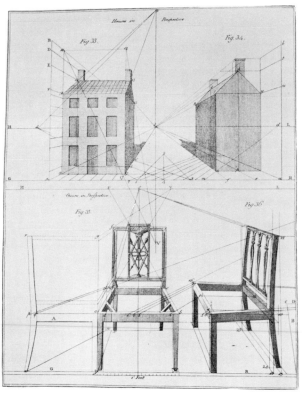

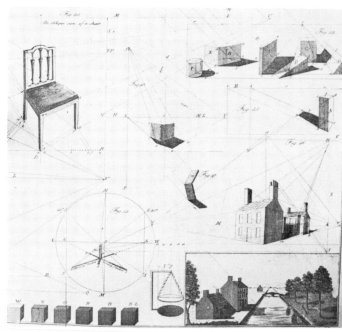

Sheraton Appendix 1802

Sheraton Encyclopaedia 1804

G. Smith 1808

G. Smith 1808

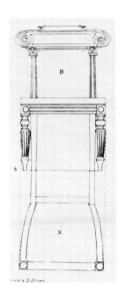

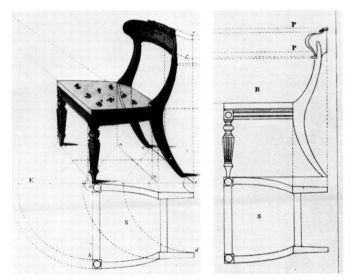

Brown 1822

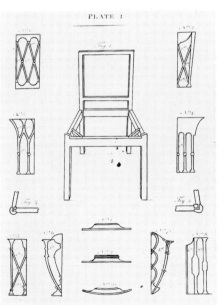

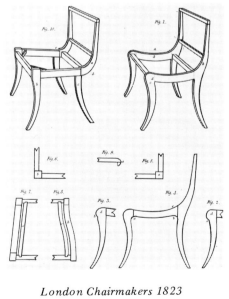

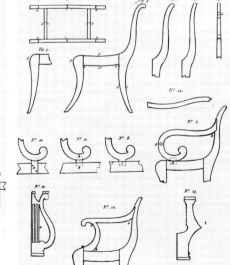

London Chairmakers 1823

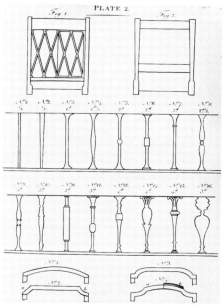

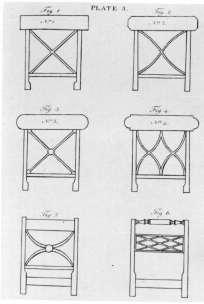

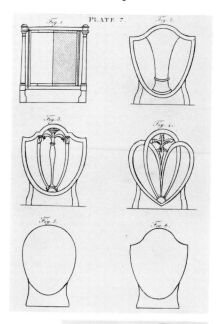

London Chairmakers 1823

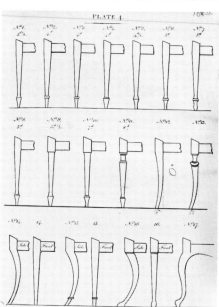

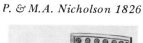

P. & M.A. Nicholson 1826

P. & M.A. Nicholson 1826

P. & M.A. Nicholson 1826

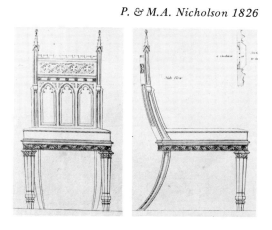

G. Smith's Guide 1826

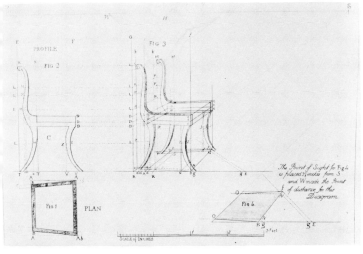

G. Smith's Guide 1826

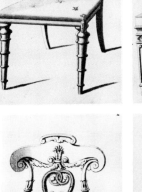

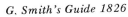

G. Smith's Guide 1826

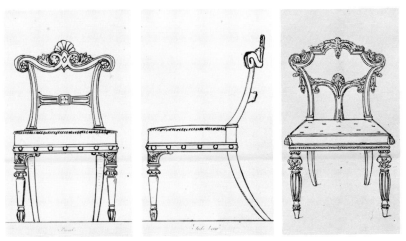

Whitaker 1825

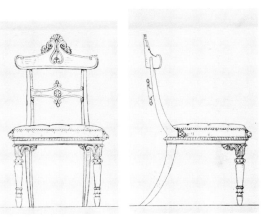

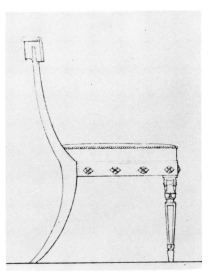

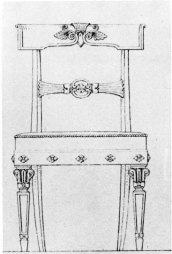

Whitaker 1825

Modern Style Exemplified 1829

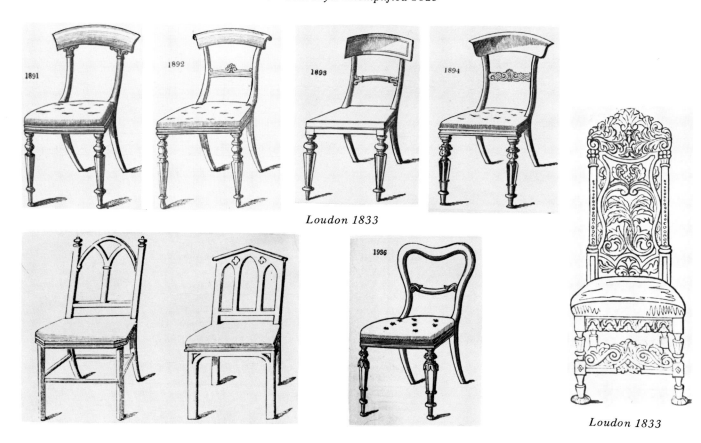

Loudon 1833

Loudon 1833

Weale 1834

T. King Cabinet Maker's Sketch Book 1835

T. King Cabinet Maker's Sketch Book 1835

LIBRARY CHAIRS.

T. King Elizabethan and Louis XIV Styles 1835

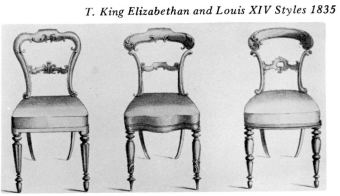

T. King Elizabethan and
Louis XIV Styles 1835

217

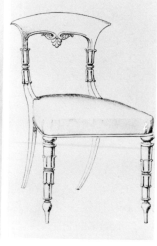

Bridgens 1838 *T. King 1840*

T. King 1840

T. King 1840

W. Toms 1840

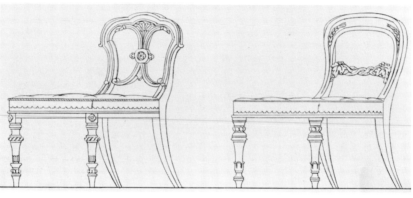

Whitaker 1847

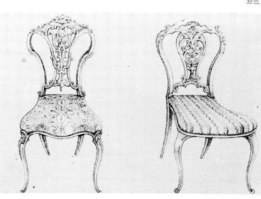

H. Wood Supplement 1848

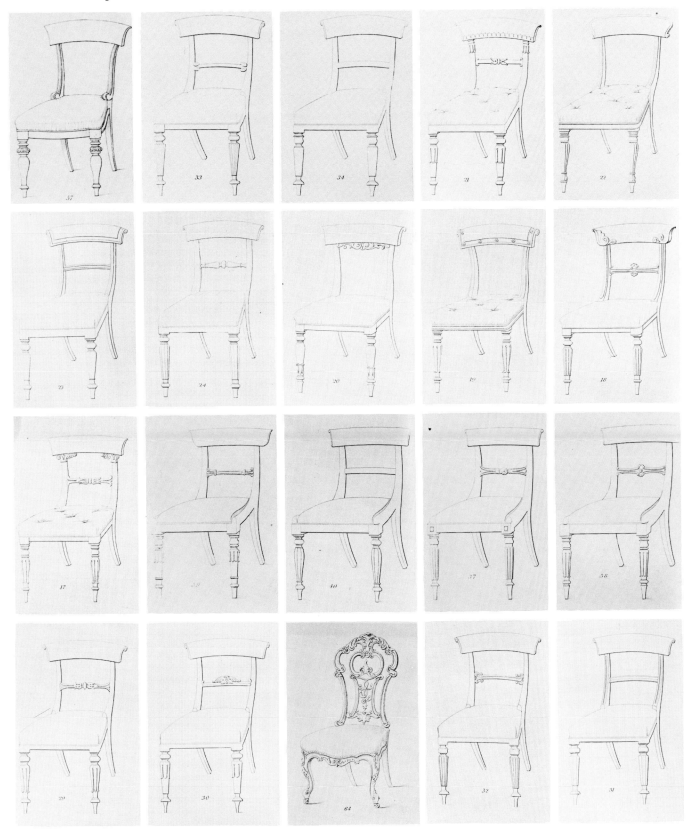

W. Smee & Sons 1850

W. Smee & Sons 1850

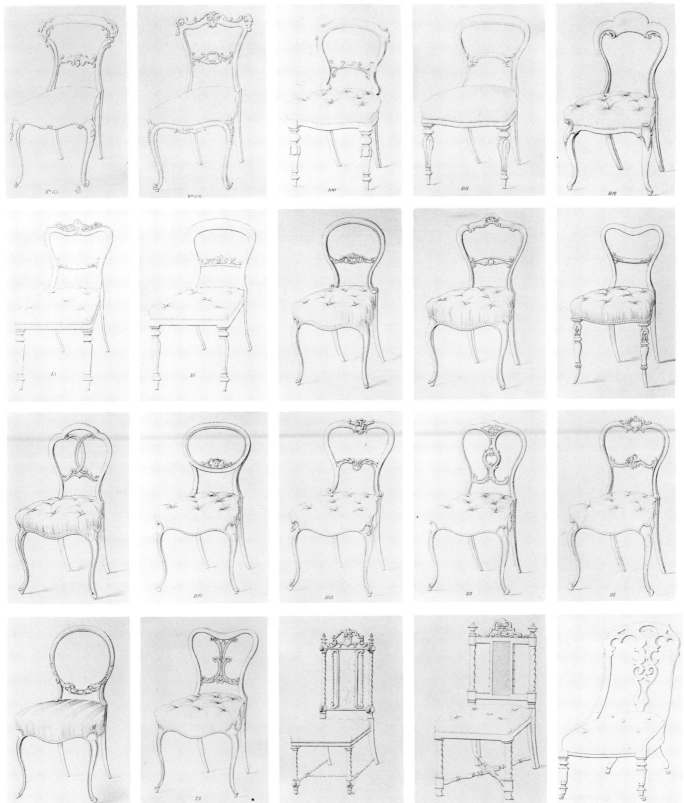

W. Smee & Sons 1850

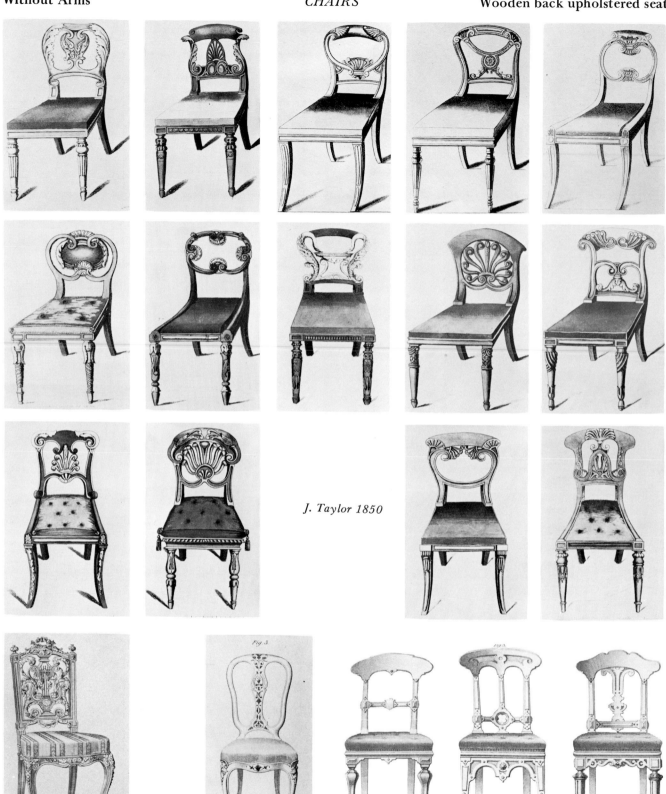

J. Taylor 1850

Braund 1858 *W. Blackie 1853*

W. Blackie 1853

Richard Charles 1866

*Shoolbred
1876*

225

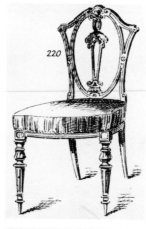

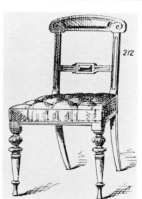

Shoolbred 1876

W. Watt 1877

226

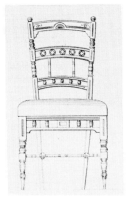

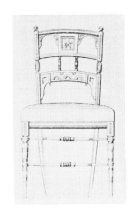

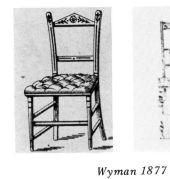

Wyman 1877

Jonquet 1879

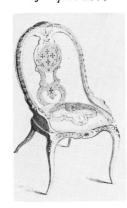

Yapp 1879

227

Yapp 1879

C. & R. Light 1881

C. & R. Light 1881

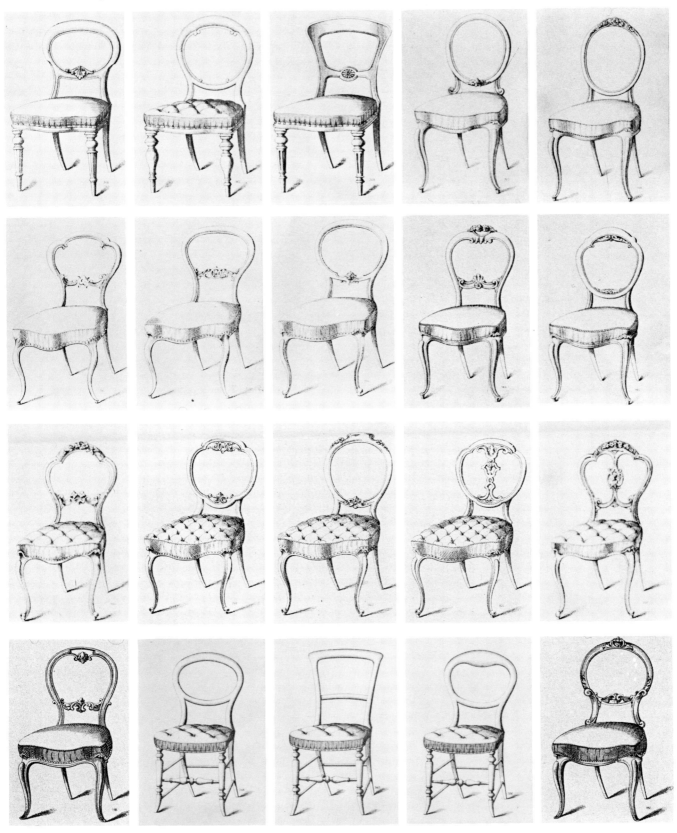

C. & R. Light 1881

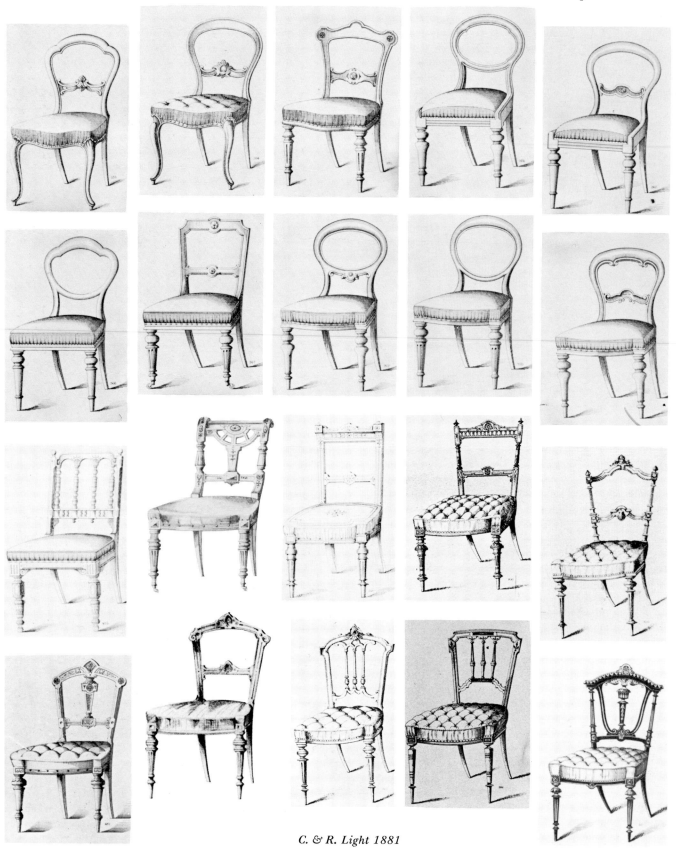

C. & R. Light 1881

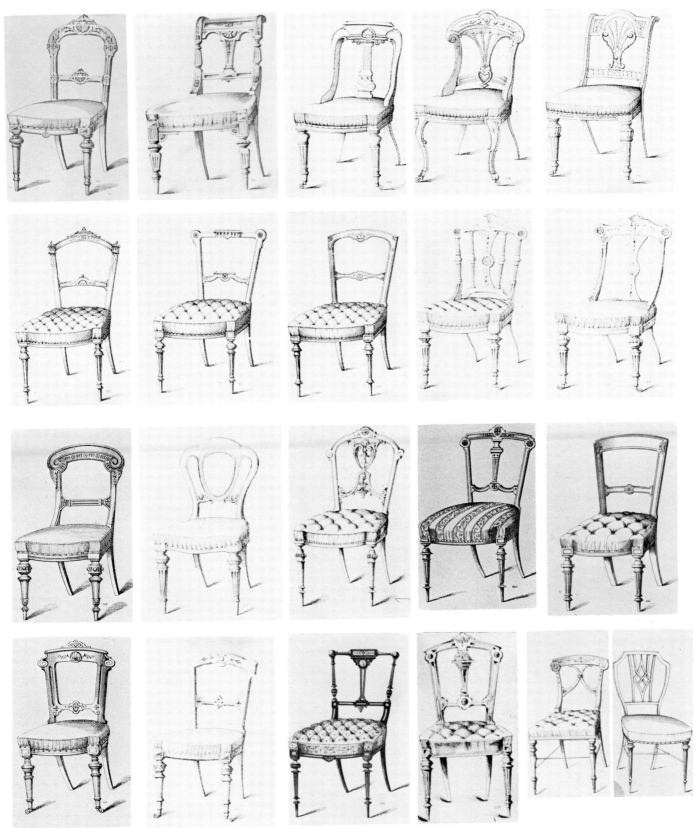

C. & R. Light 1881

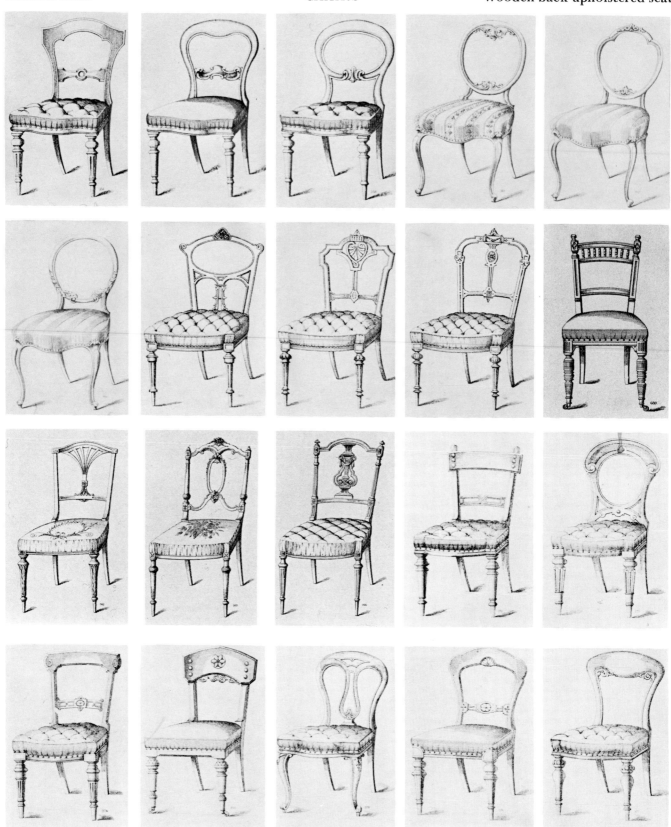

C. & R. Light 1881

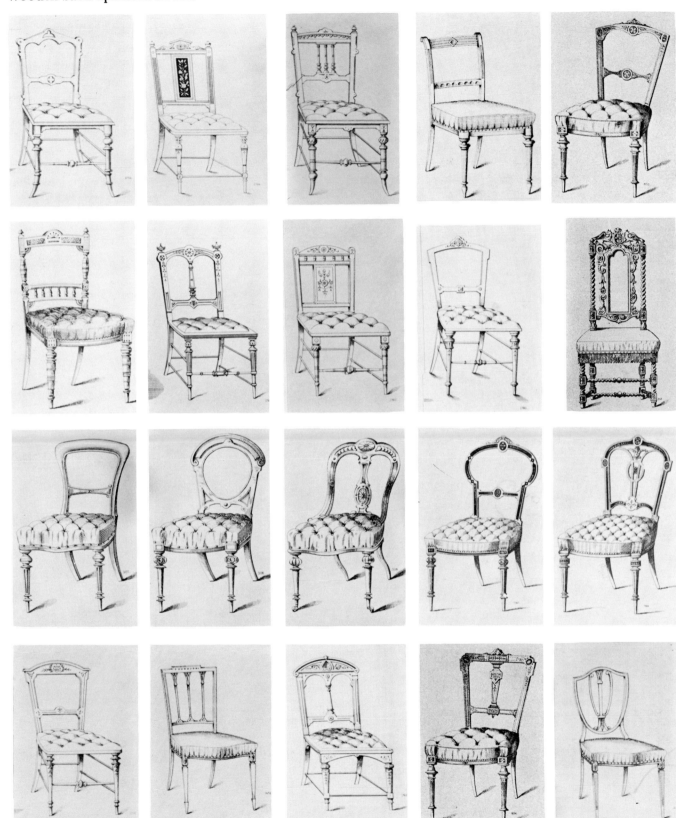

C. & R. Light 1881

Heal & Son 1884

Wyman 1886

Norman & Stacey 1910

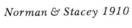

Norman & Stacey 1910

235

P. & M.A. Nicholson 1826   *G. Smith 1826*

G. Smith 1808

Modern Style Exemplified 1829

*Modern Style
Exemplified 1829*

Loudon 1833

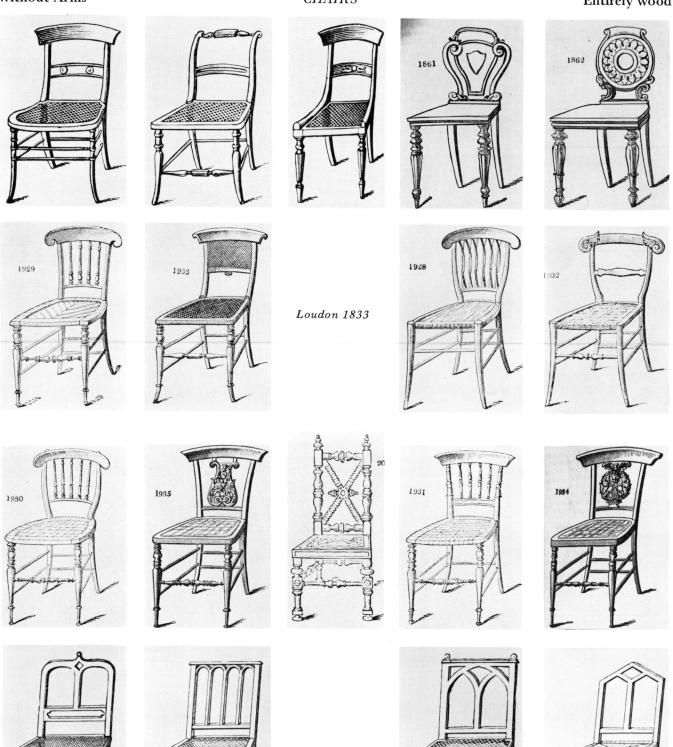

Loudon 1833

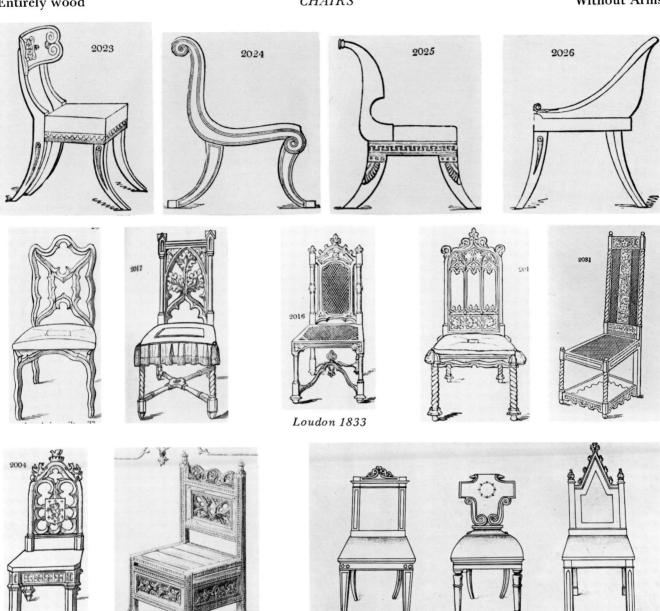

Loudon 1833

Loudon 1833

T. King Cabinet Maker's Sketch Book 1835

T. King Cabinet Maker's Sketch Book 1835

Bridgens 1838

T. King 1840

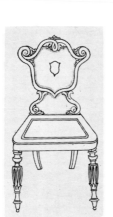

W. Toms 1840   *W. Toms 1840*   *Whitaker 1847*

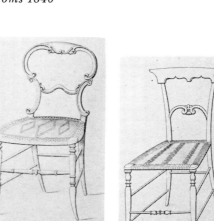

H. Wood 1848

W. Smee & Sons 1850

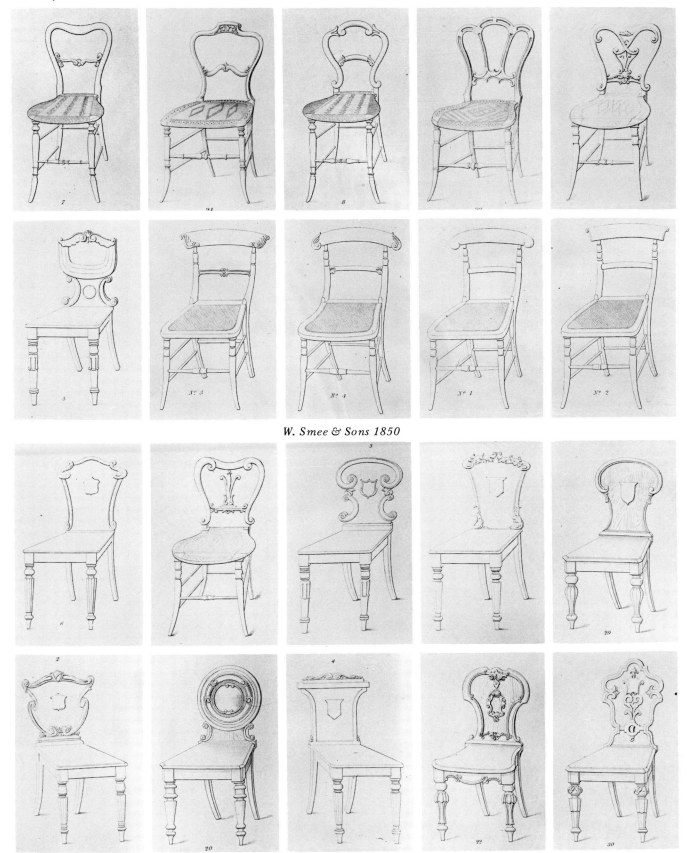

W. Smee & Sons 1850

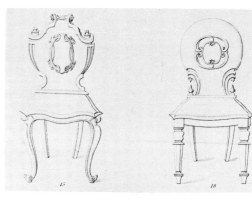

W. Smee & Sons 1850

W. Blackie 1853

Booth 1864

57.

7

2

54

5

6

8

11

9

55.

58.

10

Booth 1864

Shoolbred 1876   *W. Watt 1877*

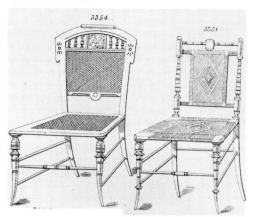

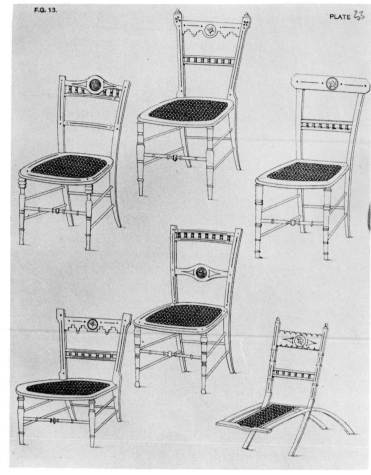

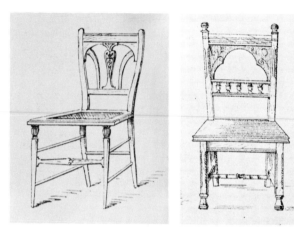

Wyman 1877

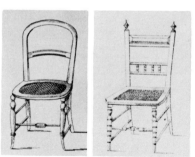

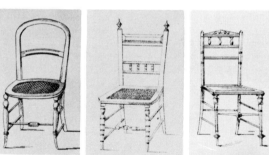

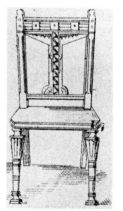

Wyman 1877

Wyman 1877   *Jonquet 1879*   *Yapp 1879*

C. & R. Light 1881

C. & R. Light 1881

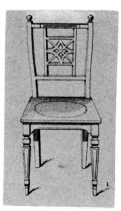
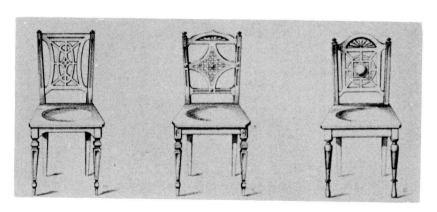

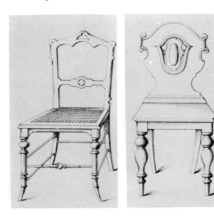
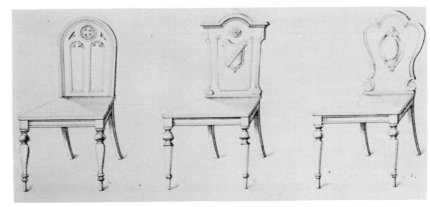

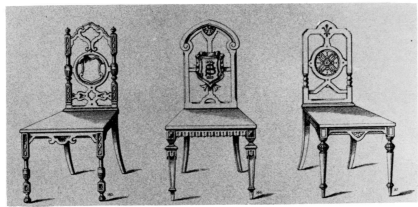

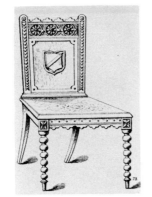

C. & R. Light
1881

C. & R. Light 1881

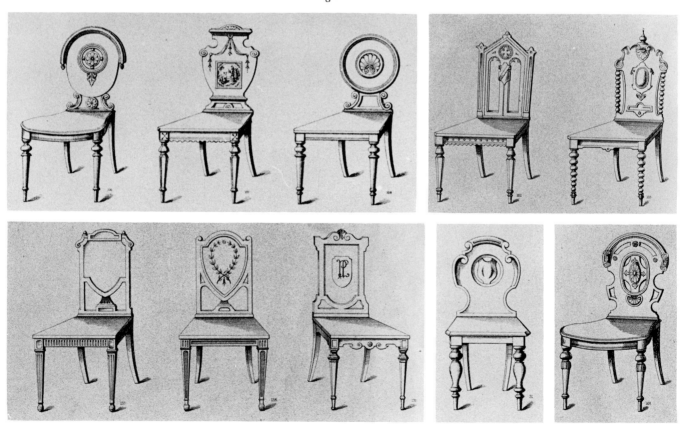

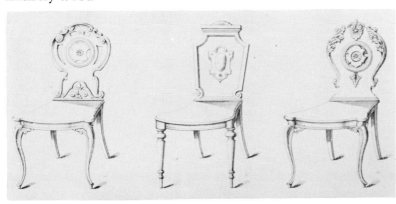

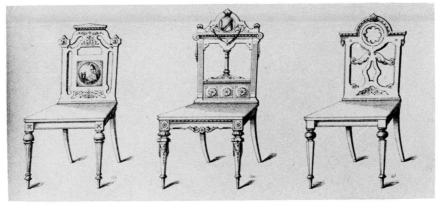

C. & R. Light 1881

Heal & Son 1884

Heal 1884

Wyman 1886

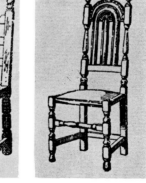

Liberty 1890

Liberty 1890

Norman & Stacey 1910

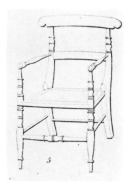

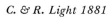

C. & R. Light 1881

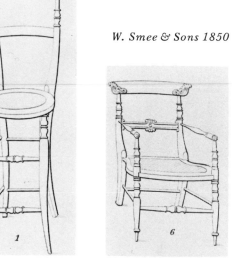

W. Smee & Sons 1850

W. Smee & Sons 1850

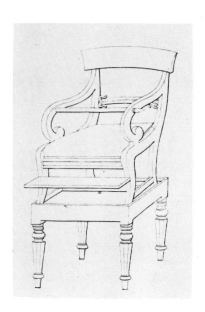

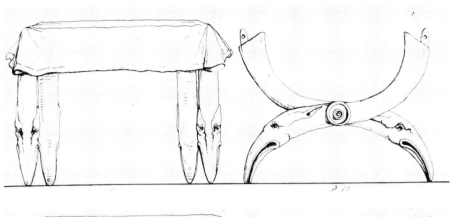

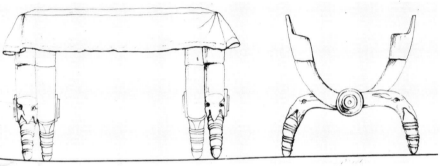

C. Tatham 1826

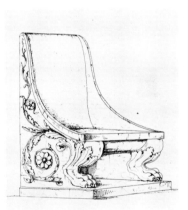

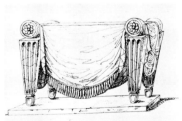

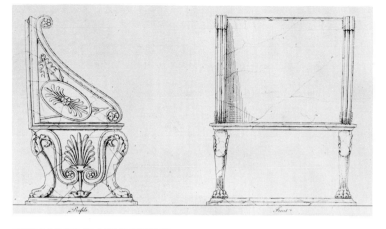

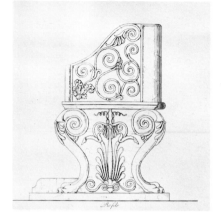

C. Tatham 1826

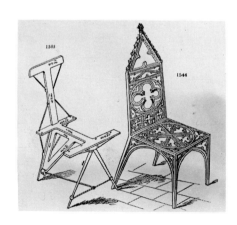

Loudon 1833

London Chairmakers 1823

Loudon 1833   *Loudon 1833*

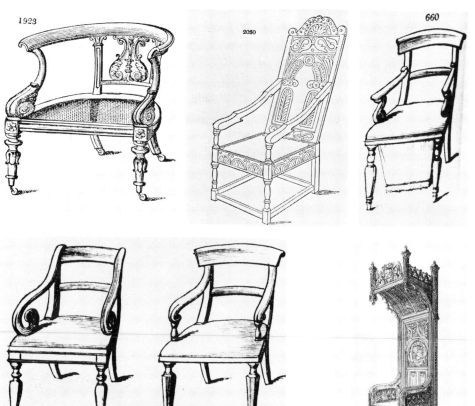

1923

2030

660

2013

Loudon 1833

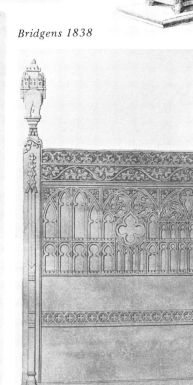

Bridgens 1838

Pugin 1835

Bridgens 1838

W. Watt 1877

J. Taylor 1850   *W. Smee & Sons 1850*

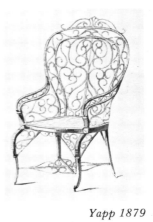

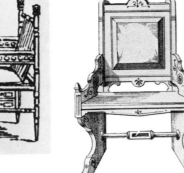

W. Watt 1877

Yapp 1879

Wyman 1886

Yapp 1879

C. & R. Light 1881

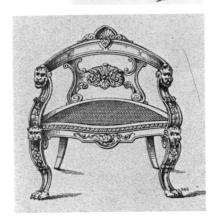

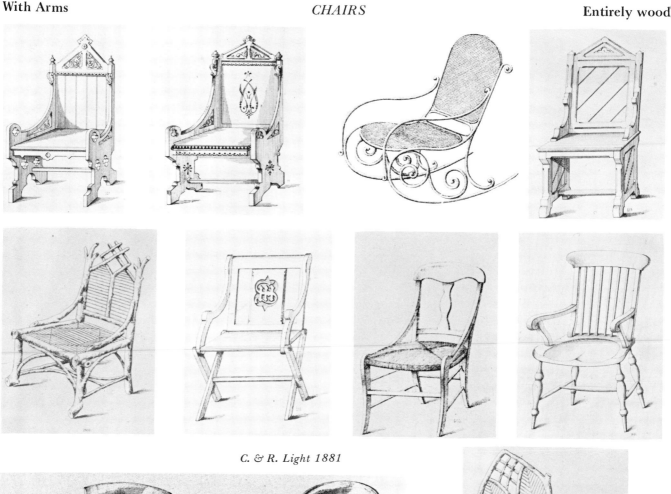

C. & R. Light 1881

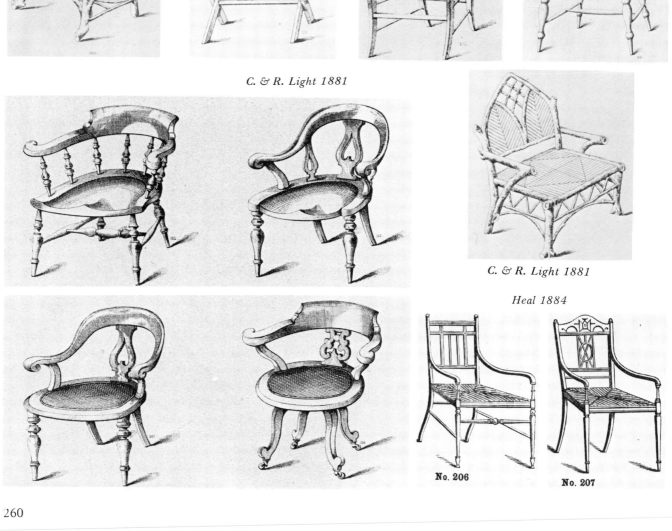

C. & R. Light 1881

Heal 1884

No. 206   No. 207

260

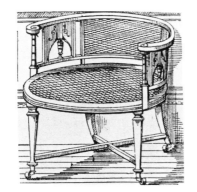

Heal 1884

Wyman 1886

Liberty 1890

Man's Chair (*black*).
Price **19/6**.

Norman & Stacey 1910

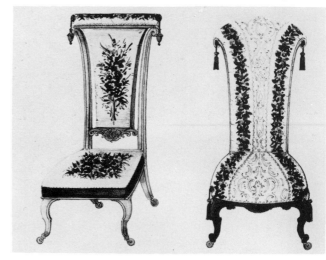

T. King 1835

Pugin 1835

H. Wood 1846

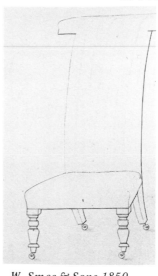

H. Wood 1846

H. Wood Supplement 1848

W. Smee & Sons 1850

Lawford 1855

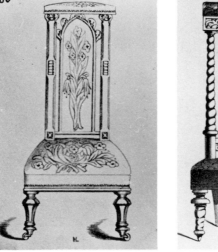

Lawford 1855

Booth 1864

Booth 1864

129

Shoolbred 1876

Yapp 1879

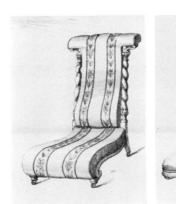

C. & R. Light 1881

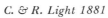

C. & R. Light 1881

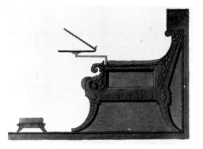

G. Smith 1808

London Chairmakers 1823

Loudon 1833

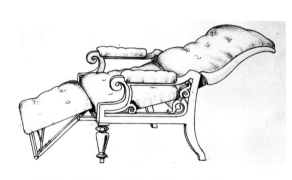

Loudon 1833

Loudon 1833

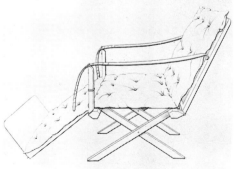

T. King Cabinet Maker's Sketch Book 1835

T. King Supplementary Plates

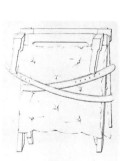

T. King 1835

W. Smee & Sons 1850

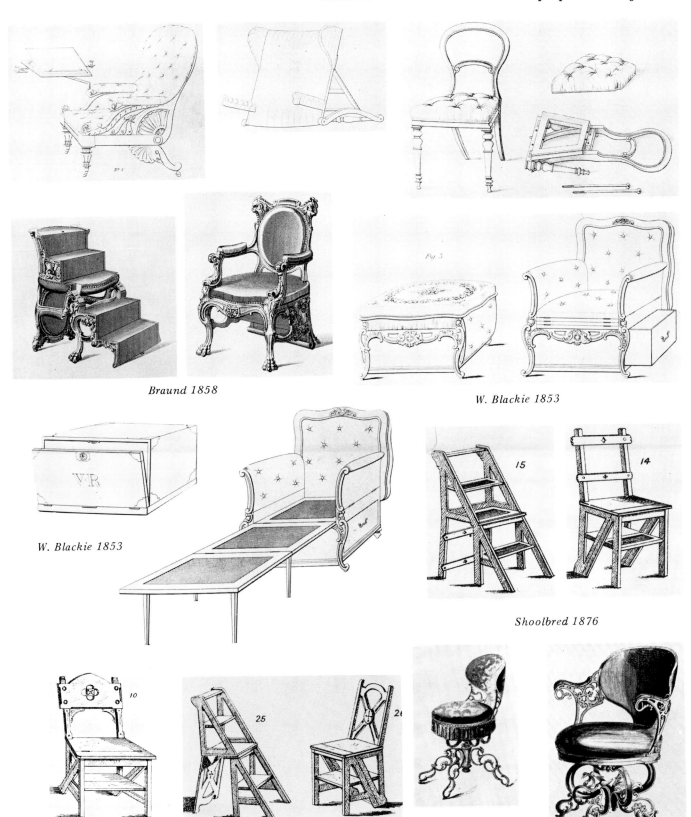

Braund 1858

W. Blackie 1853

W. Blackie 1853

Shoolbred 1876

Shoolbred 1876

Yapp 1879

Yapp 1879

C. & R. Light 1881

C. & R. Light 1881

C. & R. Light 1881   *Heal 1884*   *Norman & Stacey 1910*

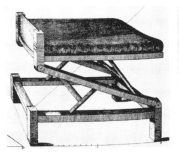

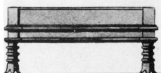

G. Smith 1808

Sheraton 1802

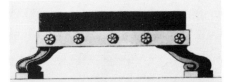

G. Smith 1808

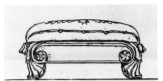

G. Smith 1808   *Brown 1822*   *Whitaker 1825*

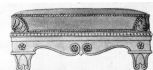

P. & M.A. Nicholson 1826

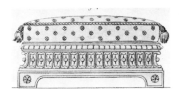

P. & M.A. Nicholson 1826   *G. Smith 1826*

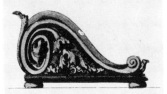

G. Smith 1826   *Loudon 1833*

267

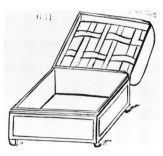
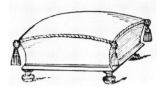

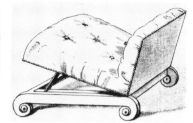

Loudon 1833

T. King Supplementary Plates

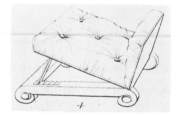

T. King Supplementary Plates

T. King 1835

T. King 1835

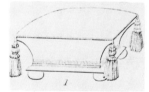
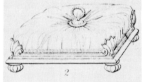
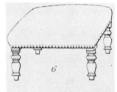
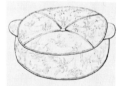
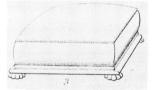

W. Smee & Sons 1850

W. Smee & Sons 1850

J. Taylor 1850

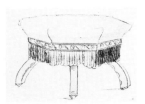

Richard Charles 1866

Wyman 1877

Yapp 1879

W. Watt 1877

C. & R. Light 1881

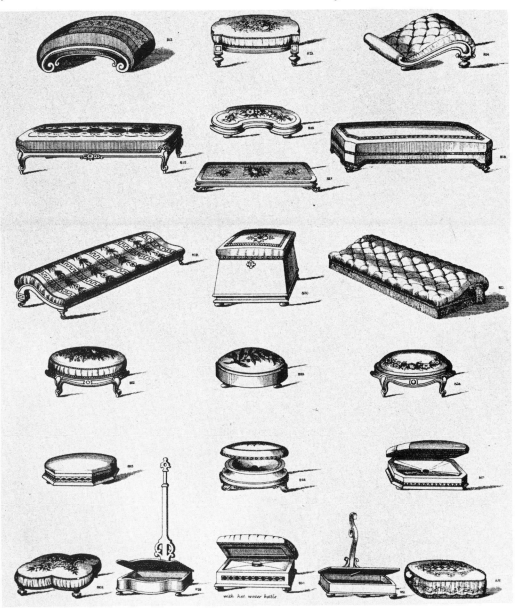

C. & R. Light 1881

with hot water bottle

P. & M.A. Nicholson 1826

G. Smith's Guide 1826

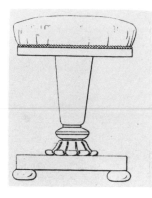

Loudon 1833

G. Smith's Guide 1826

T. King Supplementary Plates

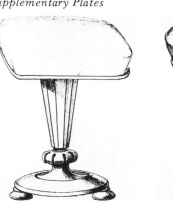

T. King Supplementary Plates

T. King Cabinet Maker's Sketch Book 1835

T. King 1835

W. Smee & Sons 1850

W. Smee & Sons 1850

W. Smee & Sons 1850

J. Taylor 1850

J. Taylor 1850

Blackie 1853

271

Blackie 1853

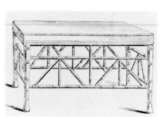

W. Watt 1877

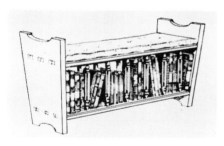

Heal 1884

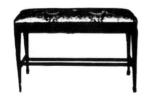

Morris 1900

Norman & Stacey 1910

Norman & Stacey 1910

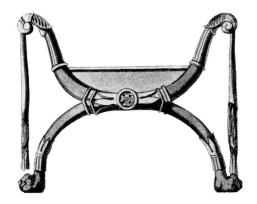

G. Smith 1808

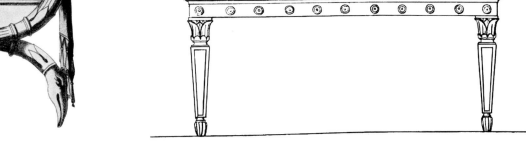

G. Smith 1808

Whitaker 1825

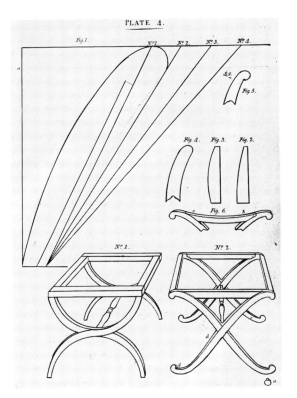

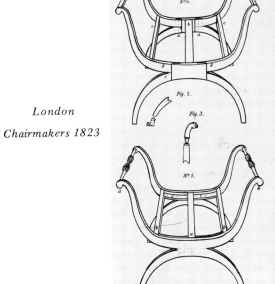

London

Chairmakers 1823

273

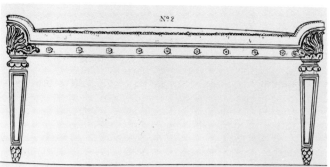
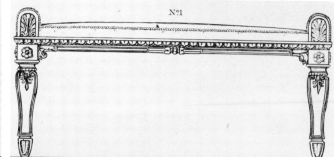

Whitaker 1825

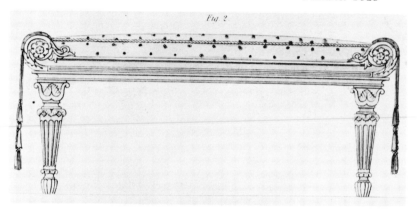

P. & M.A. Nicholson 1826   *T. King Elizabethan and Louis XIV Styles 1835*

T. King Elizabethan and Louis XIV Styles 1835

T. King Elizabethan and Louis XIV Styles 1835

Loudon 1833

H. Wood 1846

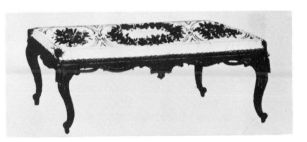

H. Wood 1846

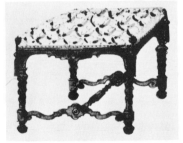

Whitaker 1847

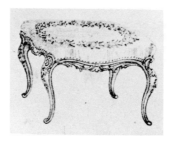

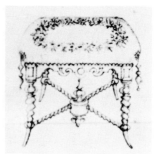

H. Wood Supplement 1848

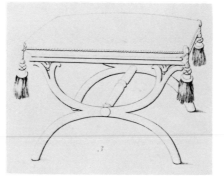

H. Wood Supplement 1848

W. Smee & Sons 1850

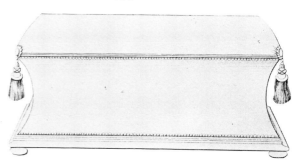

W. Smee & Sons 1850

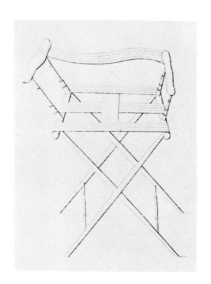
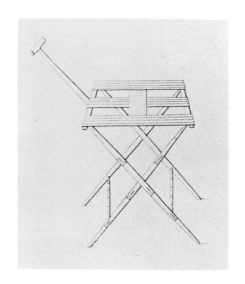
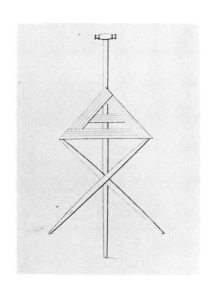

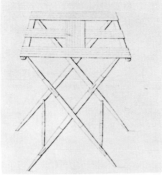

W. Smee & Sons 1850

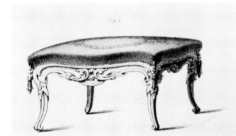

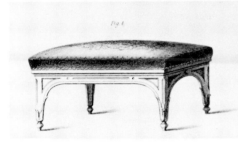

W. Blackie 1853

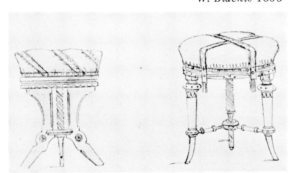

Richard Charles 1866

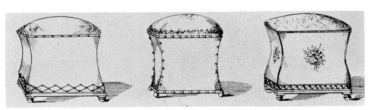
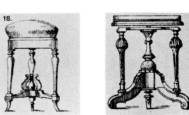

Wyman 1877

Yapp 1879

C. & R. Light 1881

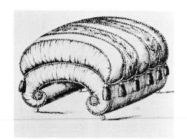

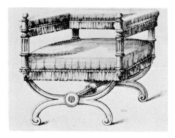

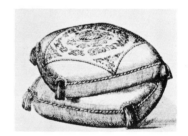

C. & R. Light 1881

C. & R. Light 1881

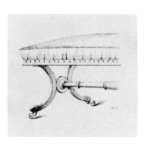
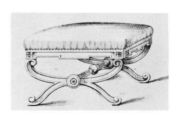

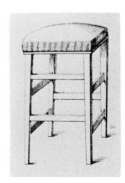

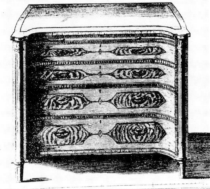

G. Smith 1808

Sheraton Appendix 1802

G. Smith's Guide 1826

Bridgens 1838

Loudon 1833

W. Smee & Sons 1850

Whitaker 1847

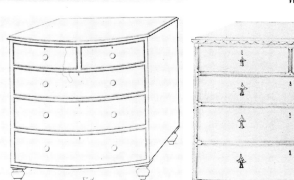

W. Smee & Sons 1850

Shoolbred 1876

W. Smee & Sons 1850

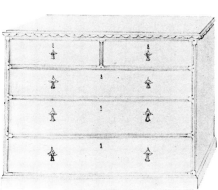

Richard Charles 1866

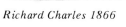

Wyman 1877

Jonquet 1879

C. & R. Light 1881

Maddox 1882

Maddox 1882

Maddox 1882

Norman & Stacey 1910

G. Smith 1808

Loudon 1833

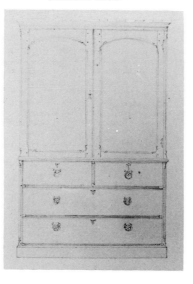

Richard Charles 1866

Booth 1864

High without stand

With drawers

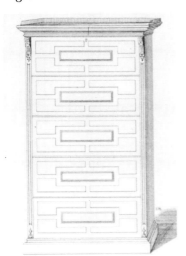

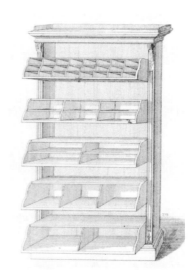

C. & R. Light 1881

High with stand

CHESTS

With drawers

Norman & Stacey 1910

Morris 1900

283

W. Smee & Sons 1850

J. Taylor 1850

J. Taylor 1850

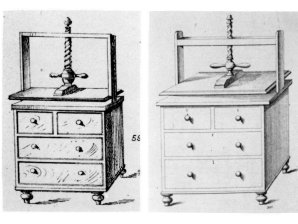

Shoolbred 1876   *C. & R. Light 1881*

C. & R. Light 1881

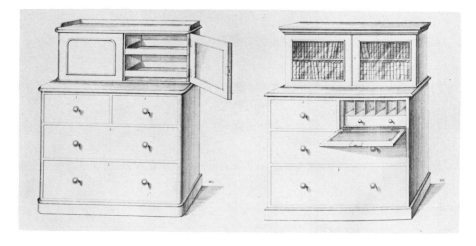

C. & R. Light 1881   *C. & R. Light 1881*

G. Smith 1808

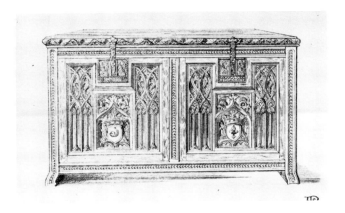

Pugin 1835

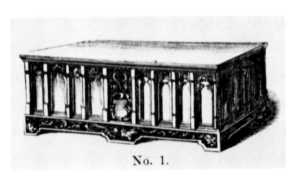

Yapp 1879

J. Talbert 1876

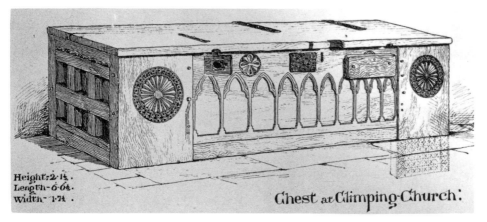

J. Talbert 1876

C. & R. Light 1881

Bridgens 1838

G. Smith 1826

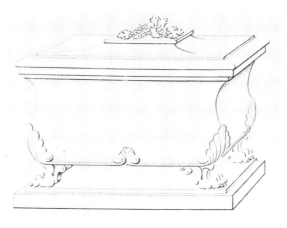

*W. Smee & Sons
1850*

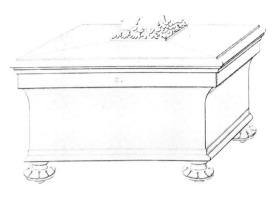

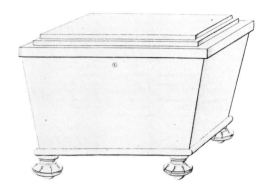

W. Smee & Sons 1850

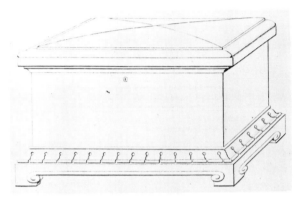

W. Smee & Sons 1850   *J. Taylor 1850*

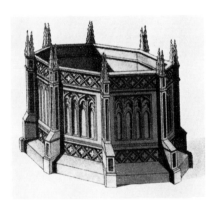

J. Taylor 1850

VENETIAN COFFER, in Chestnut-wood, in the Cinque-cento style. Date about 1560.

Yapp 1879

Morris 1890

J. Taylor 1850

C. & R. Light 1881

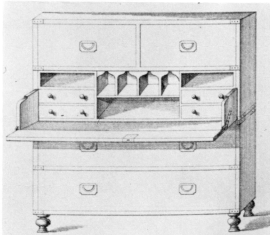

P. & M.A. Nicholson 1826

W. Smee & Sons 1850

C. & R. Light 1881

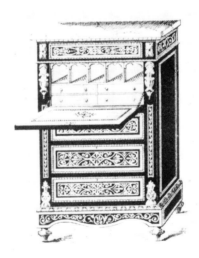

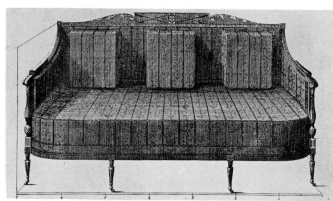

Sheraton 1802

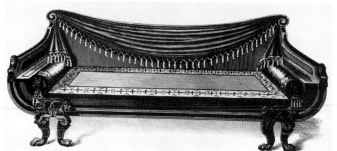

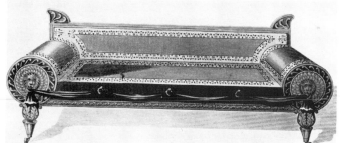

Sheraton Encyclopaedia 1804

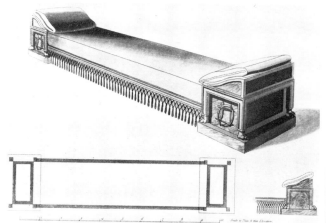

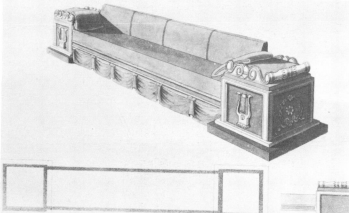

G. Smith 1808

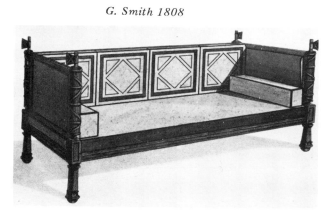

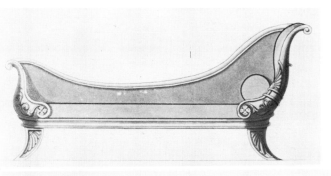

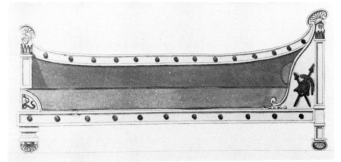

G. Smith 1808

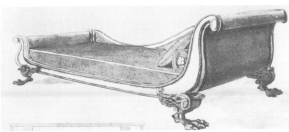

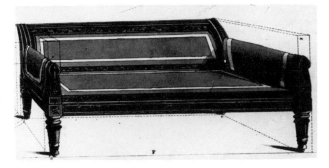

Brown 1822

G. Smith 1808

Brown 1822

London Chairmakers 1823

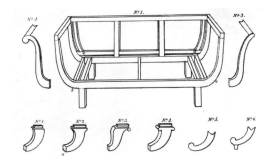

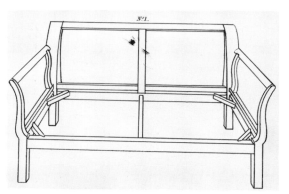

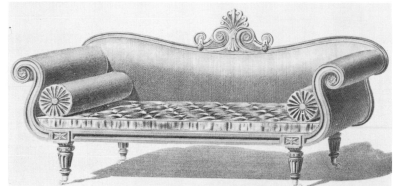

London Chairmakers 1823

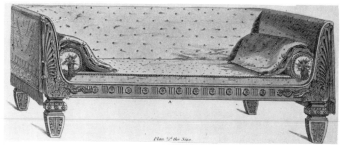

P. & M.A. Nicholson 1826

G. Smith's Guide 1826

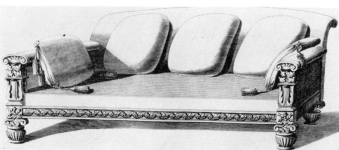

G. Smith's Guide 1826

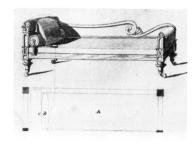

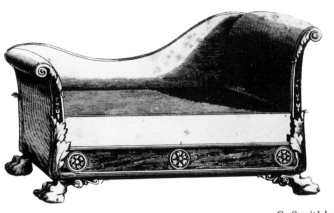

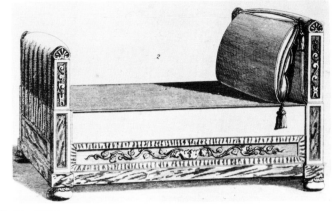

G. Smith's Guide 1826

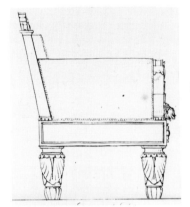

Whitaker 1825

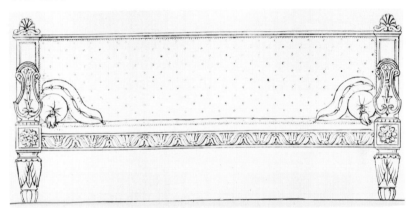

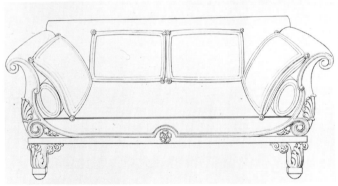

T. King Supplementary Plates

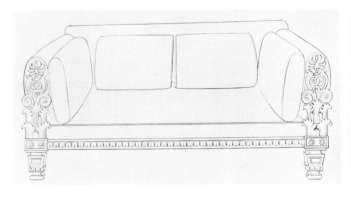

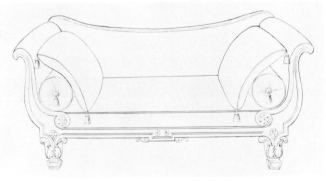

293

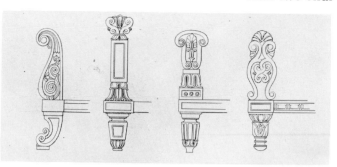

T. King Supplementary Plates

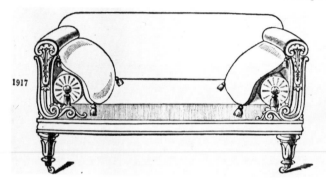

Loudon 1833

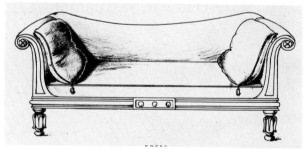

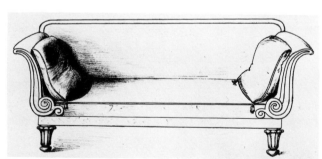

T. King

Cabinet Maker's

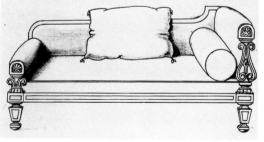

Sketch Book 1835

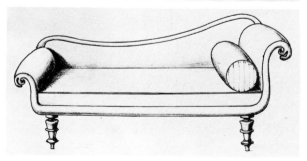

294

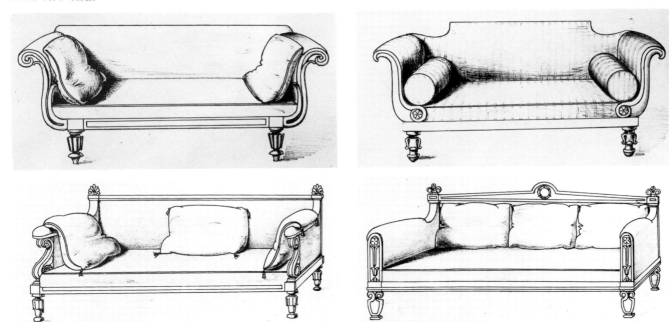

T. King Cabinet Maker's Sketch Book 1835

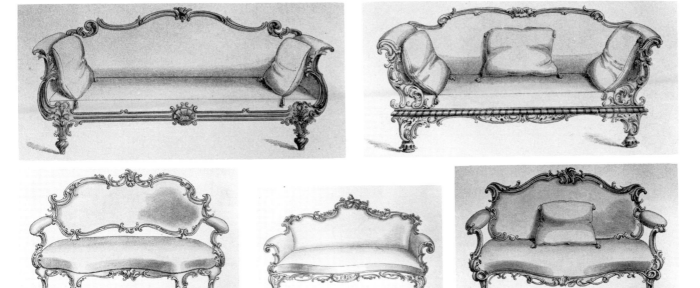

T. King Elizabethan and Louis XIV Styles 1835

Bridgens 1838

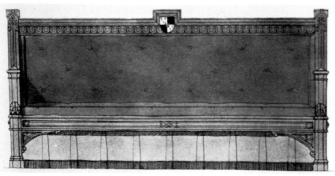

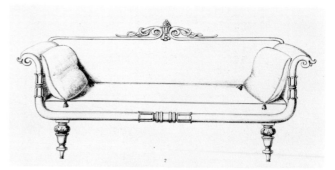

R. Bridgens 1838

T. King 1840

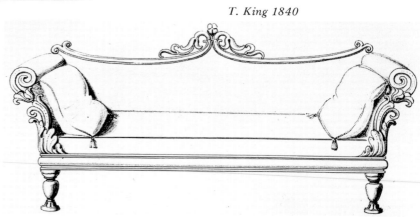

R. Bridgens 1838

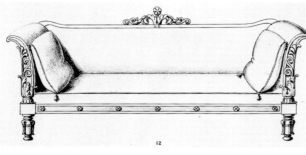

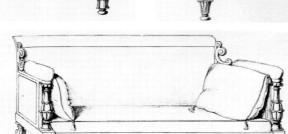

T. King 1840

T. King 1840

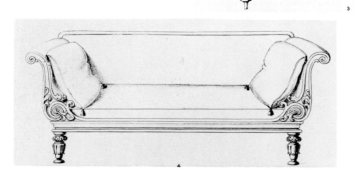

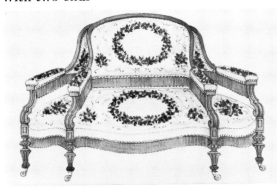

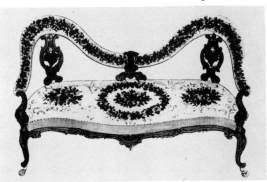

H. Wood 1846

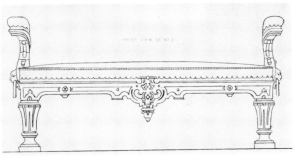

Whitaker 1847

Whitaker 1847

H. Wood Supplement 1848

H. Wood

Supplement 1848

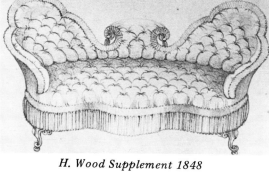

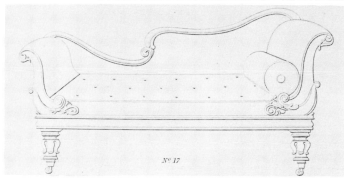

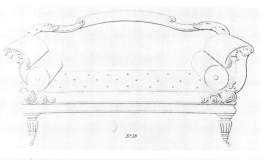

H. Wood Supplement 1848

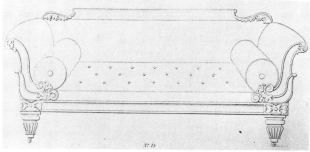

W. Smee & Sons 1850

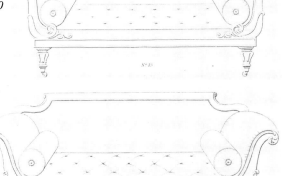

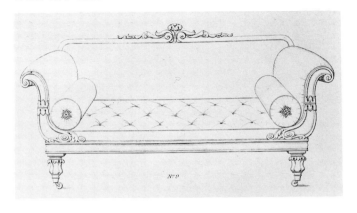

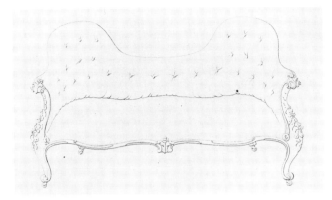

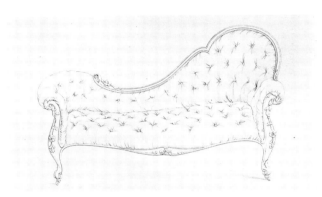

W. Smee & Sons 1850

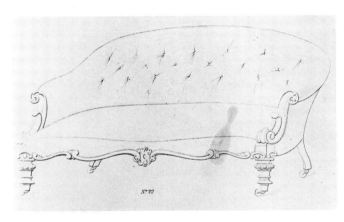

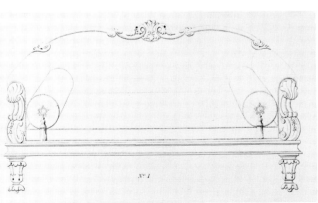

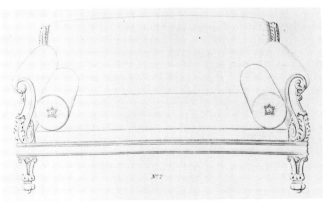

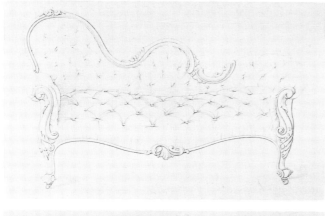

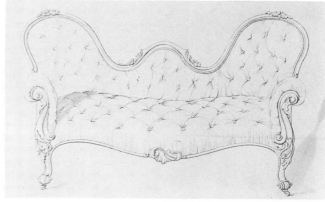

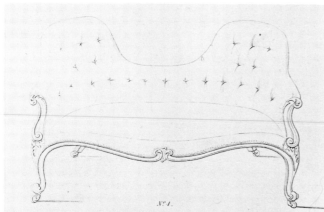

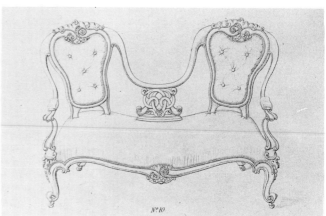

W. Smee & Sons 1850

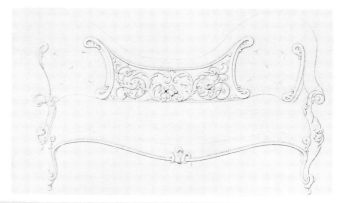

J. Taylor 1850

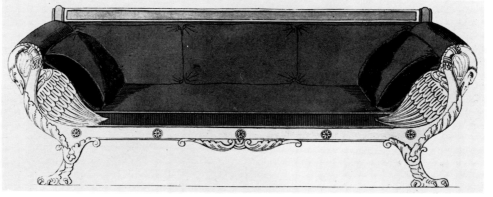

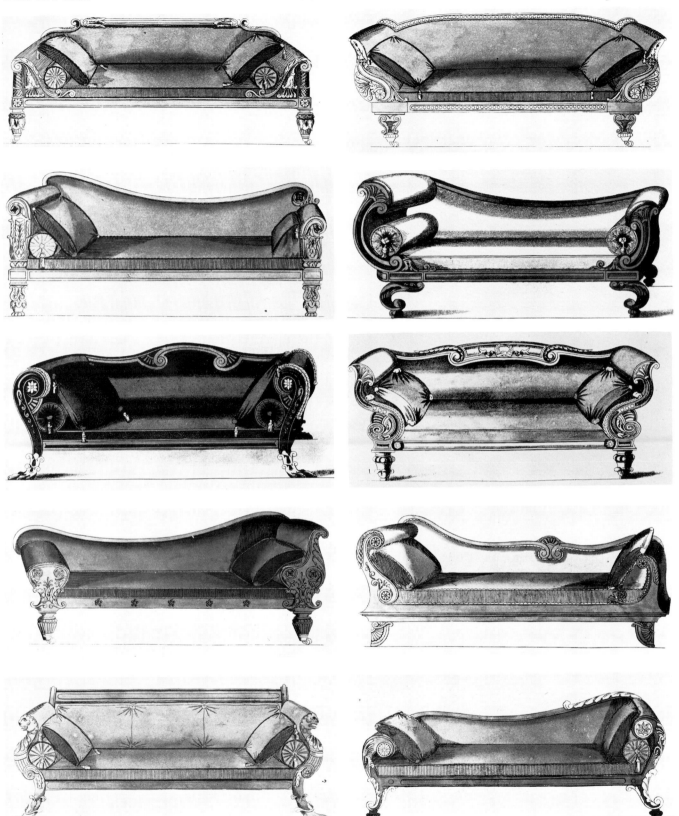

J. Taylor 1850

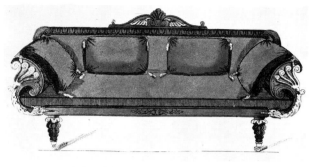

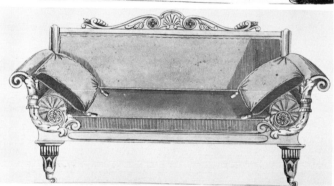

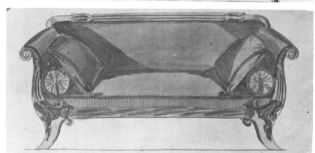

J. Taylor 1850

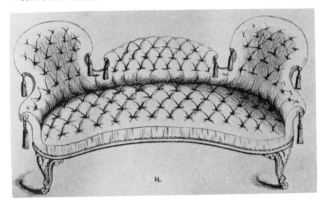

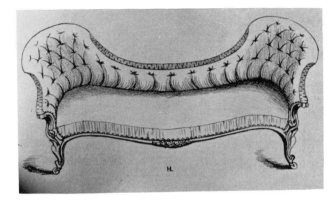

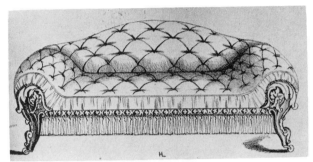

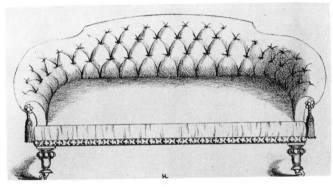

Lawford 1855

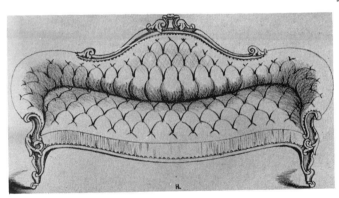

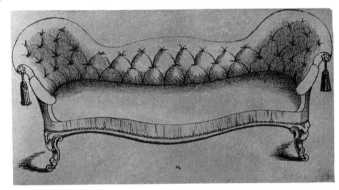

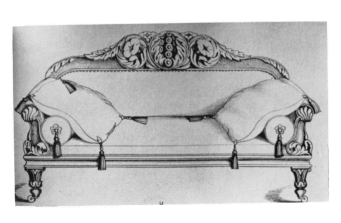

303

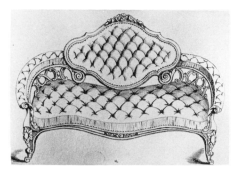

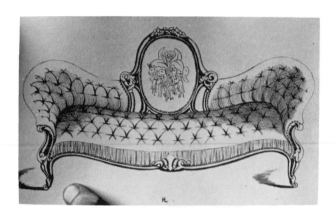
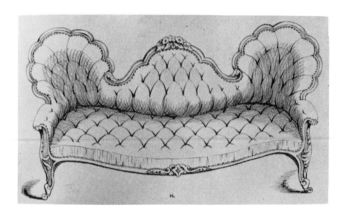

H. Lawford 1855

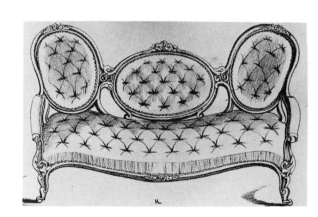

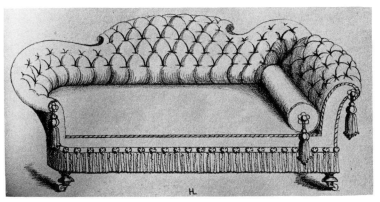

Braund 1858

H. Lawford 1855

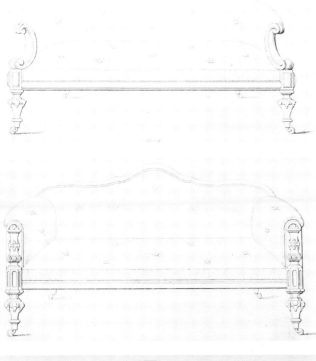

Braund 1858

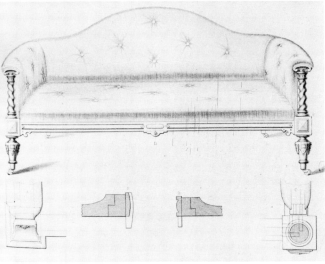

W. Blackie 1853

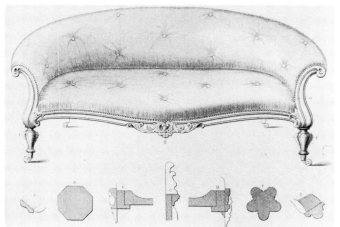

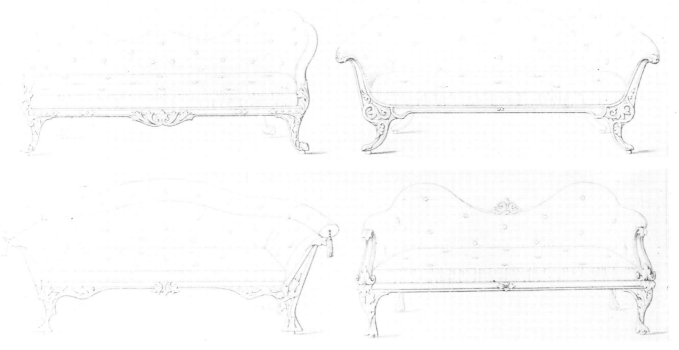

W. Blackie 1853

27.

Booth 1864

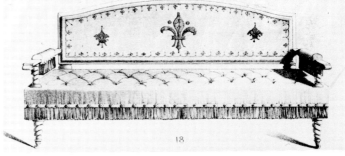

18

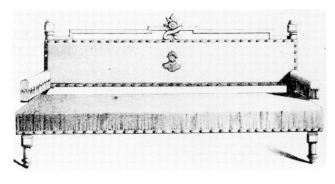

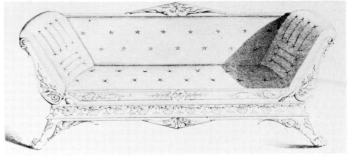

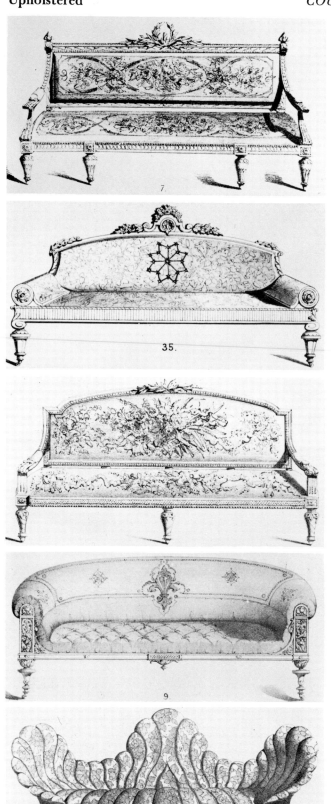

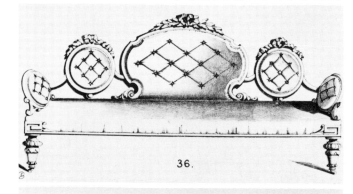

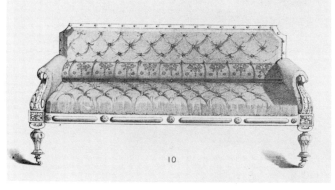

Booth 1864

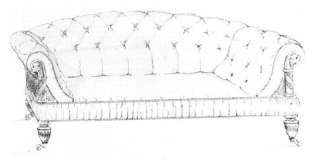

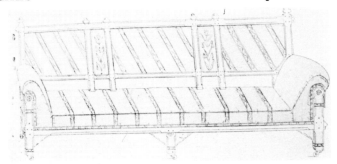

Richard Charles 1866

Shoolbred 1876

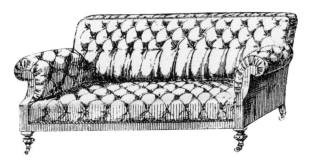

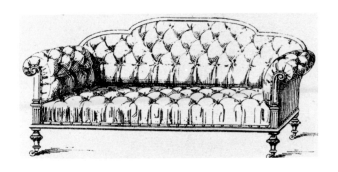

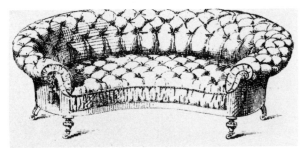

W. Watt 1877

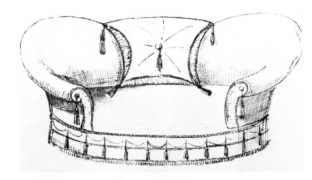

Wyman 1877   *Jonquet 1879*

309

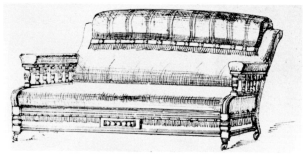

Jonquet 1879

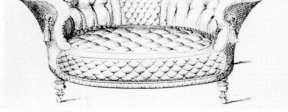

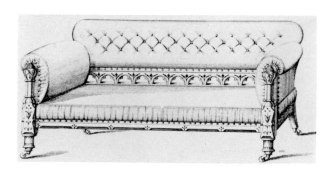

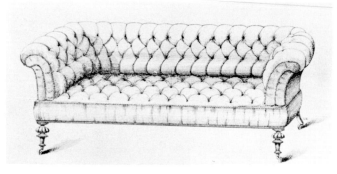

C. & R. Light 1881

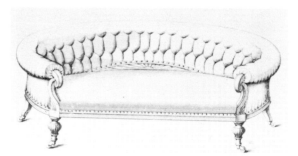

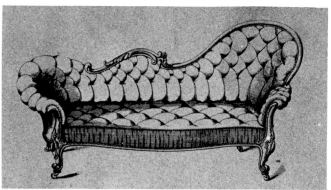

C. & R. Light 1881

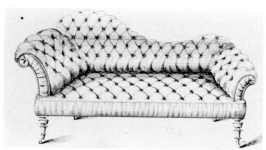

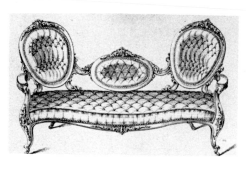

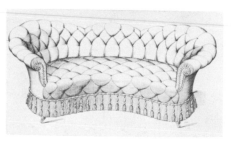

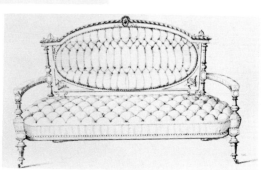

C. & R. Light 1881

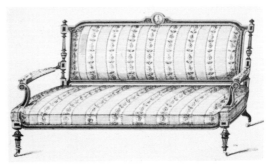

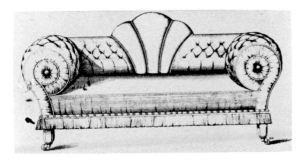

C. & R. Light 1881

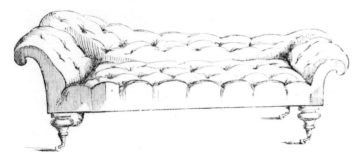

Heal 1884

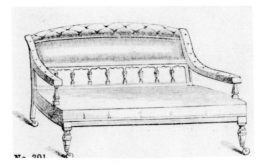

Heal 1884

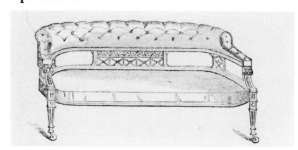

Heal 1884

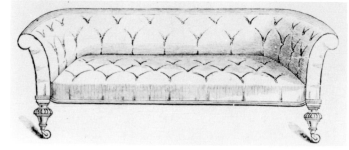

Heal 1884

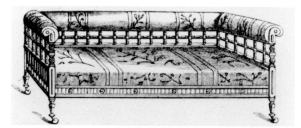

Heal 1884

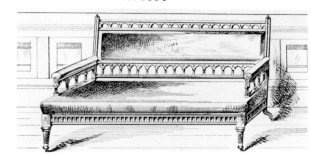

Wyman 1886

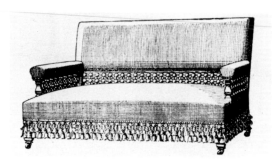

Liberty 1890

Liberty 1890

Liberty 1890

Norman & Stacey 1910

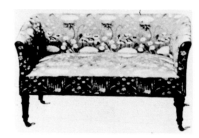

Norman & Stacey 1910

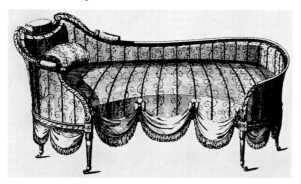

Sheraton 1802

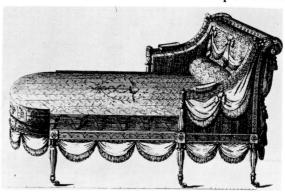

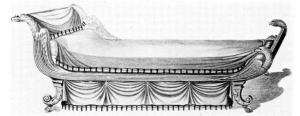

Sheraton 1804

G. Smith 1808

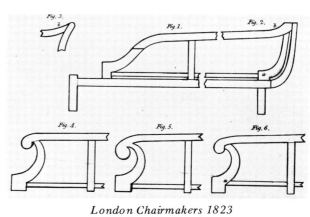

London Chairmakers 1823

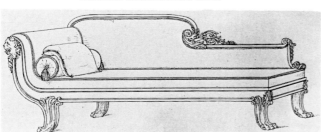

London Chairmakers 1823

Whitaker 1825

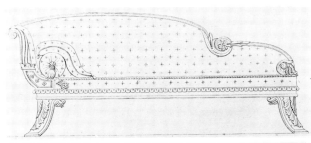

P. & M.A. Nicholson 1826

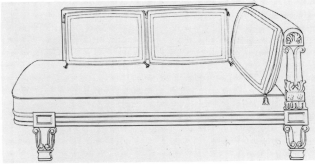

G. Smith's Guide 1826

G. Smith's Guide 1826

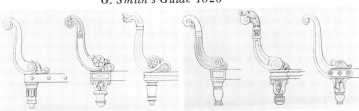

Modern Style Exemplified 1829

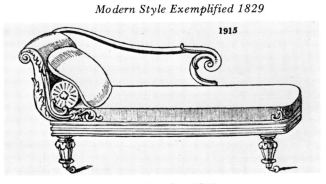

Modern Style Exemplified 1829

Modern Style Exemplified 1829

Loudon 1833

Loudon 1833

Loudon 1833

T. King Elizabethan and Louis XIV Styles 1835

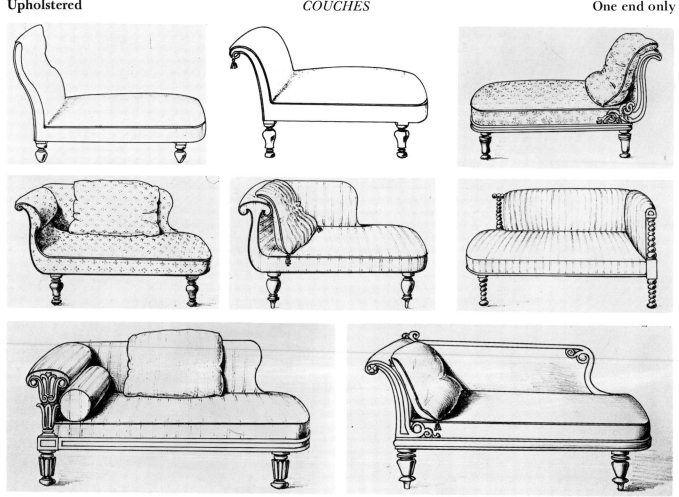

T. King Cabinet Maker's Sketch Book 1835

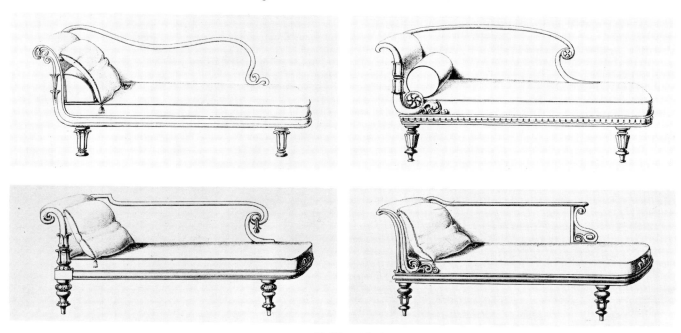

T. King 1840

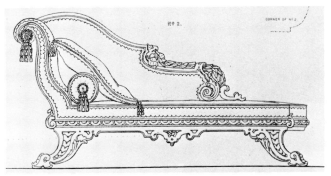

Whitaker 1847

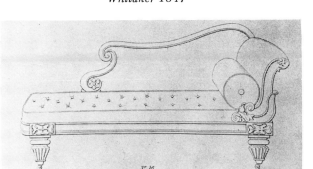

Whitaker 1847

H. Wood Supplement 1848

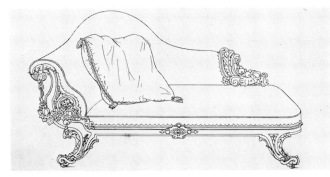

H. Wood 1848

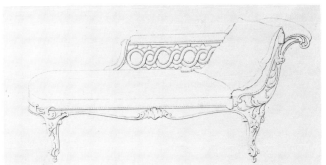

W. Smee & Sons 1850

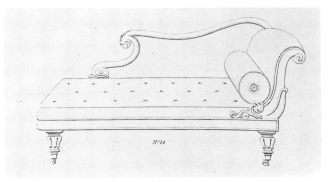

W. Smee & Sons 1850

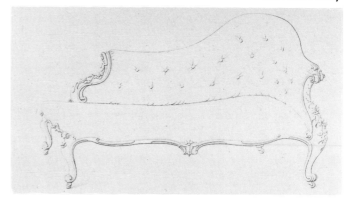

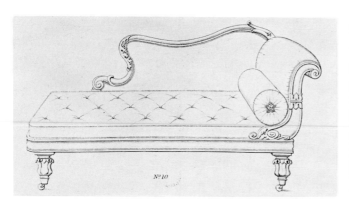

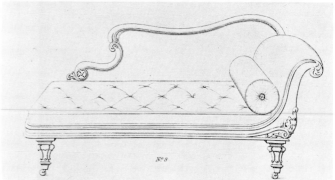

W. Smee & Sons 1850

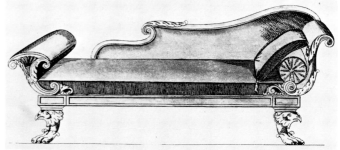

J. Taylor 1850

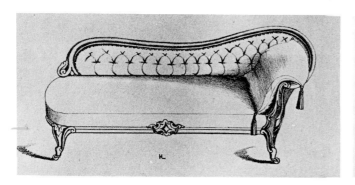

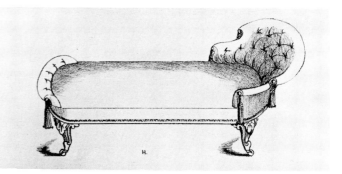

Lawford 1855

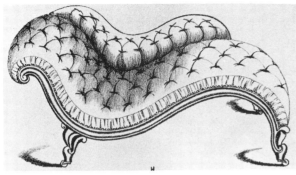

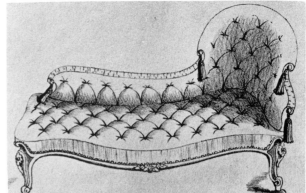

Lawford

1855

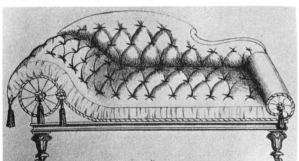

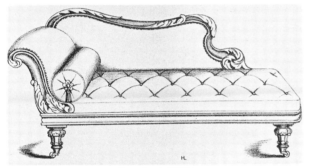

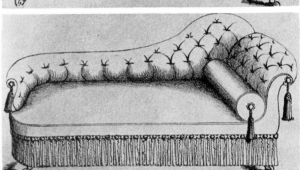

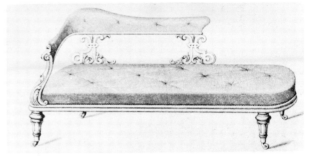

Lawford 1855

W. Blackie 1853

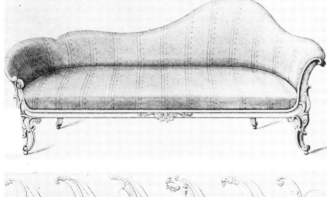

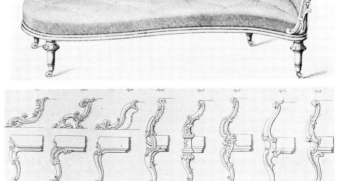

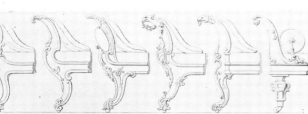

W. Blackie 1853

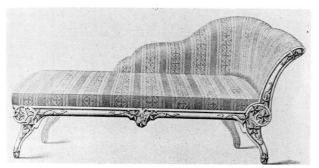

W. Blackie 1853

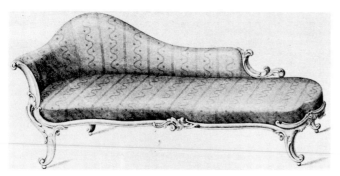

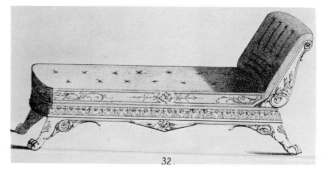

W. Blackie 1853 *Booth 1864*

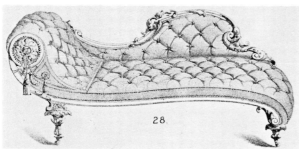

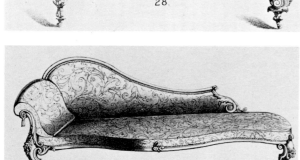

Booth 1864

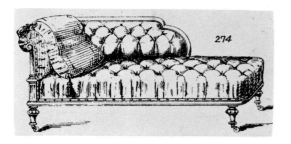

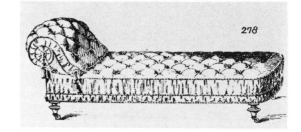

Shoolbred 1876

322

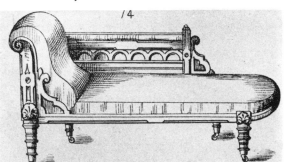

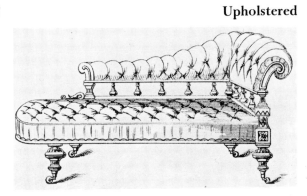

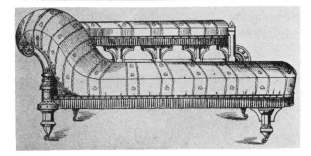

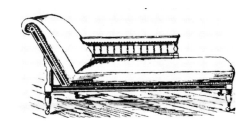

Wyman 1877

W. Watt 1877

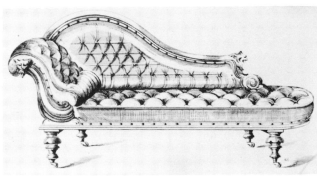

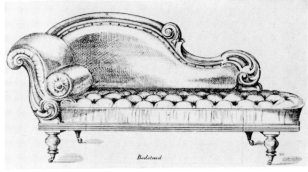

C. & R. Light 1881

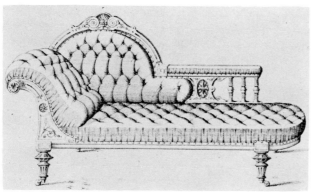

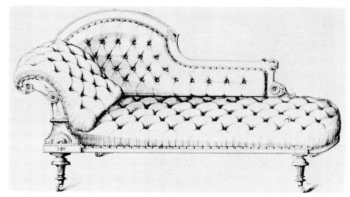

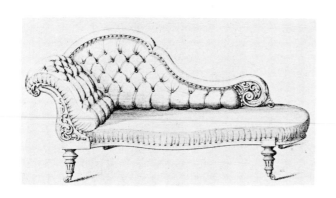

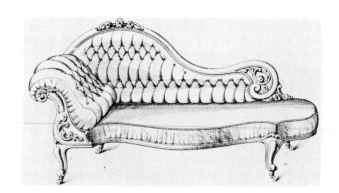

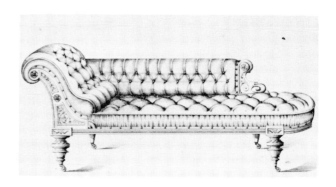

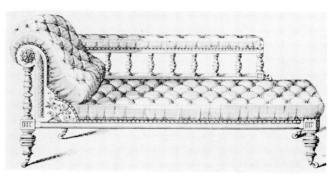

C. & R. Light 1881

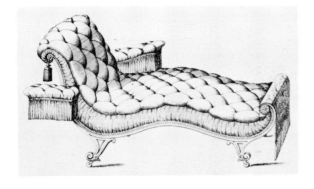

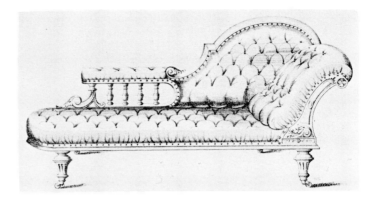

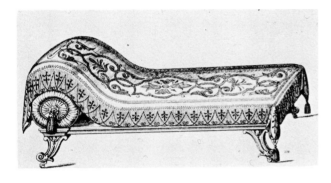

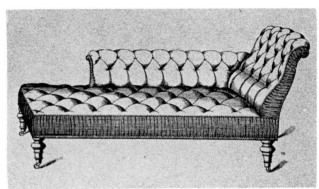

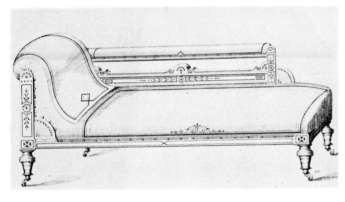

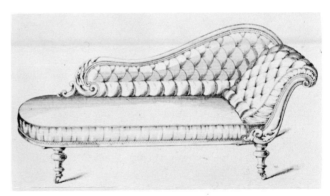

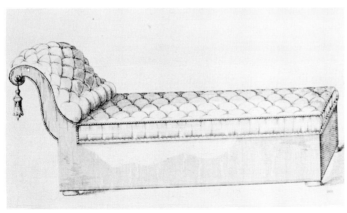

C. & R. Light 1881

Heal 1884

Wyman 1886

One end only   *COUCHES*   **Upholstered**

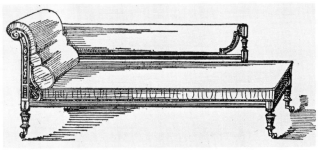

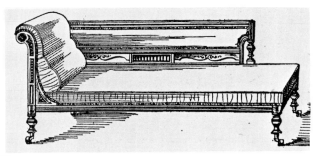

Wyman 1886

Norman & Stacey 1910

Upholstered   *COUCHES*

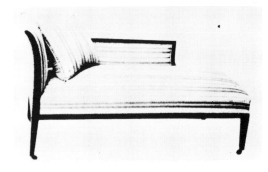

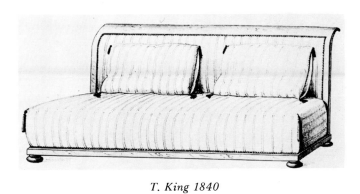

T. King 1840

T. King Elizabethan and Louis XIV Styles 1835

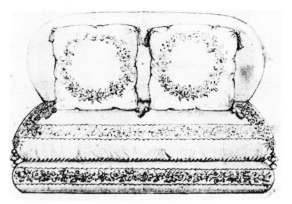

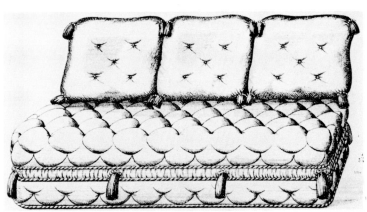

H. Wood Supplement 1848   *C. & R. Light 1881*

Sheraton 1802

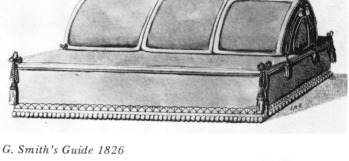

G. Smith's Guide 1826

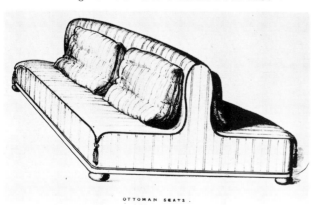

1919

1920

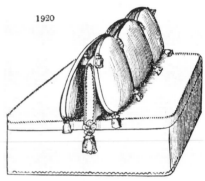

Loudon 1833

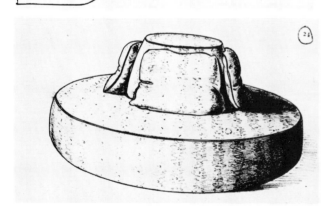

T. King Cabinet Maker's Sketch Book 1835

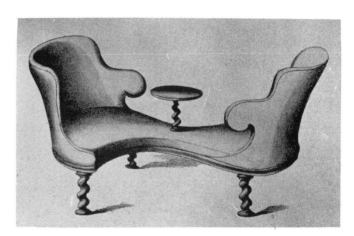

T. King Elizabethan and Louis XIV Styles 1835

OTTOMAN SEATS.

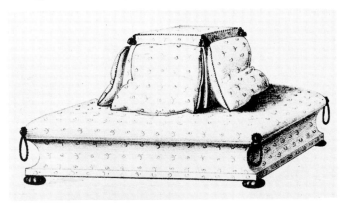

T. King Cabinet Maker's Sketch Book 1835

H. Wood 1846

Whitaker 1847

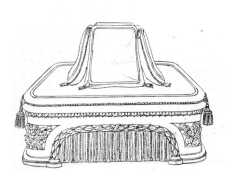

H. Wood Supplement 1848

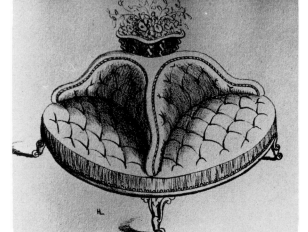

Lawford 1855

Booth 1864

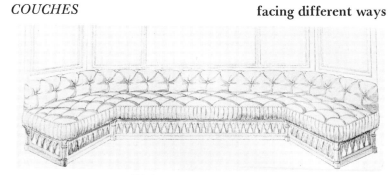

Richard Charles 1866

Jonquet 1879

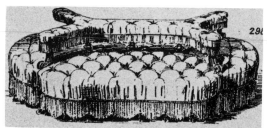

Shoolbred 1876

Shoolbred 1876

Shoolbred 1876

330

Wyman 1877

W. Watt 1877

Yapp 1879

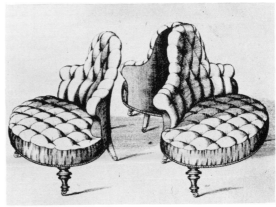

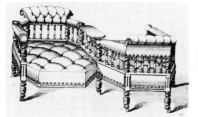

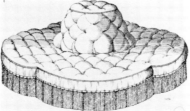

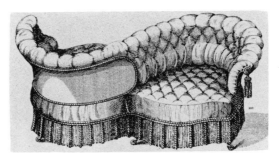

C. & R. Light 1881

*C. & R. Light
1881*

W. Smee & Sons 1850

C.R. Light 1881

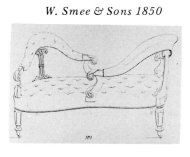

Heal 1884

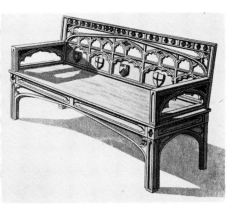

G. Smith 1808

Loudon 1833

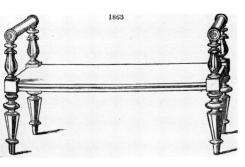

Loudon 1833

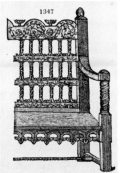

Pugin 1835

Bridgens 1838

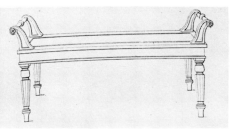

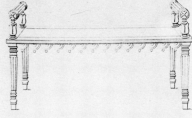

W. Smee & Sons 1850

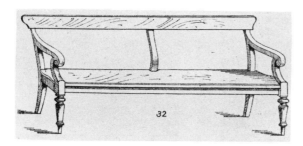

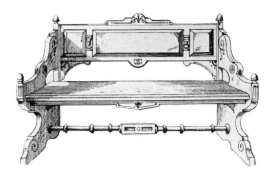

Shoolbred 1876

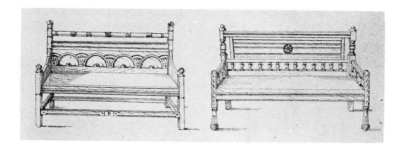

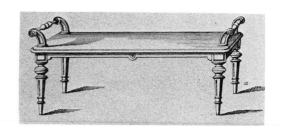

Wyman 1877

Wyman 1877

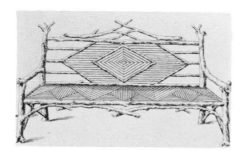

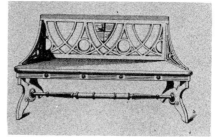

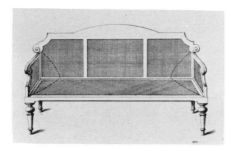

C. & R. Light 1881

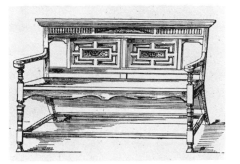

Wyman 1886

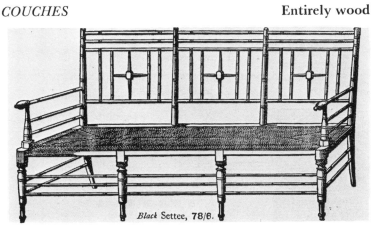

Black Settee, **78/6.**

Liberty 1890

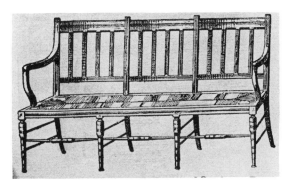

Liberty 1890

No. 38.—HALL SEAT, in

Norman & Stacey 1910

Norman & Stacey 1910

No. 47.—OAK HALL SEAT,
4 ft. wide. Can be made in any
wood. Price £2 5s.

G. Smith 1808

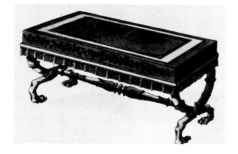

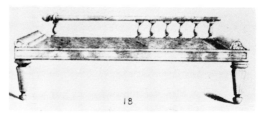

G. Smith 1826

G. Smith 1808

G. Smith 1826

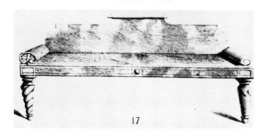

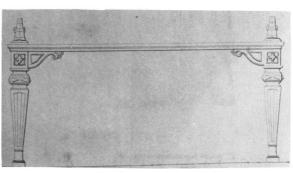

P. & M.A. Nicholson 1826

Modern Style Exemplified 1829

Loudon 1833

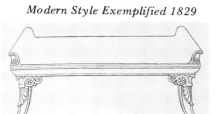

632

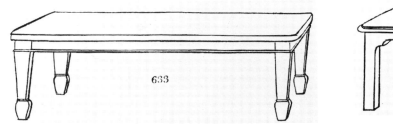

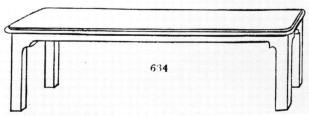

Loudon 1833

Loudon 1833

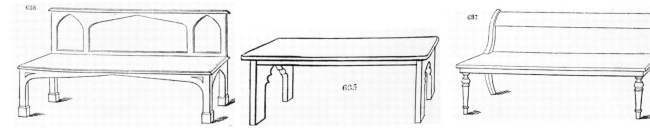

W. Blackie 1853

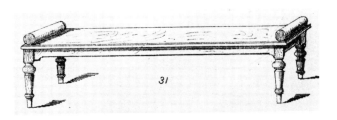

W. Blackie 1853   *Shoolbred 1876*

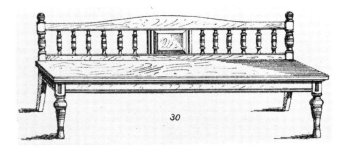

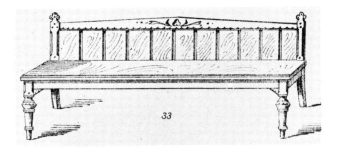

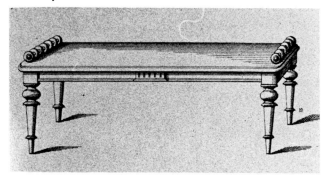

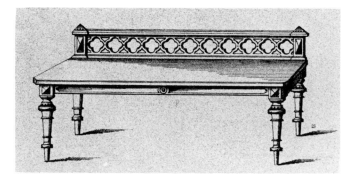

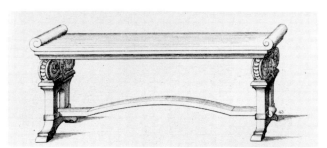

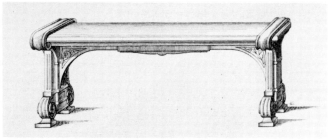

C. & R. Light 1881

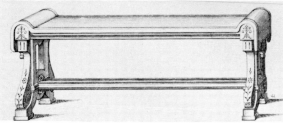

Heal 1884

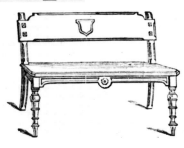

Wyman 1886

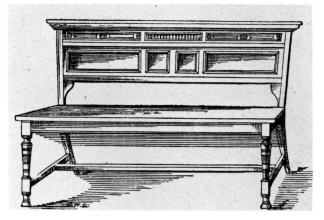

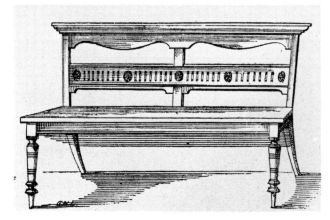

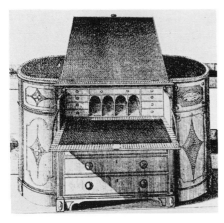

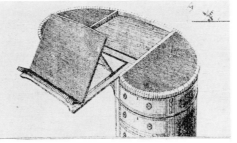

Sheraton 1802

Sheraton 1802

G. Smith 1808

Loudon 1833

T. King Elizabethan and Louis XIV Styles 1835

W. Smee & Sons 1850

J. Taylor 1850

J. Taylor 1850

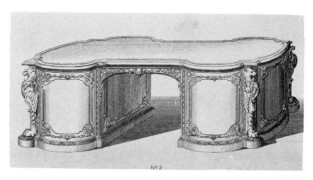

Braund 1858

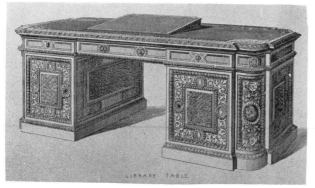

Braund 1858

W. Blackie 1853

Booth 1864

Wyman 1877

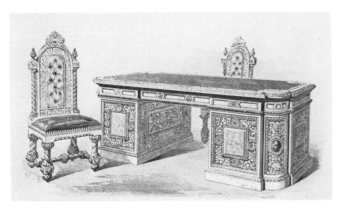

Yapp 1879

C. & R. Light 1881

C. & R. Light 1881

No. 261.—PEDESTAL WRITING

C. & R. Light 1881

Heal 1884

Wyman 1886

Norman & Stacey 1910

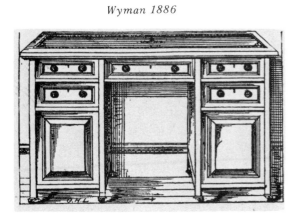

W. Smee & Sons 1850

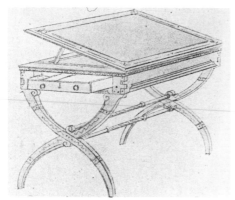

Richard Charles 1866

C. & R. Light 1881

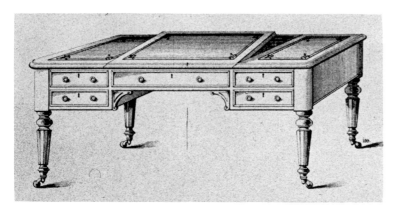

C. & R. Light 1881

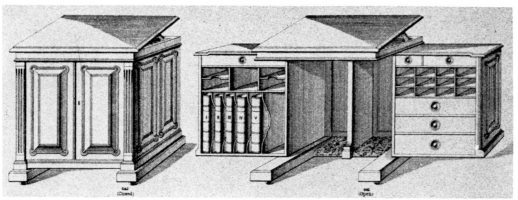

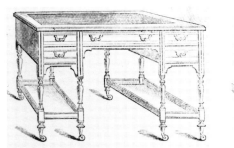
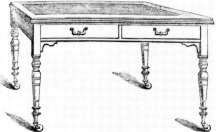

Heal 1884

Wyman 1877

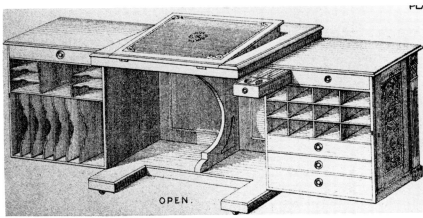

Yapp 1879

Morris 1900

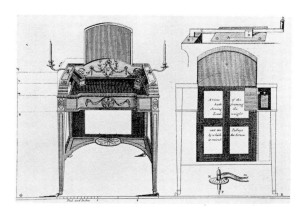

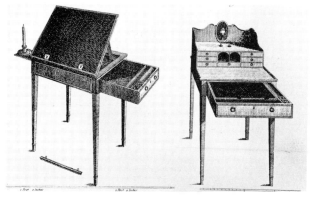

Sheraton 1802

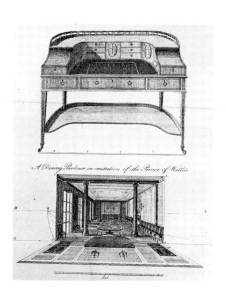

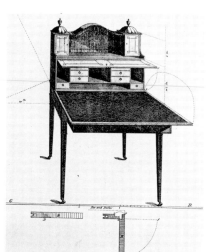

Sheraton 1802

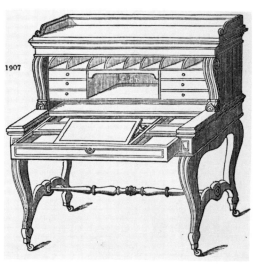

G. Smith's Guide 1826

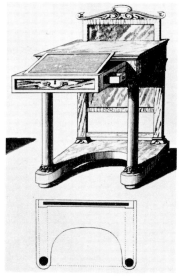

G. Smith's Guide 1826

Loudon 1833

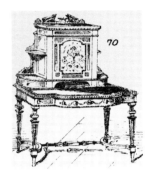

Yapp 1879

Shoolbred 1876

C. & R. Light 1881

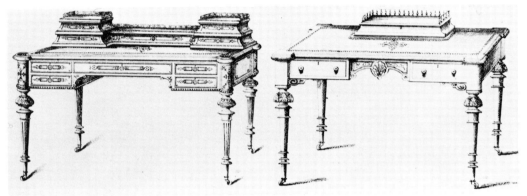

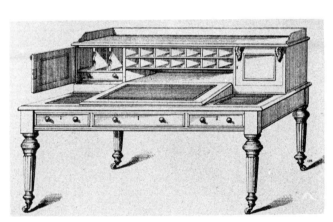

Heal 1884

C. & R. Light 1881

Heal 1884

Heal 1884

Heal 1884

345

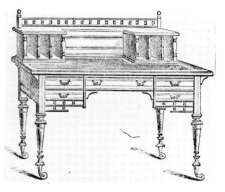

Heal 1884

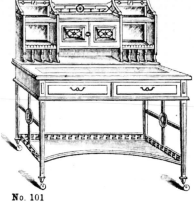

No. 101

Heal 1884

Heal 1884

Norman & Stacey 1910

Norman & Stacey 1910

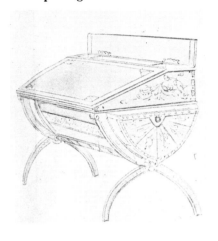

Richard Charles 1866

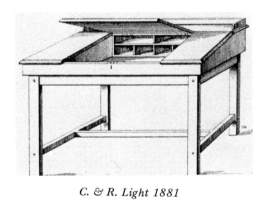

C. & R. Light 1881

Richard Charles 1866

Lawford 1867

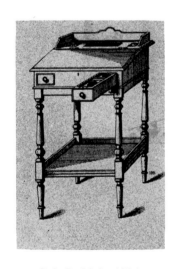

Norman & Stacey 1910

C. & R. Light 1881

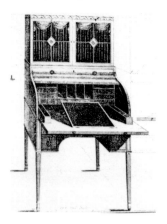

Sheraton Appendix 1802

H. Lawford 1867

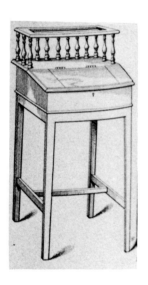

C. & R. Light 1881

Loudon 1833   *T. King Supplementary Plates*

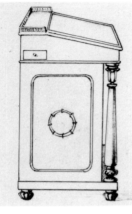

T. King Supplementary Plates

T. King Cabinet Maker's Sketch Book 1835

Pugin 1835

W. Smee & Sons 1850

Braund 1858

J. Taylor 1850

Booth 1864

Blackie 1853

Booth 1864   *Richard Charles 1866*

Shoolbred 1876

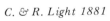

C. & R. Light 1881

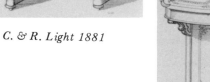

C. & R. Light 1881

Wyman 1886

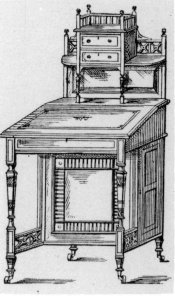

Norman & Stacey 1910

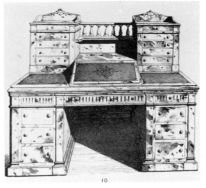

W. Blackie 1853

Booth 1864

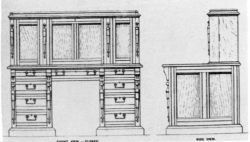

Richard Charles 1866

Wyman 1877

Yapp 1879

C. & R. Light 1881

353

C. & R. Light 1881

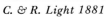

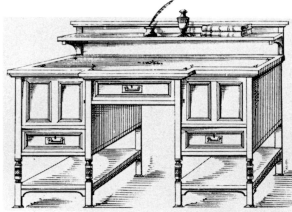

Wyman 1886

Wyman 1886

Morris 1900

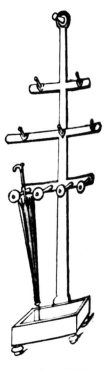

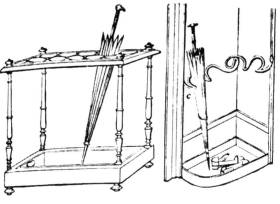

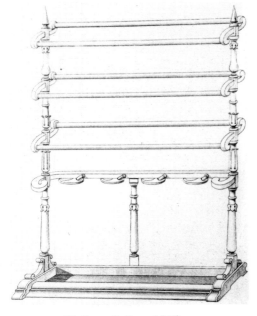

Loudon 1833

Loudon 1833

W. Smee & Sons 1850

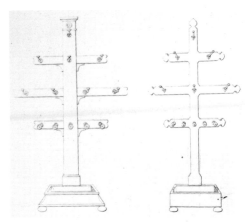

W. Smee & Sons 1850

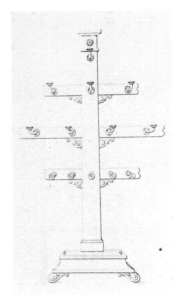

355

Blackie 1853

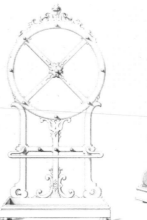

Blackie 1853

Booth 1864

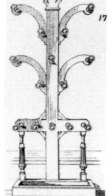

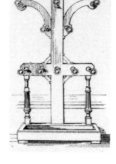

Waring 1862

Shoolbred 1876

Booth 1864

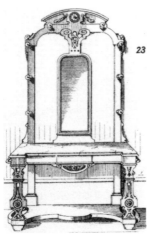
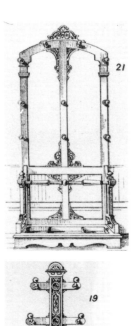

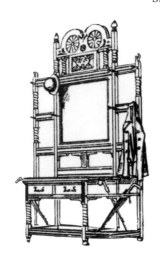
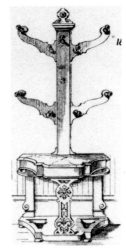

Shoolbred 1876

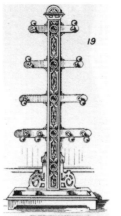
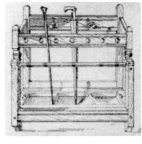

Shoolbred 1876

W. Watt 1877

Wyman 1877

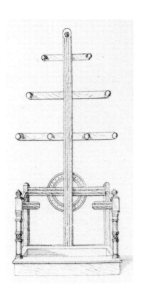
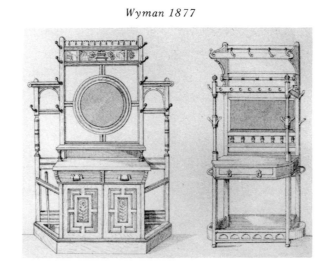
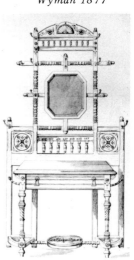

Wyman 1877

Wyman 1877

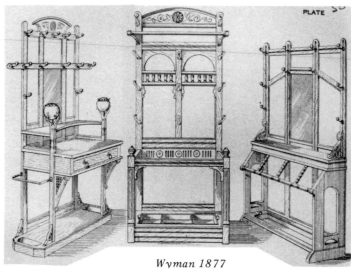

Wyman 1877

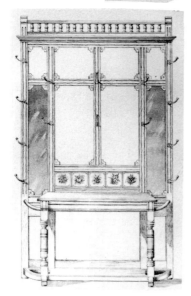

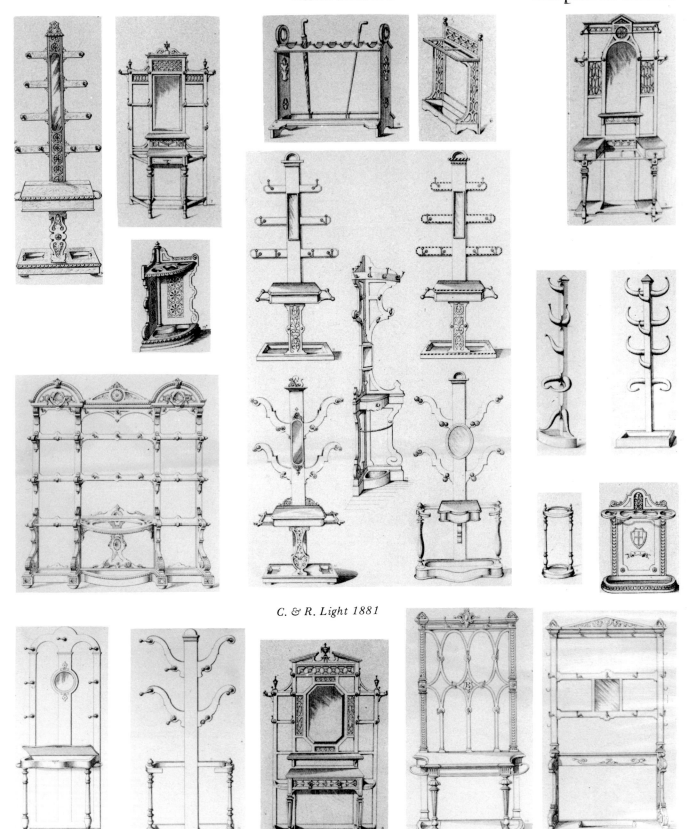

C. & R. Light 1881

With place for umbrella   *HALL STANDS*

C. & R. Light 1881

C. & R. Light 1881

C. & R. Light 1881

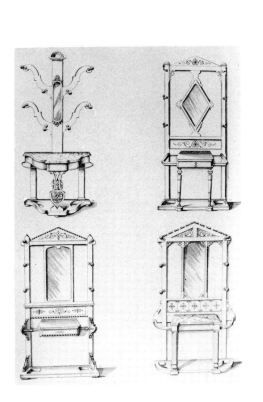

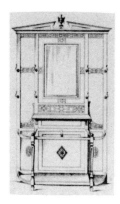

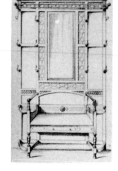

C. & R. Light 1881

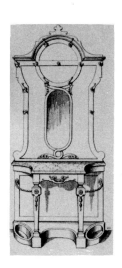

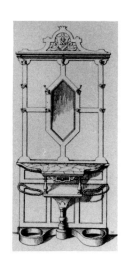

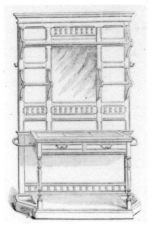

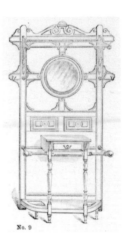

Heal 1884

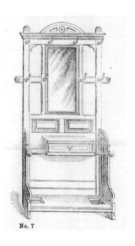

No. 7

No. 6

Hat and Umbrella Stand, Mahogany.

No. 8

No. 9

Heal 1884

Heal 1884

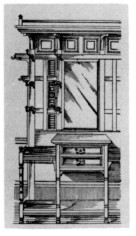

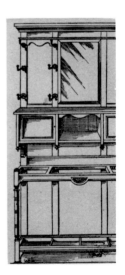

Wyman 1886

363

With place for umbrella

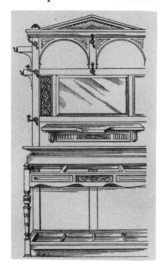

Wyman 1886

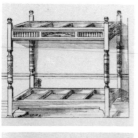

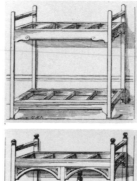

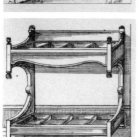

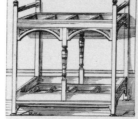

Wyman 1886

Norman & Stacey 1910

Norman & Stacey 1910

Wyman 1877

H. Wood Supplement 1848

Shoolbred 1876

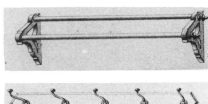

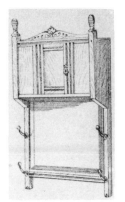

Wyman 1877

C. & R. Light 1881

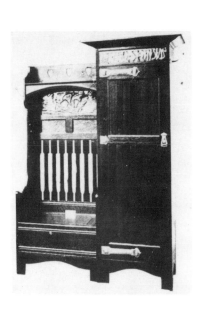

Norman & Stacey 1910

G. Smith 1808

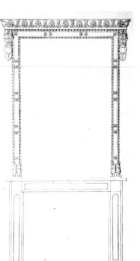

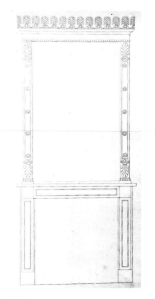

T. King 1830

Braund 1858

Braund 1858

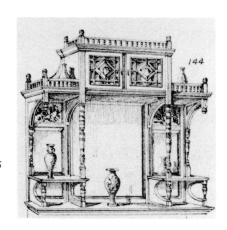

Shoolbred 1876

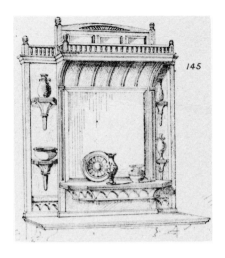

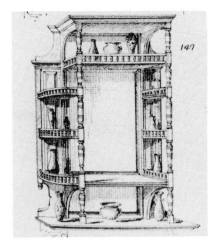

Shoolbred 1876

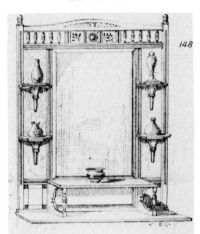

W. Watt 1877

Shoolbred 1876

W. Watt 1877

Wyman 1877

Jonquet 1879

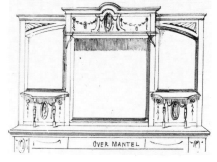

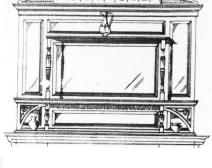

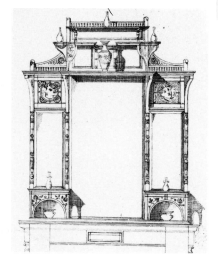

Jonquet 1879   *C. & R. Light 1881*

C. & R. Light 1881

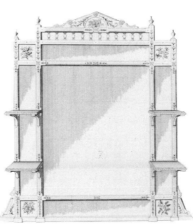

Heal 1884

C. & R. Light 1881

Heal 1884

Heal 1884

Heal 1884

369

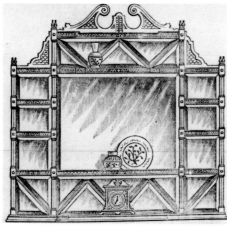

Heal 1884

Wyman 1886

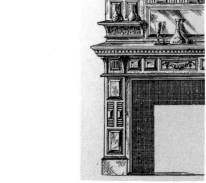

Wyman 1886

Liberty 1890   Morefque Overmantel.

Liberty 1890

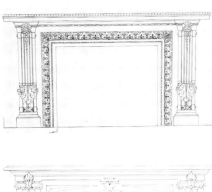

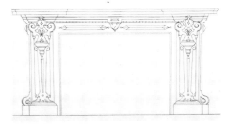

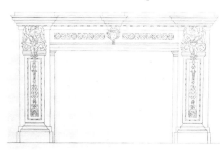

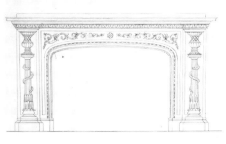

Whitaker 1847

Whitaker 1847

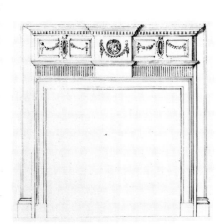

Jonquet 1879

T. King 1830

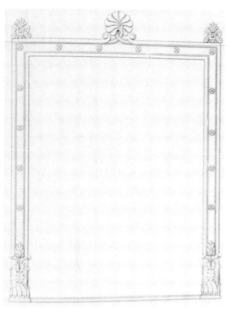

T. King 1830

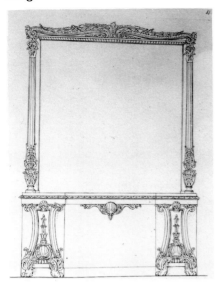

Whitaker 1825

Whitaker 1825

G. Smith's Guide 1826

T. King 1830

T. King 1830

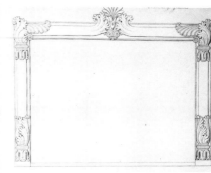

T. King 1830

Loudon 1833

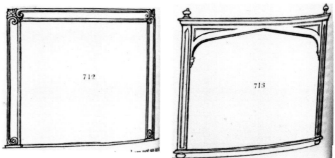

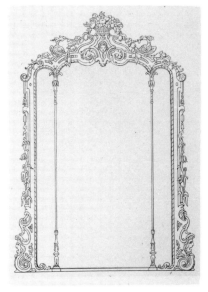

Whitaker 1847

W. Smee & Sons
1850

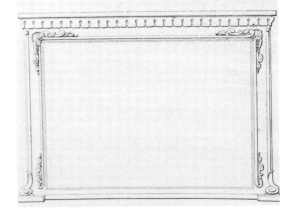

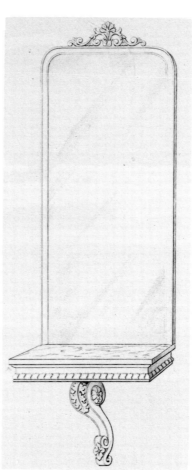

W. Smee & Sons 1850

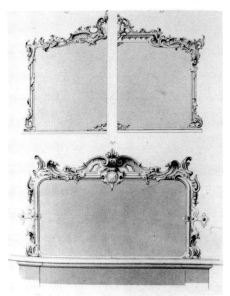

W. Blackie 1853

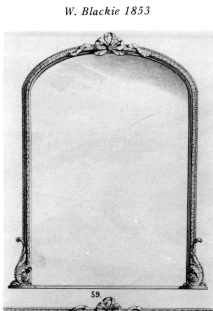

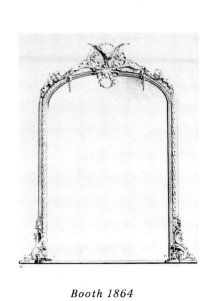

Booth 1864

Booth 1864

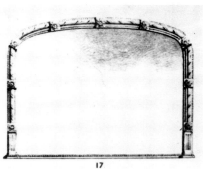

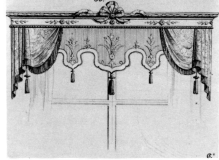

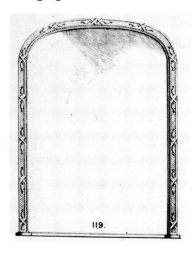

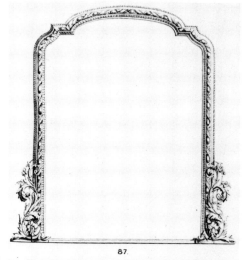

119.

87.

120.

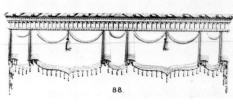

88.

71.

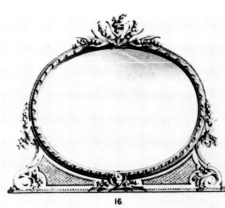

91.

Booth 1864

72.

16.

15.

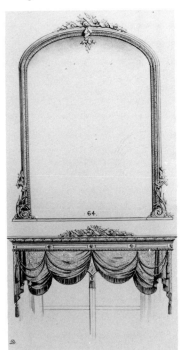

Booth 1864

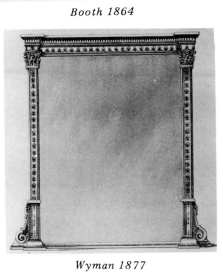

Wyman 1877

Yapp 1879

*Yapp
1879*

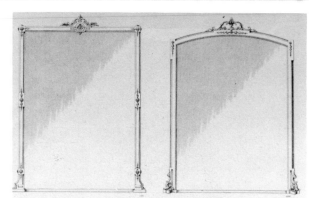

C. & R. Light

1881

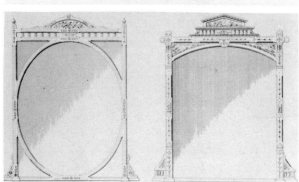

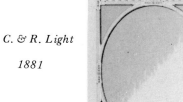

Morris 1900

G. Smith 1808

W. Smee & Sons 1850

W. Smee & Sons 1850

Booth 1864

Booth 1864

Wyman 1877

Booth 1864

Wyman 1877

Wyman 1877

C. & R. Light 1881

Yapp 1879

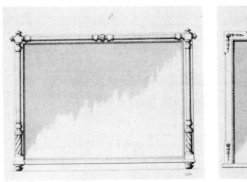

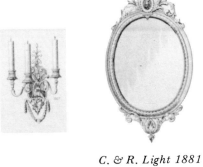

C. & R. Light 1881

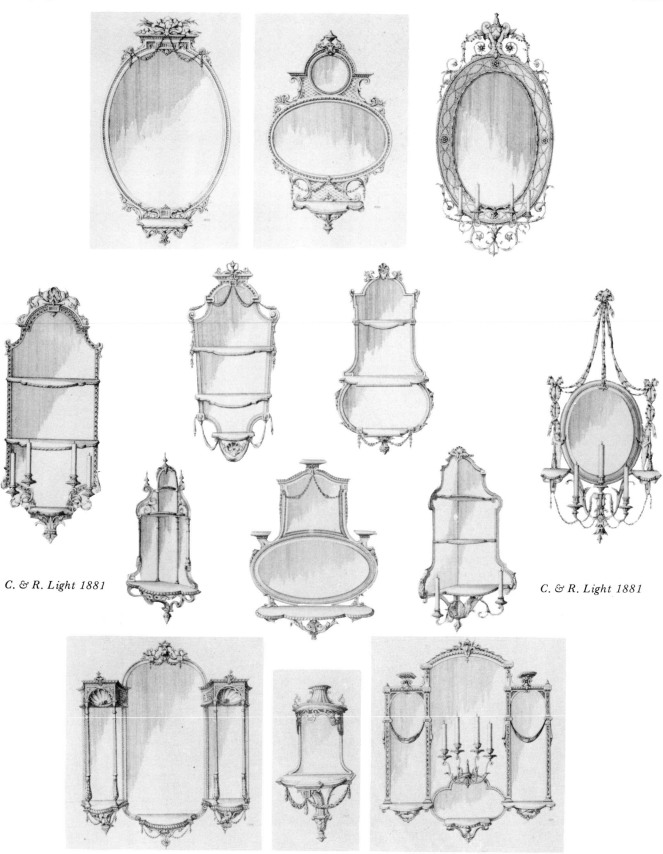

C. & R. Light 1881

C. & R. Light 1881

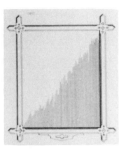

C. & R. Light 1881

No. 12

Heal 1884

No. 10

Heal 1884

Syrian Wall Mirrors.
Inlaid with pearl or ivory.
From 21/-

Liberty 1890

No. 13

Heal 1884

NO. 505. INLAID MAHOGANY OCTAGON
HANGING MIRROR. 28 IN.

£6 15 0.

Morris 1900

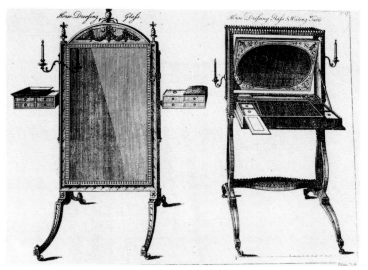

Sheraton 1802   *G. Smith 1808*

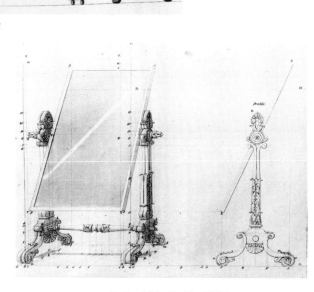

G. Smith 1808

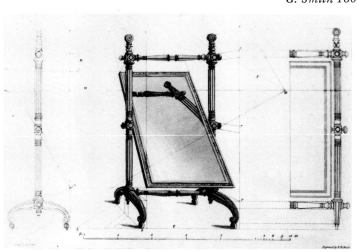

Brown's Rudiments 1822   *G. Smith's Guide 1826*

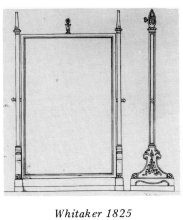

Whitaker 1825

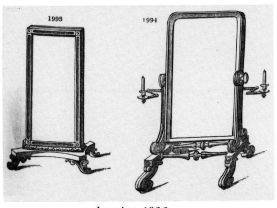

Loudon 1833

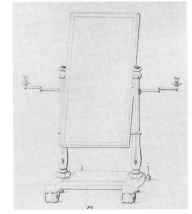

W. Smee & Sons 1850

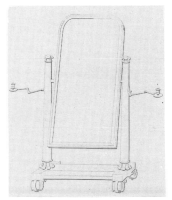

W. Smee & Sons 1850

Booth 1864

Shoolbred 1876

C. & R. Light 1881

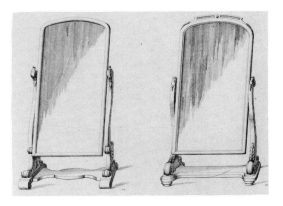

MIRRORS

Norman & Stacey 1910

W. Smee & Sons 1850

Shoolbred 1876

Norman & Stacey 1910

Loudon 1833

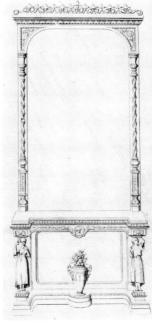

W. Smee & Sons 1850

W. Blackie 1853

W. Smee & Sons 1850

Booth 1864

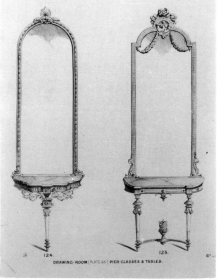

Booth 1864

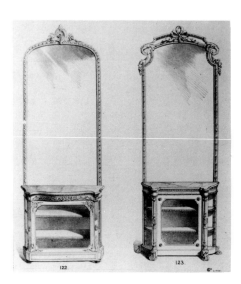

Booth 1864

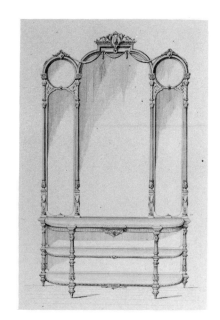

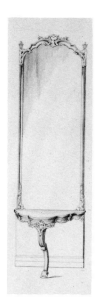

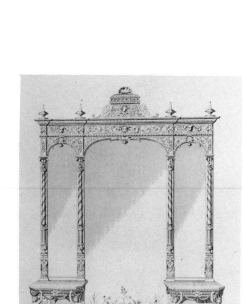

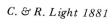

C. & R. Light 1881

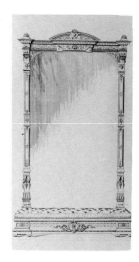

G. Smith 1808

Whitaker 1825

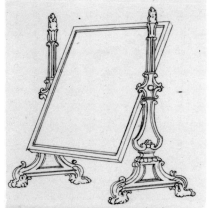

Whitaker 1825

G. Smith 1826

P. & M.A. Nicholson 1826

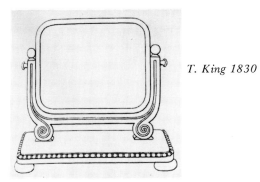

T. King 1830

T. King 1830

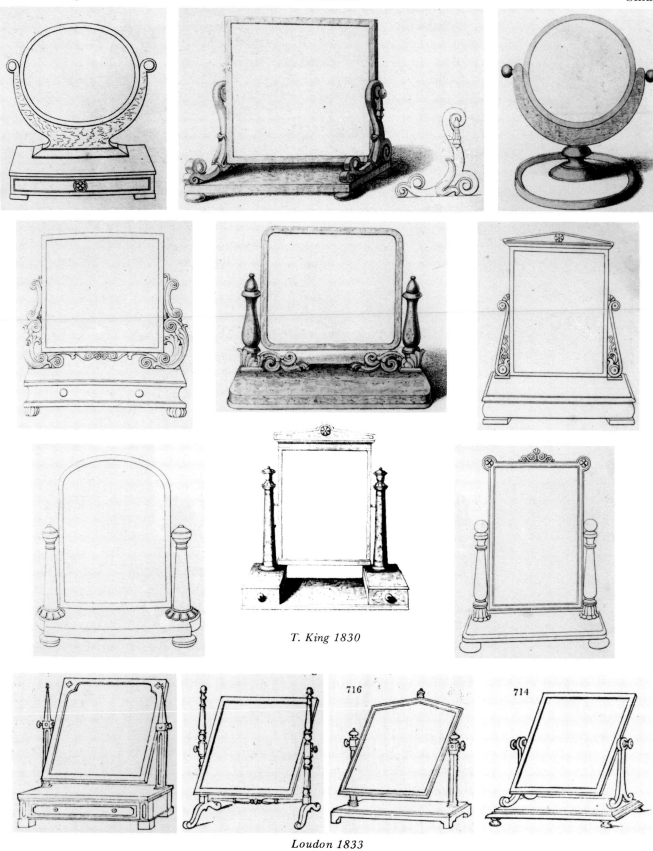

T. King 1830

Loudon 1833

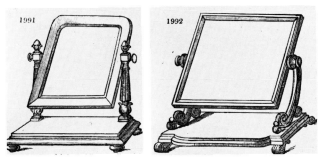

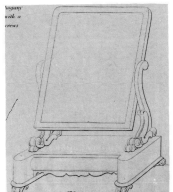

Loudon 1833

W. Smee & Sons 1850

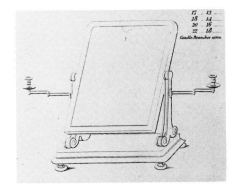

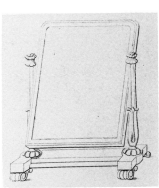

W. Smee & Sons 1850

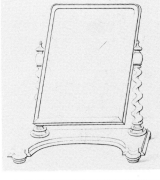

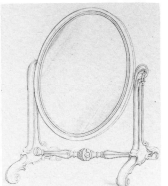

W. Smee & Sons 1850

Braund 1858

Booth 1864

Wyman 1877

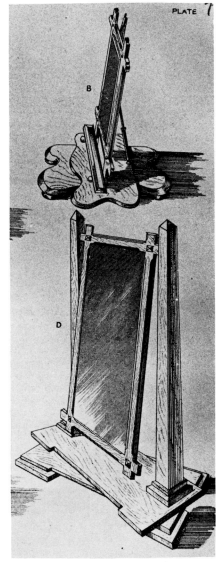

Wyman 1877

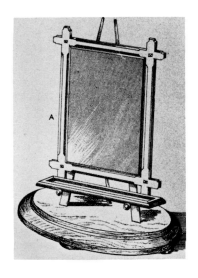

A. Jonquet 1879

Wyman 1877

G. Maddox 1882

Sheraton Appendix 1802   *G. Smith 1808*

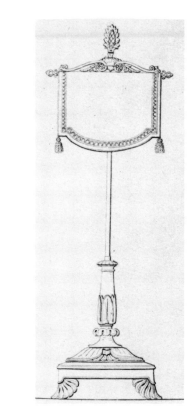
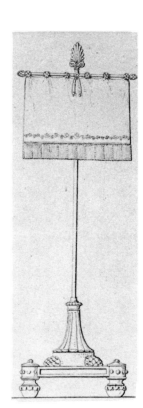

G. Smith 1808   *Whitaker 1825*

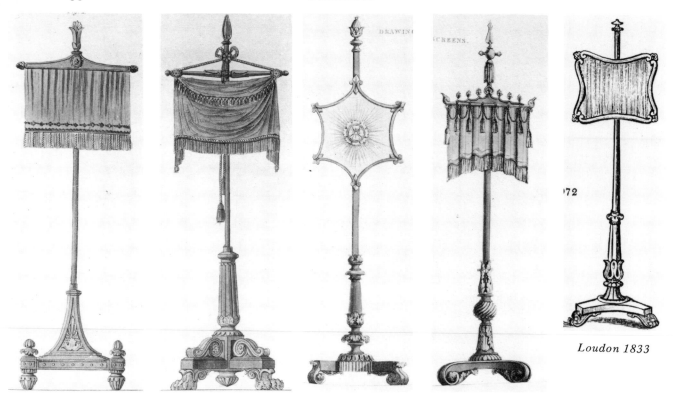

P. & M.A. Nicholson 1826   *G. Smith 1826*

Loudon 1833

Loudon 1833

T. King 1835

Bridgens 1838

Henry Wood 1846

T. King 1835

Whitaker 1847

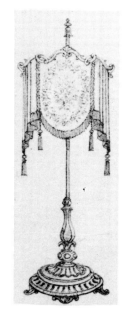

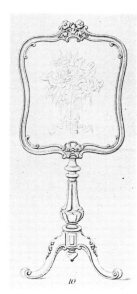

H. Wood 1848

W. Smee & Sons 1850

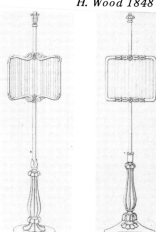

W. Smee & Sons 1850

J. Taylor 1850

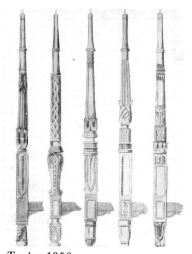

J. Taylor 1850

Blackie 1853

Blackie 1853

Booth 1864

Wyman 1877

Yapp 1879

Vertical, folding panels

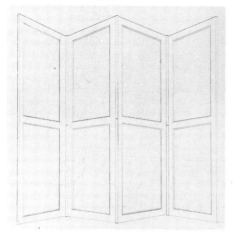

W. Smee & Sons 1850

SCREENS

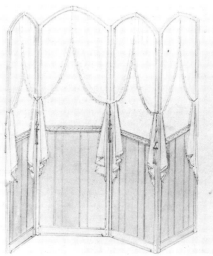

Richard Charles 1866

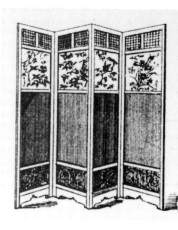

W. Watt 1877

C. & R. Light 1881

C. & R. Light 1881

Liberty 1890

Liberty 1890

Liberty 1890

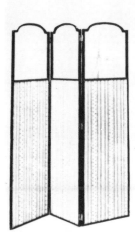

Liberty 1890

Norman & Stacey 1910

Detachable

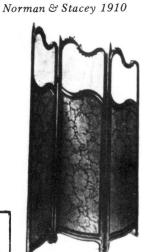

Norman & Stacey 1910

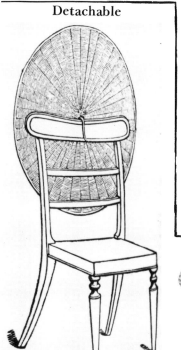

Norman & Stacey 1910

Loudon 1833

W. Smee & Sons 1850

Norman & Stacey 1910

407

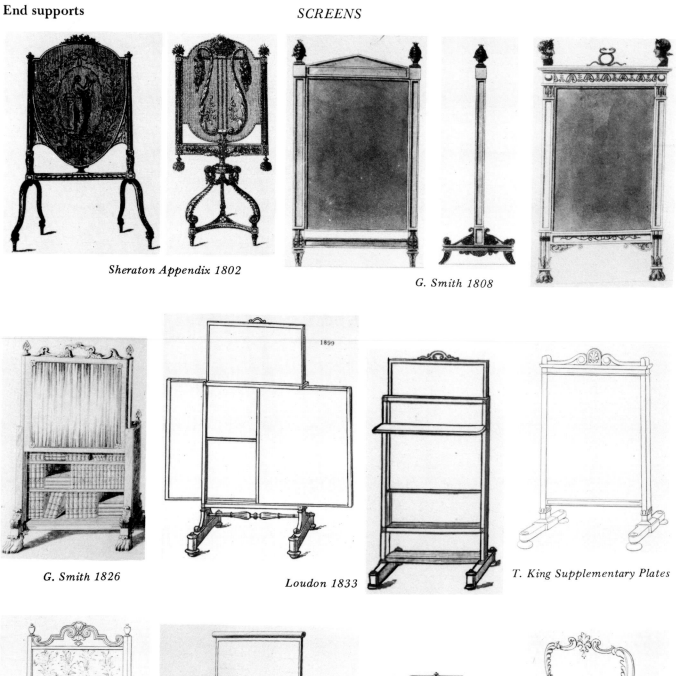

Sheraton Appendix 1802

G. Smith 1808

G. Smith 1826

Loudon 1833

T. King Supplementary Plates

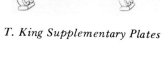

T. King Supplementary Plates

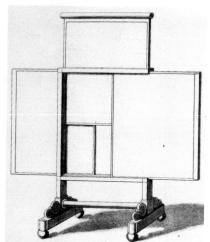

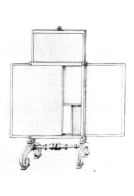

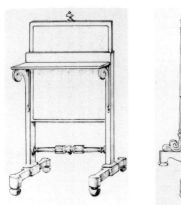

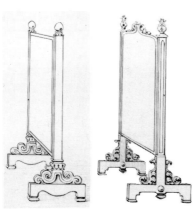

T. King 1835

T. King 1835

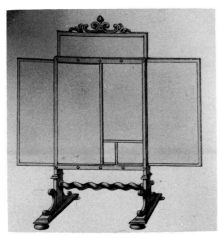

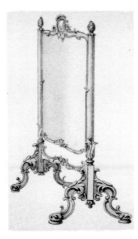

T. King 1835

T. King 1835

Pugin 1835

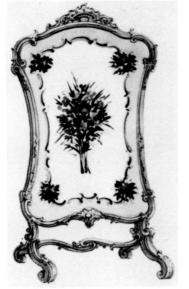

H. Wood 1846

Whitaker 1847

409

H. Wood 1848

Whitaker 1847

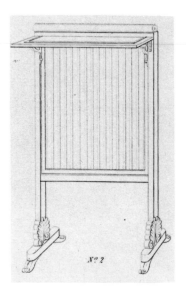

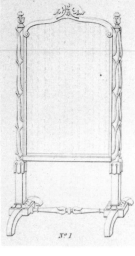

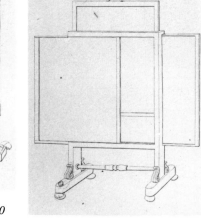

Blackie 1853

W. Smee & Sons 1850

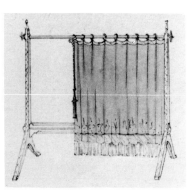

Shoolbred 1876

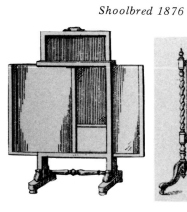

Booth 1864

Richard Charles 1866

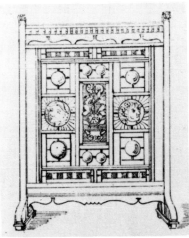

Wyman 1877

A. Jonquet 1879

Yapp 1879

Yapp 1879

C. & R. Light 1881

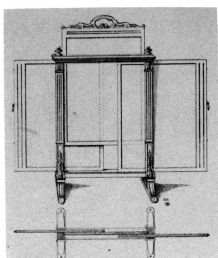

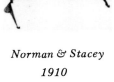

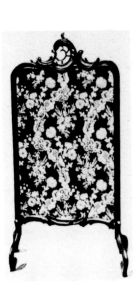

C. & R. Light 1881

*Norman & Stacey
1910*

G. Smith 1808

T. King 1830

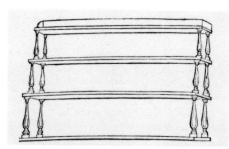

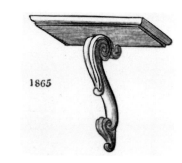

Loudon 1833

1865

1866

1867

Loudon 1833

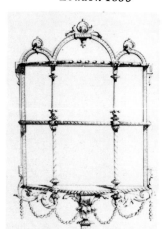

20

Booth 1864

21

Shoolbred 1876

53

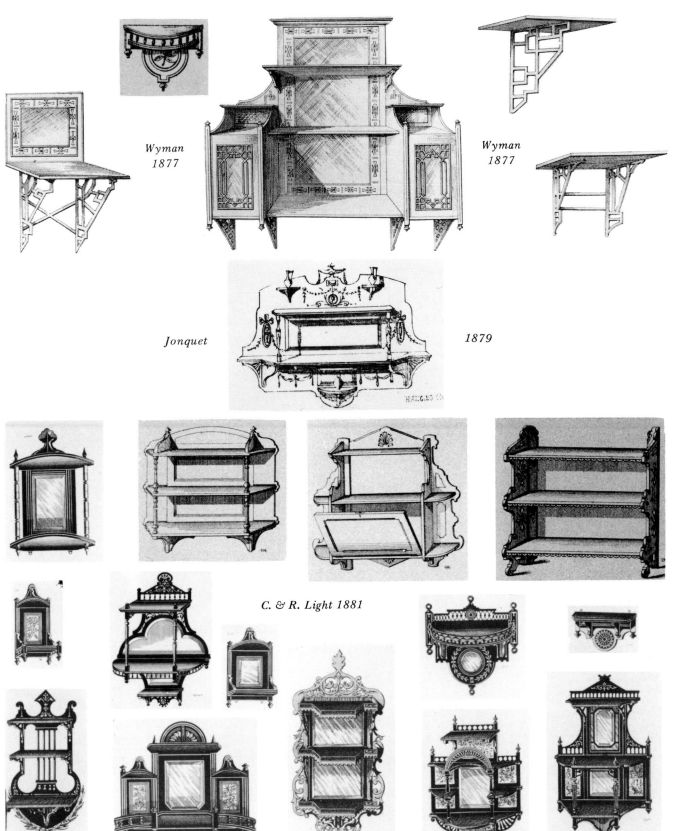

Wyman
1877

Wyman
1877

Jonquet   *1879*

C. & R. Light 1881

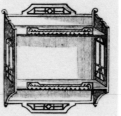
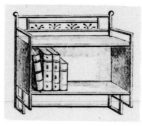

C. & R. Light 1881

Heal 1884

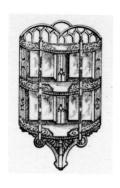
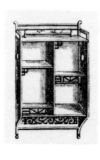

Heal 1884

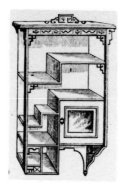

Heal 1884   *Liberty 1890*

SHELVES

Central support

T. King 1835

Booth 1864

Shoolbred 1876

C. & R. Light 1881

C. & R. Light 1881

Horizontal

SHELVES

Mobile

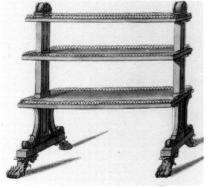

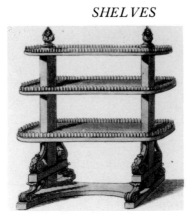

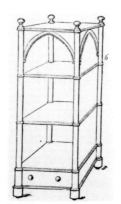

Loudon 1833

G. Smith 1808

T. King Supplementary Plates

415

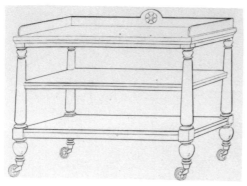

T. King Supplementary Plates

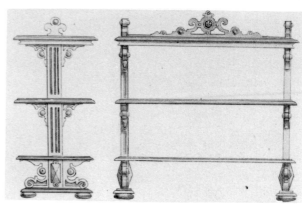

T. King 1835

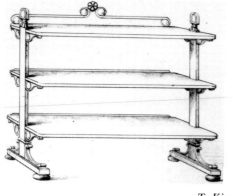

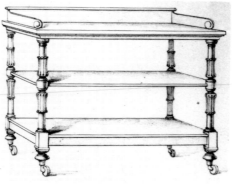

T. King 1835

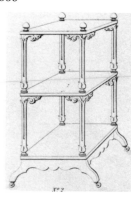

W. Smee & Sons 1850

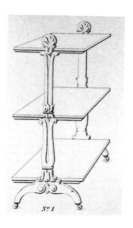

W. Smee & Sons 1850

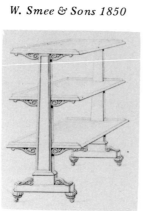

416

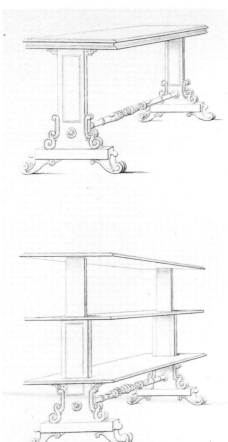

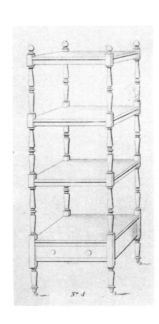

W. Smee & Sons 1850

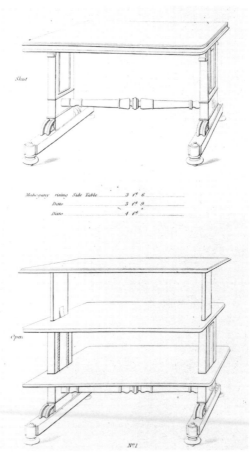

W. Blackie 1853

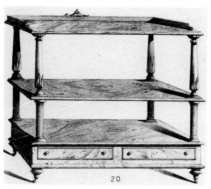

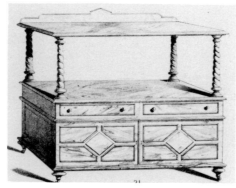

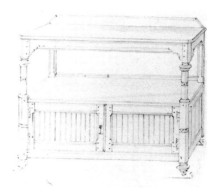

Booth 1864   *Richard Charles 1866*

Richard Charles 1866

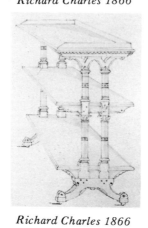

Richard Charles 1866

Shoolbred 1876

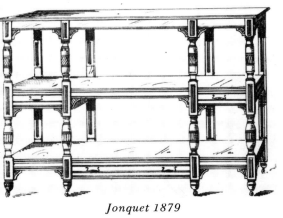

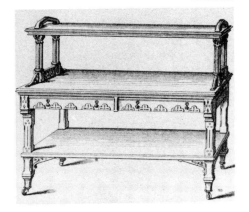

Jonquet 1879   *Yapp 1879*   *C. & R. Light 1881*

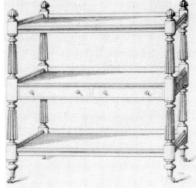

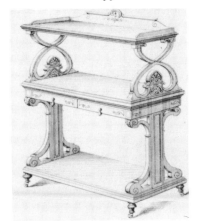

C. & R. Light 1881

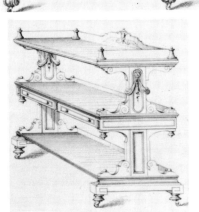

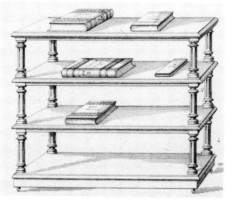

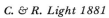

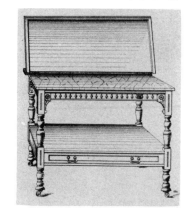

C. & R. Light 1881

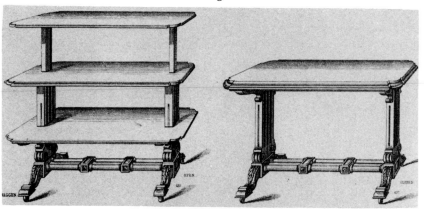

C. & R. Light 1881

C. & R. Light 1881

Heal 1884

Heal 1884

Heal 1884

Wyman 1886

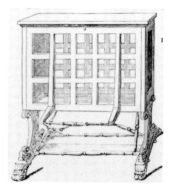
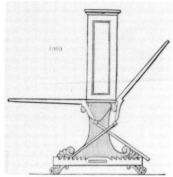

G. Smith 1808   *Loudon 1833*

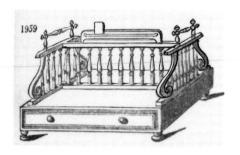
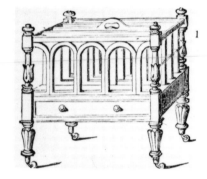

Loudon 1833

T. King Supplementary Plates   *W. Smee & Sons 1850*

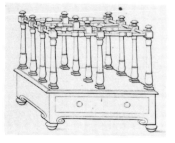

W. Smee & Sons 1850

W. Smee & Sons 1850

W. Blackie 1853

W. Blackie 1853   *Booth 1864*   *W. Watt 1877*

C. & R. Light 1881

Wyman 1886

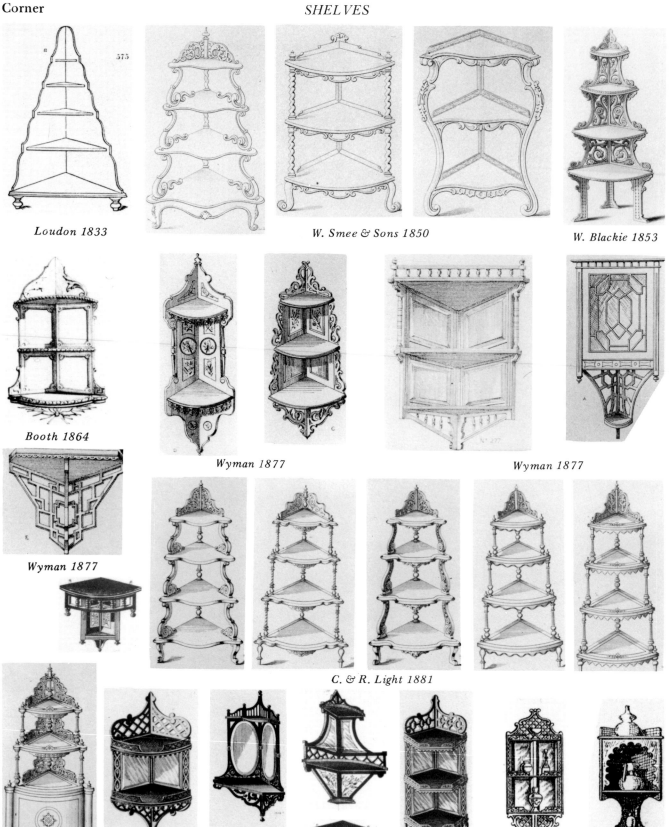

Loudon 1833

W. Smee & Sons 1850

W. Blackie 1853

Booth 1864

Wyman 1877

Wyman 1877

Wyman 1877

C. & R. Light 1881

C. & R. Light 1881

Heal 1884

Liberty 1890

C. & R. Light 1881

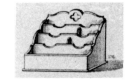

C. & R. Light 1881

C. & R. Light 1881

Morris 1900

Sheraton 1802

Sheraton 1802

Sheraton Encyclopaedia 1804

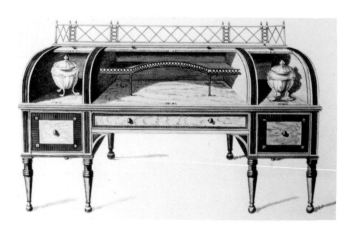

Sheraton Encyclopaedia 1804

Sheraton Encyclopaedia 1804

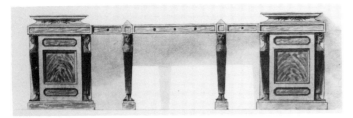

G. Smith 1808

G. Smith 1808

G. Smith 1808

Brown's Rudiments 1822

P. & M.A. Nicholson

P. & M.A. Nicholson 1826

P. & M.A. Nicholson 1826

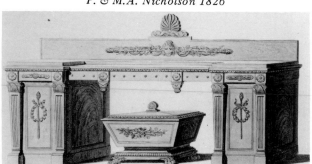

P. & M.A. Nicholson 1826

G. Smith's Guide 1826

G. Smith's Guide 1826

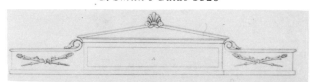

G. Smith's Guide 1826

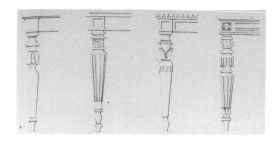

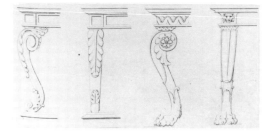

G. Smith's Guide 1826

Whitaker 1825

Whitaker 1825

Whitaker 1825

Modern Style Exemplified 1829

Whitaker 1825

Modern Style Exemplified 1829

Modern Style Exemplified 1829

Modern Style Exemplified 1829

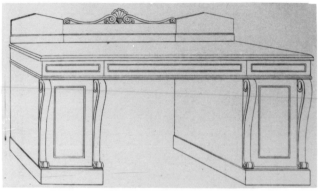

Modern Style Exemplified 1829

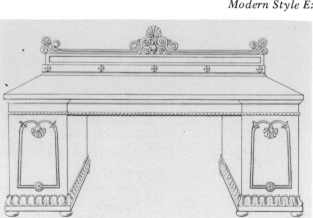

Bridgens 1838

Modern Style Exemplified 1829

Bridgens 1838

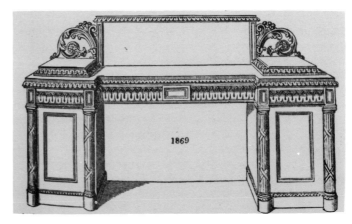

Loudon 1833

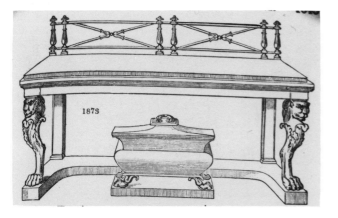

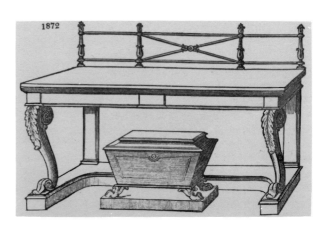

Loudon 1833

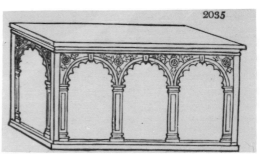

431

T. King Elizabethan and Louis XIV Styles 1835

T. King Elizabethan and Louis XIV Styles 1835

T. King Cabinet Maker's Sketch Book 1835

T. King Cabinet Maker's Sketch Book 1835

T. King Cabinet Maker's Sketch Book 1835

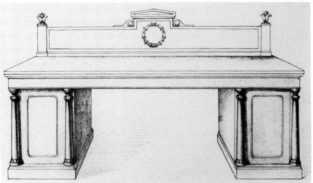

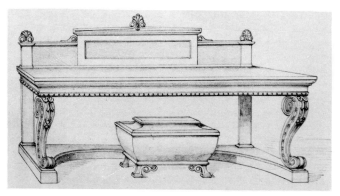

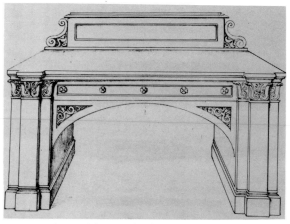

T. King Cabinet Maker's Sketch Book 1835

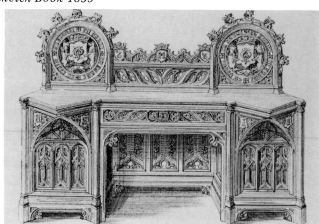

T. King Cabinet Maker's Sketch Book 1835

Pugin 1835

Whitaker 1847

Whitaker 1847

Whitaker 1847

H. Wood Supplement 1848

W. Smee & Sons 1850

W. Smee & Sons 1850

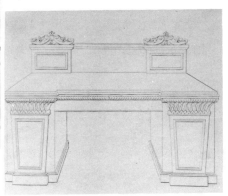

W. Smee & Sons 1850

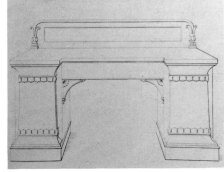

W. Smee & Sons 1850

435

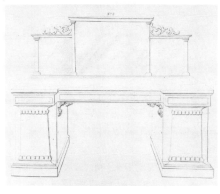

W. Smee & Sons 1850

W. Smee & Sons 1850

W. Smee & Sons 1850

W. Smee & Sons 1850

J. Taylor 1850

J. Taylor 1850

J. Taylor 1850

J. Taylor 1850

Blackie 1853

Blackie 1853

J. Taylor 1850

Blackie 1853

Blackie 1853

Blackie 1853

437

W. Blackie — 1853

W. Blackie 1853

Booth 1864

Booth 1864

Booth 1864

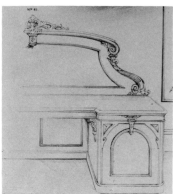

Booth 1864

Richard Charles 1866

Richard Charles 1866

Richard Charles 1866

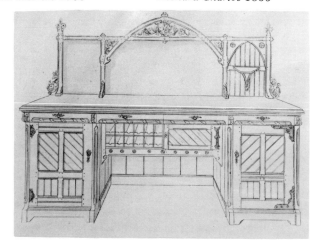

Richard Charles 1866

Richard Charles 1866

Richard Charles 1866

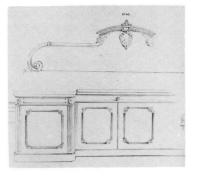

Richard Charles 1866

Shoolbred 1876

W. Watt 1877

Yapp 1879

Yapp 1879

Yapp 1879

Yapp 1879

Yapp 1879

Yapp 1879

Yapp 1879

C. & R. Light 1881

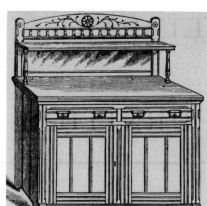

Heal 1884

Heal 1884

Heal 1884

Heal 1884

Heal 1884

Heal 1884

Heal 1884

Heal 1884

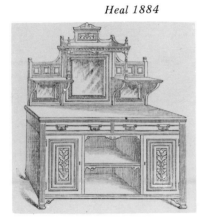

Heal 1884

Heal 1884

Norman & Stacey 1910

Norman & Stacey 1910

No. 75. MAHOGANY SIDEBOARD New Design
5 ft. wide. Price £25 18s. 6d.

Norman & Stacey 1910

Norman & Stacey 1910

Norman & Stacey 1910

441

G. Smith 1808

Whitaker 1825

Loudon 1833

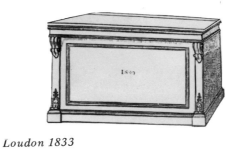

Loudon 1833

T. King Supplementary Plates

T. King Cabinet Maker's Sketchbook 1835

T. King
Cabinet Maker's Sketchbook 1835

T. King
Elizabethan and
Louis XIV Styles
1835

T. King Elizabethan and Louis XIV Styles 1835

H. Wood 1848

T. King 1835

W. Smee & Sons 1850

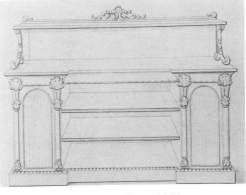

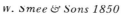

W. Smee & Sons 1850

W. Smee & Sons 1850

J. Taylor 1850

Blackie 1853

445

Blackie 1853

Richard Charles 1866

Shoolbred 1876

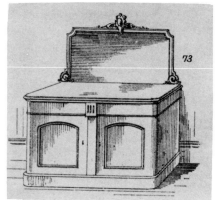

Yapp 1879

C. & R. Light 1881

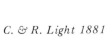
C. & R. Light 1881

C. & R. Light 1881

C. & R. Light 1881

Liberty 1890

G. Smith 1808

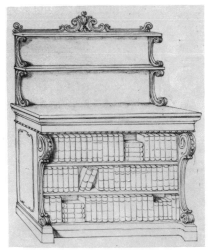

Loudon 1833   *T. King 1835*   *W. Smee & Sons 1850*

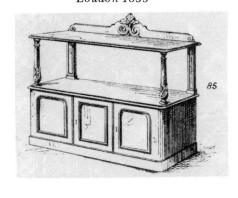

Shoolbred 1876

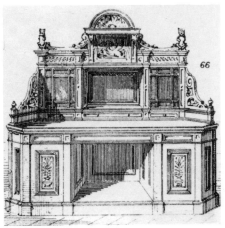

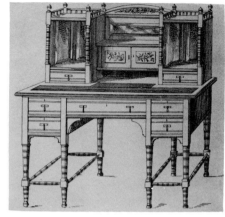

Wyman 1877

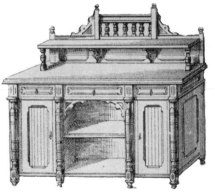

Yapp 1879

Wyman 1877

C. & R. Light 1881

C. & R. Light 1881

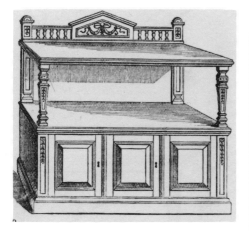

Heal 1884

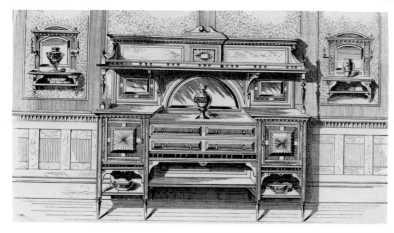

Wyman 1886

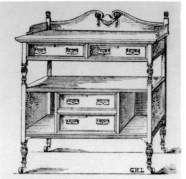

Brown 1822

P. & M.A. Nicholson 1826

Modern Style Exemplified 1829

Modern Style Exemplified 1829

Whitaker 1847

Whitaker 1847

Whitaker 1847

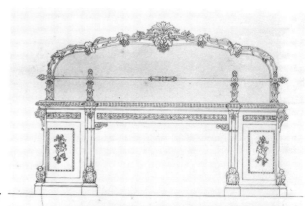

Whitaker 1847

Whitaker 1847

*H. Wood
Supplement 1848*

H. Wood Supplement 1848

W. Smee & Sons 1850   *W. Smee & Sons 1850*

W. Smee & Sons 1850   *J. Taylor 1850*

Braund 1858

Braund 1858

W. Blackie 1853

W. Blackie 1853

Waring 1862

Booth 1864

Waring 1862

Waring 1862

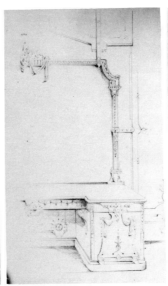

Richard Charles 1866

Richard Charles 1866

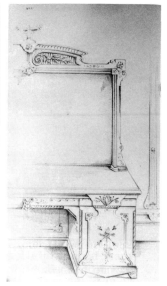

Richard Charles 1866

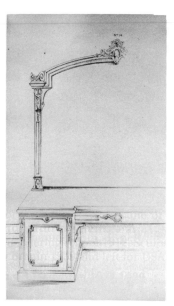
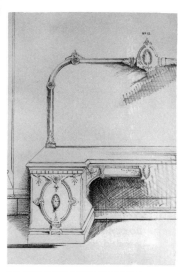

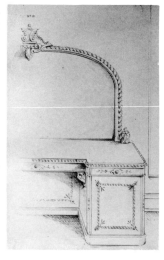
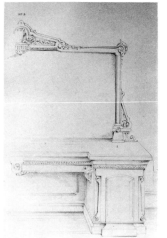

Richard Charles 1866

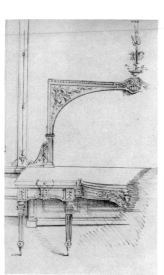

Richard Charles 1866

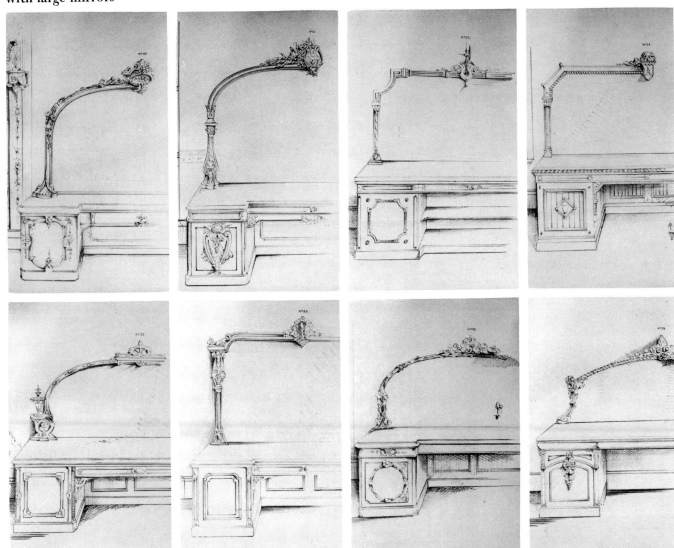

Richard Charles 1866

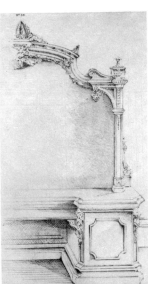

461

Richard Charles
1866

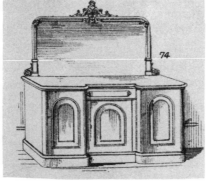

Shoolbred 1876

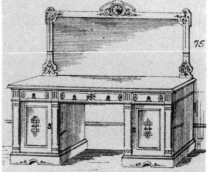

Shoolbred 1876

Shoolbred 1876

463

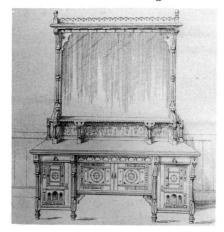

Wyman 1886

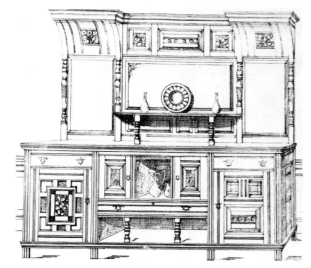

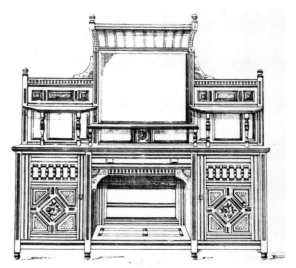

Jonquet 1879   *Jonquet 1879*

Yapp 1879   *Yapp 1879*

Yapp 1879

Yapp 1879

C. & R. Light 1881

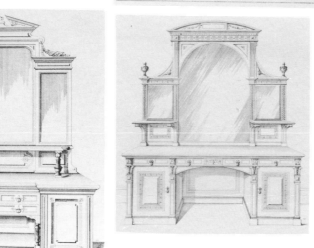

C. & R. Light 1881

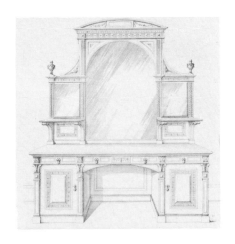

C. & R. Light 1881

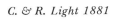

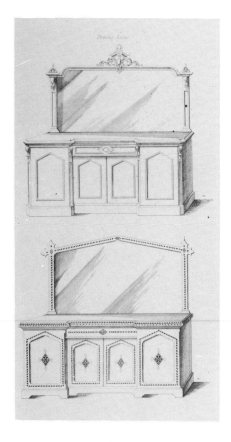

C. & R. Light 1881

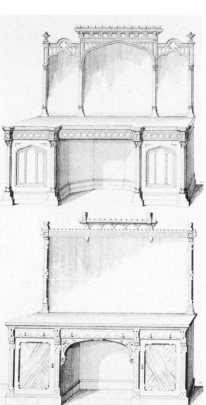

C. & R. Light 1881

Heal 1884

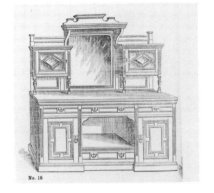

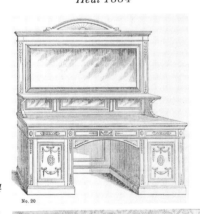

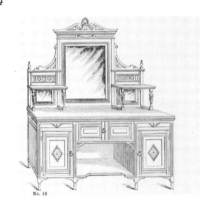

Heal 1884

Heal 1884

Wyman 1886

Wyman 1886

469

Wyman 1886

Wyman 1886

Wyman 1886

Norman & Stacey 1910

Norman & Stacey 1910

Norman & Stacey 1910

Norman & Stacey 1910

No. 94.—A SOLID SIDEBOARD in Fumed Oak or Walnut. 4 ft. 6 in. wide. Well constructed and of a compact design. Price £3 18s. 6d.

No. 81.—FUMED OAK SIDEBOARD, of solid construction. 5 ft. wide. Price £11 5s.

Norman & Stacey 1910

No. 78.—A FINELY CARVED

Norman & Stacey 1910

No. 72.—INLAID MAHOGANY SHERATON SIDEBOARD. 5 ft. wide. Price £29 10s.

471

No. 85.—SOLID FUMED OAK SIDEBOARD.
5 ft. wide. An original design. Price £27.

No. 87.—A GOOD DESIGN, in Fumed Oak, Walnut

Norman & Stacey 1910

Braund 1858

W. Blackie 1853

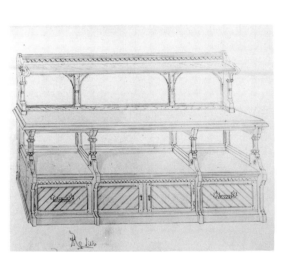

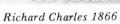

Richard Charles 1866

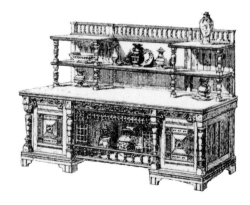

Shoolbred 1876

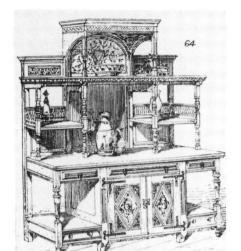

Shoolbred 1876

W. Watt 1877

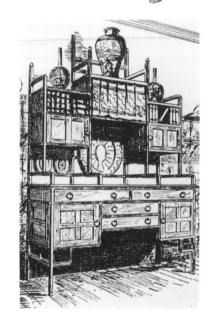

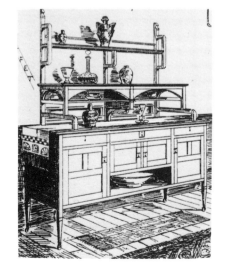

W. Watt 1877

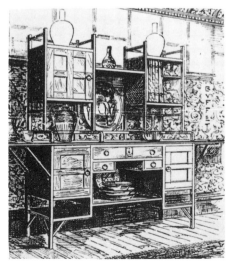

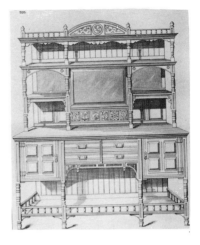

Wyman 1877

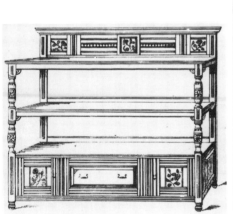

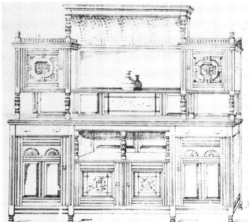

Jonquet 1879　　　　　　　　　　　　　　　*Yapp 1879*

Yapp 1879

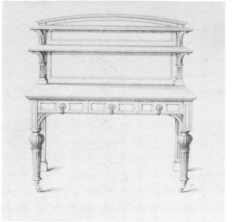

C. & R. Light 1881   *Heal 1884*

No. 22   No. 21   No. 24

Heal 1884

Wyman 1886

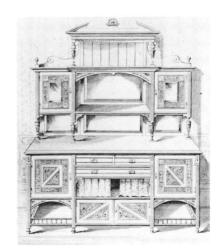

Wyman 1886

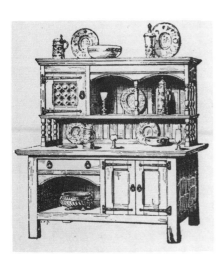

Liberty 1890

Morris 1900

No. 85.—SIDEBOARD in Solid Fumed Oak. 6 ft. wide. A very good

Morris 1900

Norman & Stacey 1910

G. Smith 1808

Pugin 1835

Waring 1862

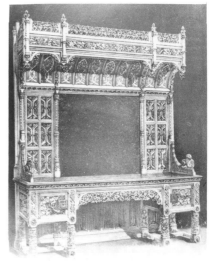

Waring 1862

J. Talbert 1876

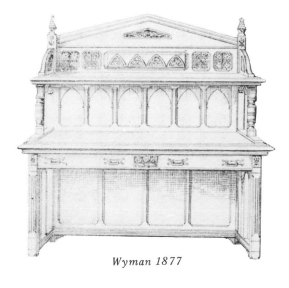

Wyman 1877

Yapp 1879

Yapp 1879

C. & R. Light 1881

Wyman 1886

Norman & Stacey 1910

G. Smith 1808

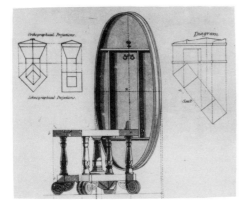

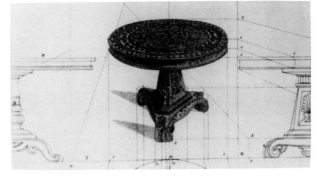

Brown's Rudiments 1822

Whitaker 1825

Brown's Rudiments 1822

G. Smith's Guide 1826

P. & M.A. Nicholson 1826

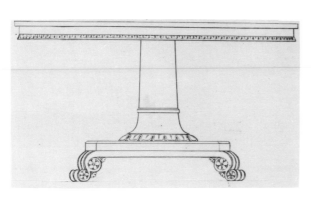

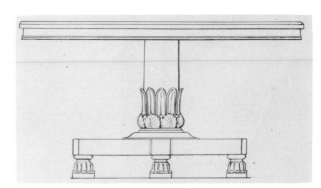

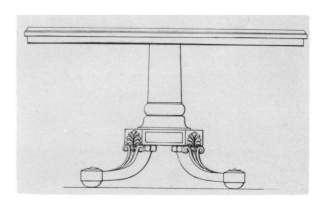

Loudon 1833

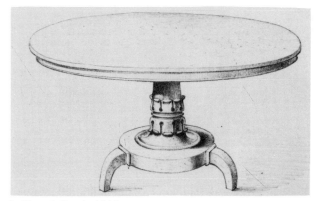

T. King Cabinet Maker's Sketch Book 1835

T. King Elizabethan and Louis XIV Styles 1835

Whitaker 1847

W. Smee & Sons 1850

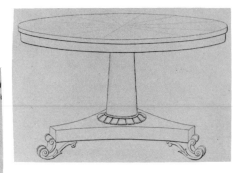

W. Smee & Sons 1850

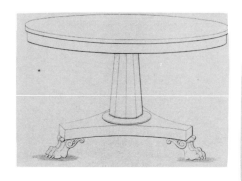

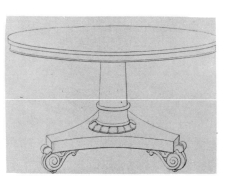

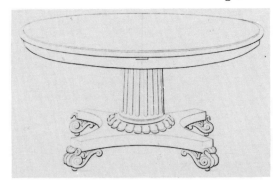

W. Smee & Sons 1850

W. Blackie 1853

Booth 1864

Yapp 1879

Booth 1864   *C. & R. Light 1881*

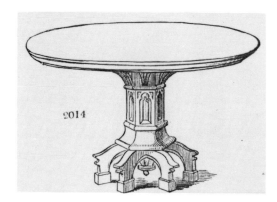

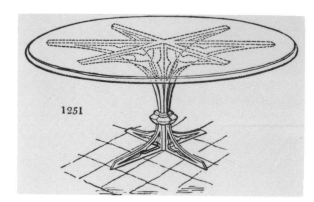

Loudon 1833

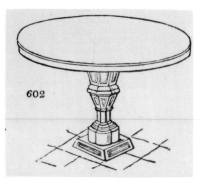

Loudon 1833

Whitaker 1847

Whitaker 1847

H. Wood Supplement 1848

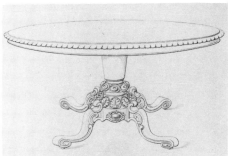

*W. Smee
& Sons
1850*

J. Taylor 1850

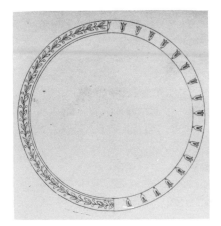

Braund 1858

W. Blackie 1853

Blackie 1853

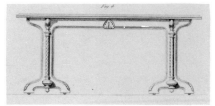

Blackie 1853

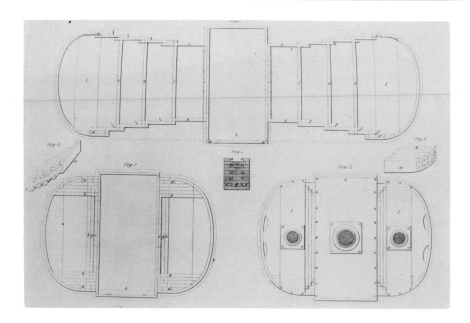

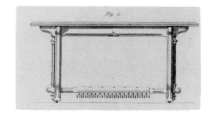

Blackie 1853

Waring 1862

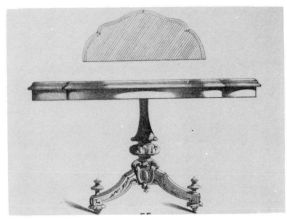

Booth 1864

Yapp 1879   *C. & R. Light 1881*

C. & R. Light 1881

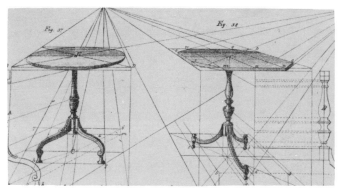

Sheraton 1802

G. Smith 1808

G. Smith 1808

G. Smith 1808

Whitaker 1825

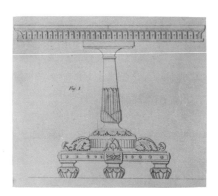

P. & M.A. Nicholson 1826

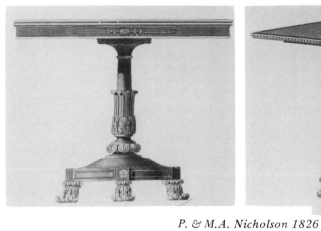

T. King 1830

P. & M.A. Nicholson 1826

G. Smith 1826

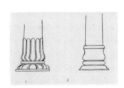

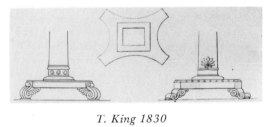

T. King 1830   *T. King 1830*

T. King 1830

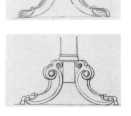

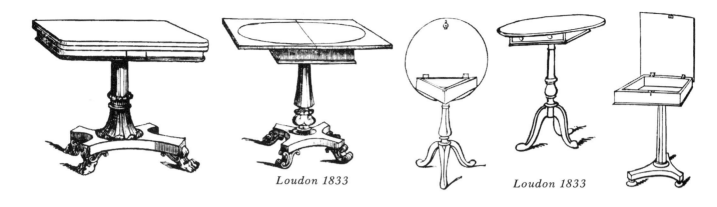

Loudon 1833 *Loudon 1833*

Loudon 1833

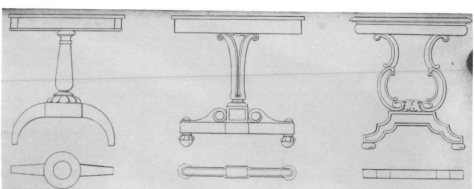

T. King Supplementary Plates

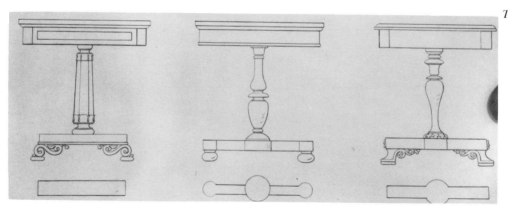

T. King Elizabethan and Louis XIV Styles 1835 *T. King 1835*

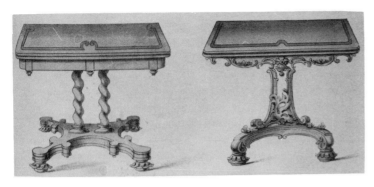

T. King Elizabethan and Louis XIV Styles 1835

T. King 1835

T. King Cabinet Maker's Sketch Book 1835

*T. King Cabinet Maker's
Sketch Book 1835*

Whitaker 1847

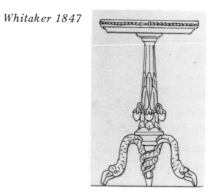

494

W. Smee & Sons
1850

W. Smee & Sons 1850

J. Taylor 1850

Braund 1858

W. Blackie 1853

H. Lawford 1867

Shoolbred 1876

Booth 1864

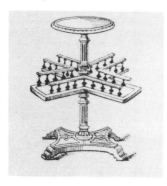

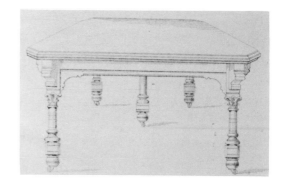

Wyman 1877

Jonquet 1879

Yapp 1879

Yapp 1879

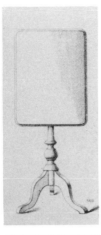

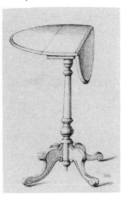

C. & R. Light 1881

Heal 1884

Liberty 1890

Pugin 1835

H. Wood Supplement 1848

H. Wood Supplement 1848

J. Taylor 1850

J. Taylor 1850

W. Smee & Sons 1850

W. Blackie 1853

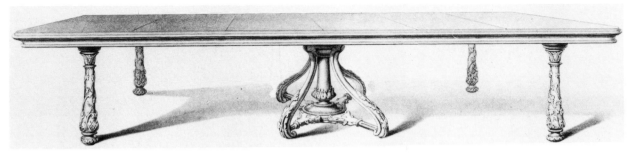

W. Blackie l853

W. Blackie 1853

Waring 1862

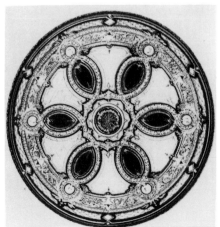

Booth 1864

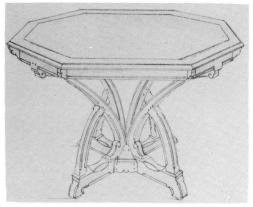

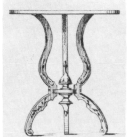

Richard Charles 1866

Shoolbred 1876

Wyman 1877

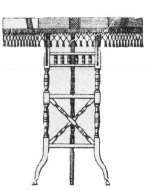

Wyman 1877

Yapp 1879

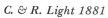

C. & R. Light 1881

C. & R. Light 1881

503

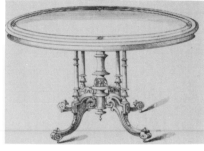

C. & R. Light 1881

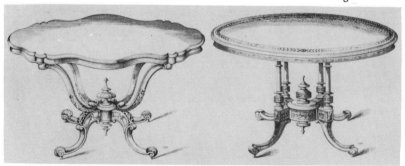

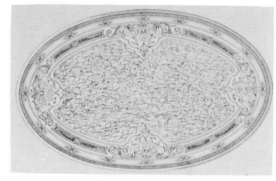

C. & R. Light 1881

Norman & Stacey 1910

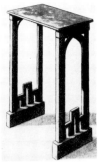

G. Smith 1808

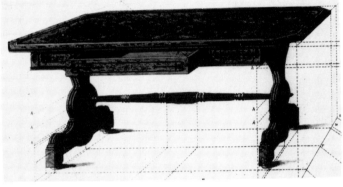

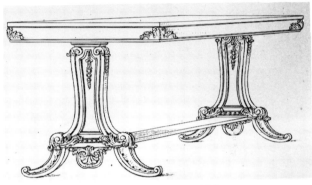

Brown's Rudiments 1822

Whitaker 1825

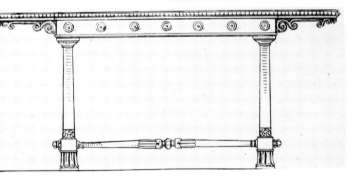

G. Smith's Guide 1826

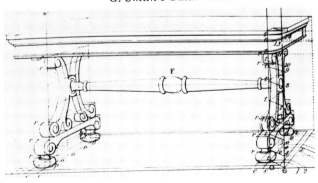

G. Smith's Guide 1826

505

G. Smith's Guide 1826

Modern Style

Exemplified 1829

Loudon 1833

1952

1951

1950

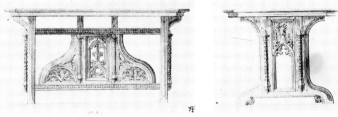

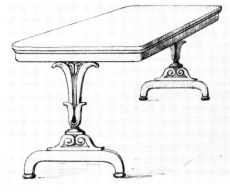

Pugin 1835

T. King Cabinet Maker's Sketch Book 1835

T. King
Elizabethan and Louis XIV Styles 1835

507

T. King Elizabethan and Louis XIV Styles 1835

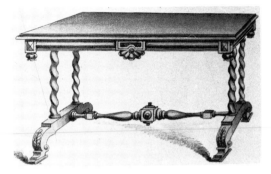

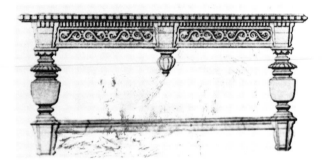

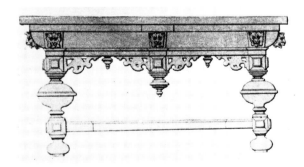

Bridgens 1838

Bridgens 1838

Bridgens 1838

Whitaker 1847

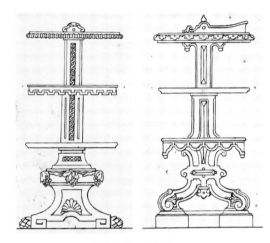

Whitaker 1847

H. Wood Supplement 1848

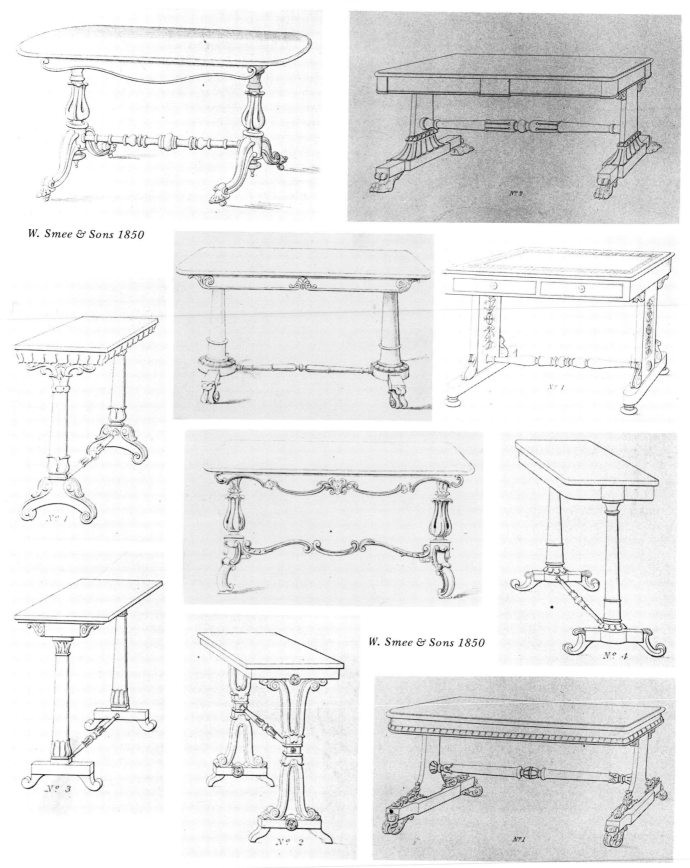

W. Smee & Sons 1850

W. Smee & Sons 1850

W. Blackie 1853

W. Blackie 1853

Booth 1864

Richard Charles 1866

Yapp 1879

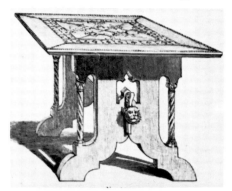

Yapp 1879

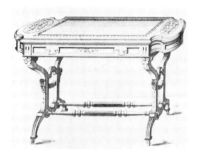

C. & R. Light 1881

Yapp 1879

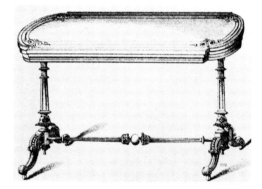

C. & R. Light 1881

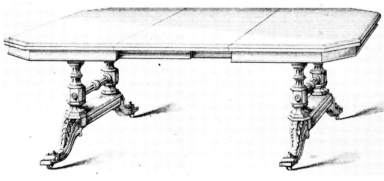

C. & R. Light 1881

Heal 1884

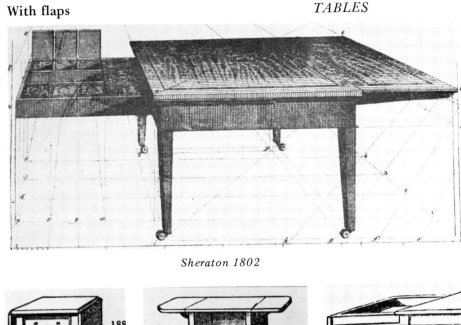

Loudon 1833

Sheraton 1802

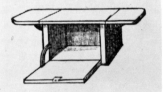

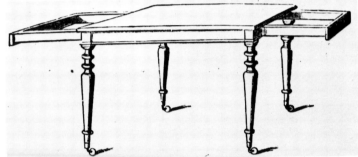

Loudon 1833

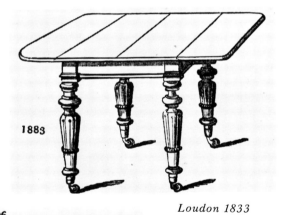

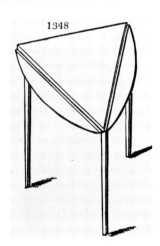

1882

1883

1348

Loudon 1833

606

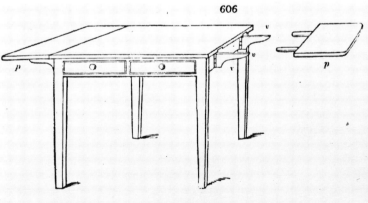

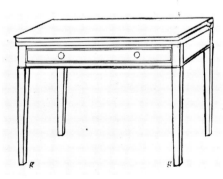

W. Smee & Sons 1850

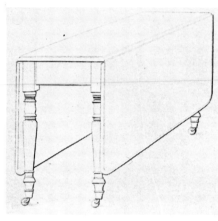

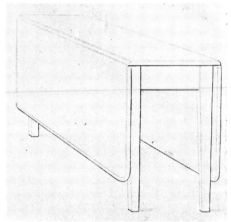

C. & R. Light 1881

Booth 1864

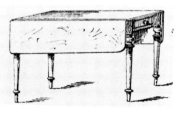

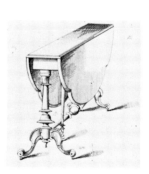

Shoolbred 1876

C. & R. Light 1881

C. & R. Light 1881

C. & R. Light 1881

Heal 1884

Heal 1884

Norman & Stacey 1910

Sheraton 1802

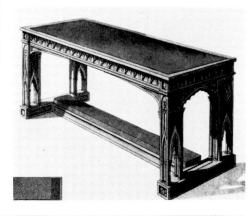

G. Smith 1808

G. Smith 1808

G. Smith 1808

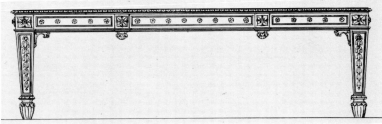

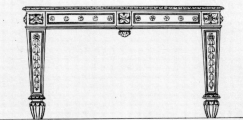

Whitaker 1825

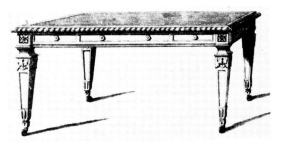

G. Smith's Guide 1826

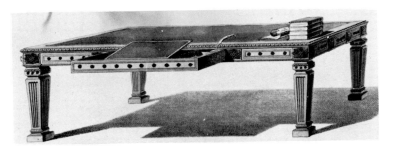

P. & M.A. Nicholson 1826

Loudon 1833

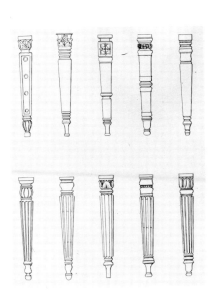

Modern Style Exemplified 1829

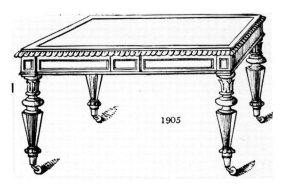

1905

Loudon 1833

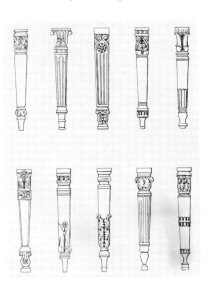

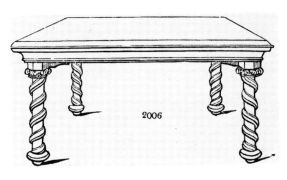

2006

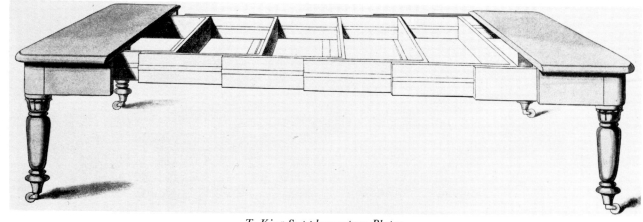

T. King Supplementary Plates

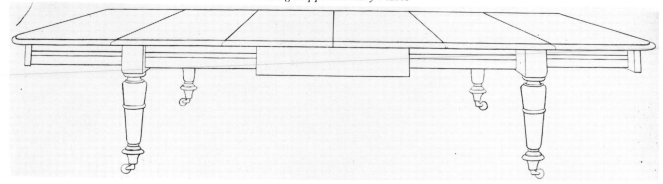

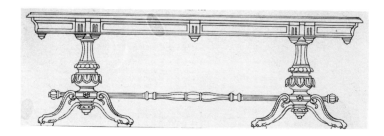

Whitaker 1847

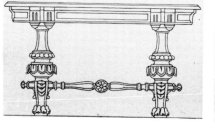

T. King Elizabethan and Louis XIV Styles 1835

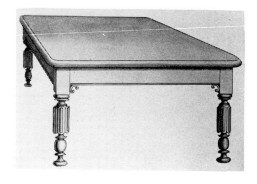

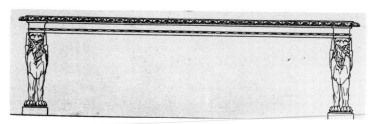

W. Smee & Sons 1850

Braund 1858

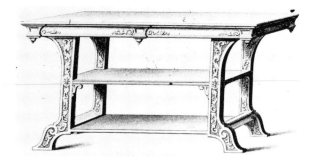

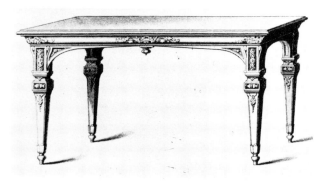

W. Blackie 1853

W. Blackie 1853

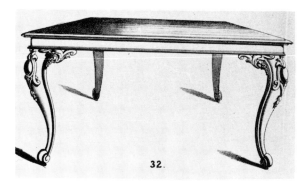

32.

Booth 1864

Booth 1864

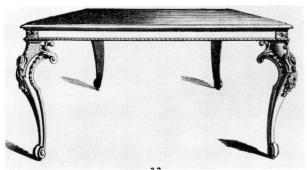

Booth 1864

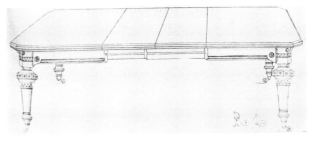

Richard Charles 1866

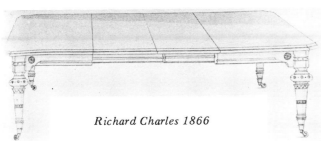

Richard Charles 1866

H. Lawford 1867

H. Lawford 1867

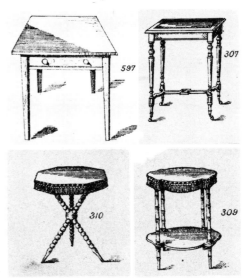

Shoolbred 1876

Wyman 1877

Yapp 1879

Jonquet 1879

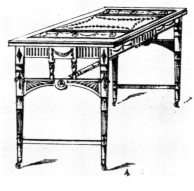
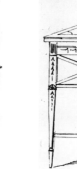

Jonquet 1879

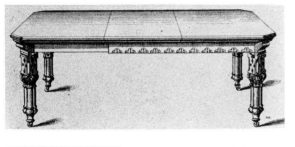

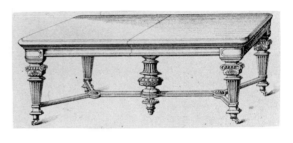

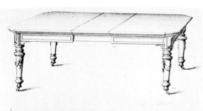

C. & R. Light 1881

C. & R. Light 1881

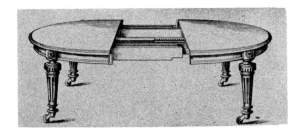
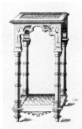
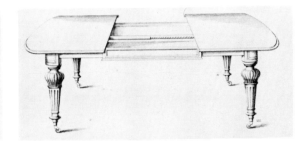

C. & R. Light 1881

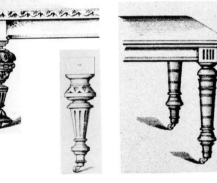
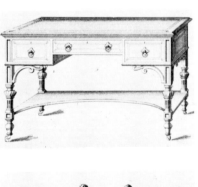

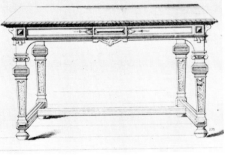

C. & R. Light 1881

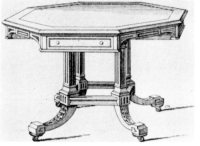

C. & R. Light 1881

C. & R. Light 1881

Maddox 1882

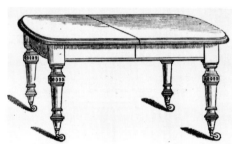

Heal 1884

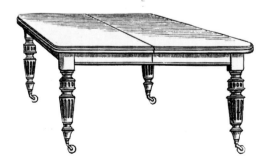

Heal 1884

Heal 1884

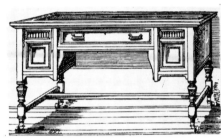

Wyman 1886

Wyman 1886

Liberty 1890

Morris 1900

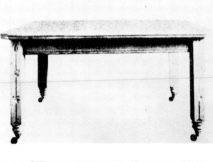

No. 123.—AN INEXPENSIVE TABLE, with stained legs and plain top. Sizes and Prices £. s. d.

No. 124.—SOLID OAK, Walnut or Mahogany Extending Table, Sizes and Prices—

Norman & Stacey 1910

No. 192.—INLAID MAHO-

No. 194.

No. 195.

Norman & Stacey 1910

529

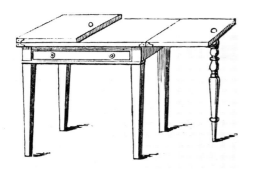

Loudon 1833

W. Smee & Sons 1850

Booth 1864

Shoolbred 1876

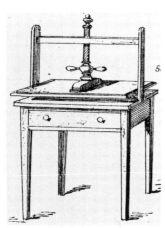

C. & R. Light 1881

Shoolbred 1876

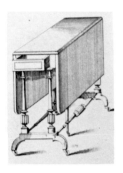

C. & R. Light 1881

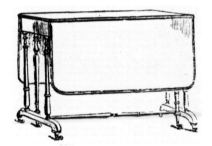

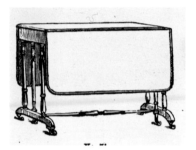

Maddox 1882   *Maddox 1882*

Norman & Stacey 1910

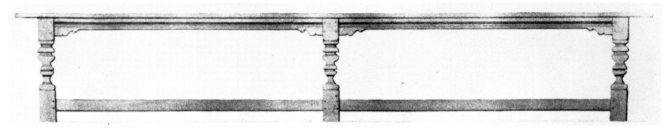

Bridgens 1838

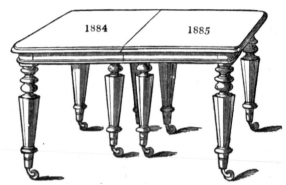

Loudon 1833

W. Watt 1877

Liberty 1890

Yapp 1879

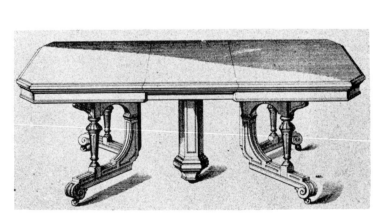

C. & R. Light 1881

Norman & Stacey 1910

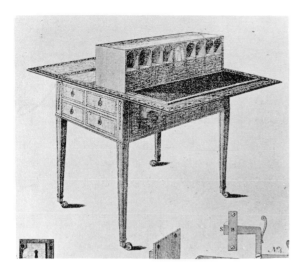

Sheraton 1802

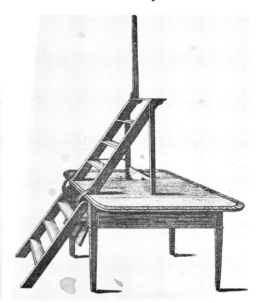

Sheraton 1802

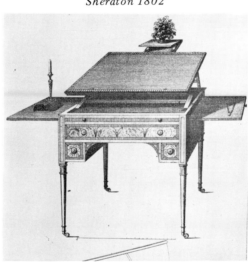

G. Smith 1808

G. Smith 1808

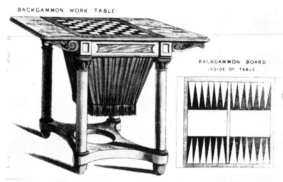

Whitaker 1825

G. Smith's Guide 1826

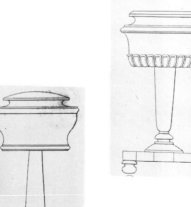

Modern Style Exemplified 1829

Loudon 1833

Loudon 1833

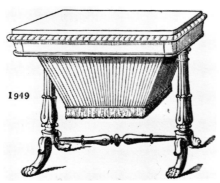

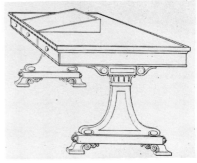

Loudon 1833

T. King Supplementary Plates

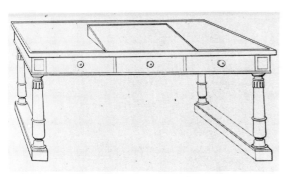

T. King Supplementary Plates

T. King 1835

T. King 1835

T. King 1835

W. Smee & Sons 1850

W. Smee & Sons 1850

W. Smee & Sons 1850

J. Taylor 1850

W. Blackie 1853

J. Taylor 1850

W. Blackie 1853

Waring 1862

Booth 1864

Richard Charles 1866

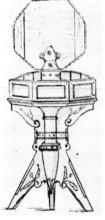

Richard Charles 1866

Lawford 1867

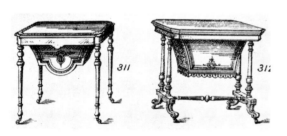

W. Watt 1877

Shoolbred 1876

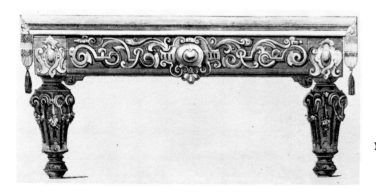

Yapp 1879

Yapp 1879

C. & R. Light 1881

C. & R. Light 1881

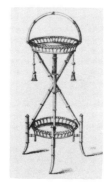

C. & R. Light 1881

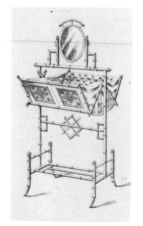

No. 104   No. 105

Heal 1884

Norman & Stacey 1910

G. Smith 1808

Whitaker 1825

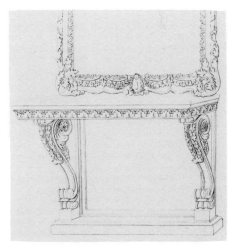

G. Smith's Guide 1826

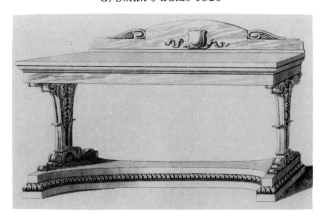

G. Smith's Guide 1826

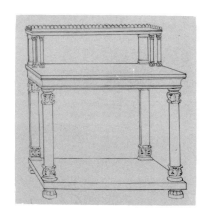

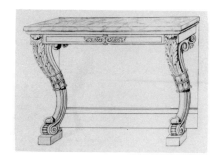

Modern Style Exemplified 1829

Bridgens 1838

T. King 1835

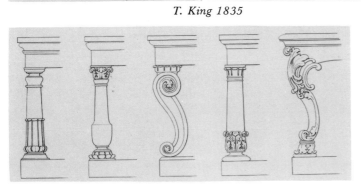

T. King 1835

Whitaker 1847

Whitaker 1847

Whitaker 1847

W. Blackie 1853

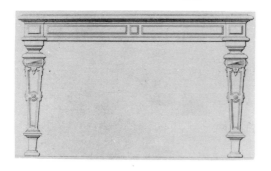

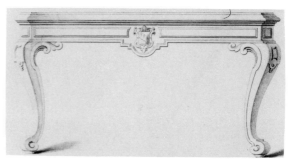

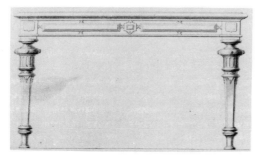

Booth 1864

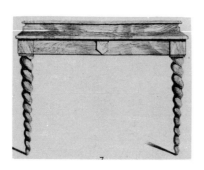

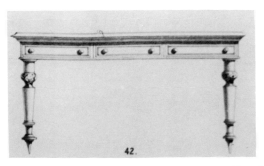
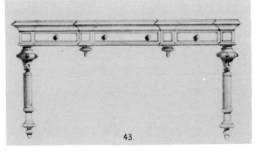

Booth 1864

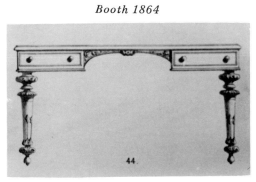

Shoolbred 1876   *Shoolbred 1876*

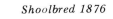

Yapp 1879

Wyman 1877

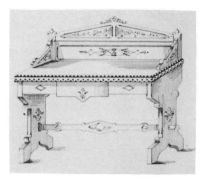

C. & R. Light 1881

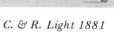

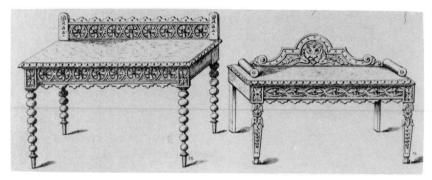

C. & R. Light 1881

Heal 1884

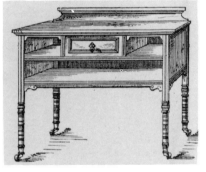

Heal 1884

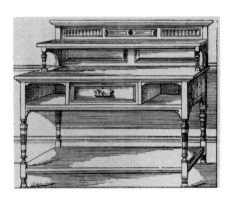

Wyman 1886

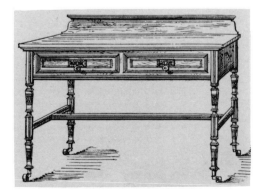

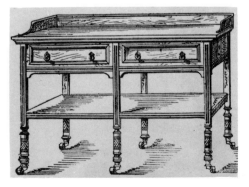

Wyman 1886

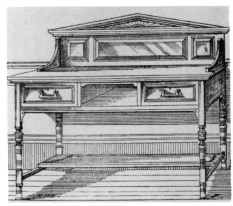

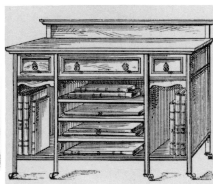

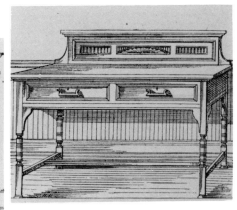

Norman & Stacey 1910

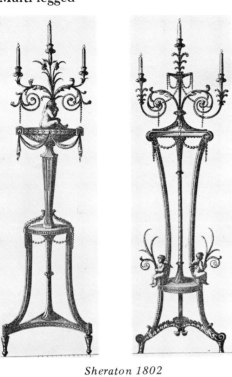

G. Smith 1808

G. Smith's Guide 1826

Sheraton 1802

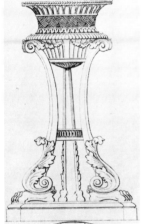

G. Smith's Guide 1826

T. King 1830

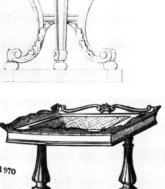

T. King 1830

1970

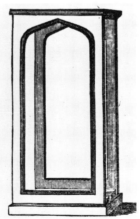

Loudon 1833

Loudon 1833

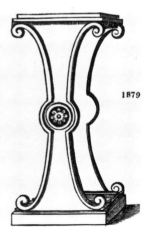

1879

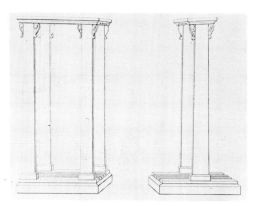

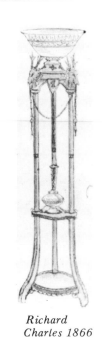

W. Smee & Sons 1850

W. Smee & Sons 1850

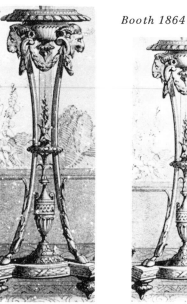

Booth 1864

Booth 1864

Booth 1864

Richard Charles 1866

Braund 1858

588

Shoolbred 1876

5

5

H. Lawford 1867

Shoolbred 1876

W. Watt 1877

Yapp 1879

C. & R. Light 1881

C. & R. Light 1881

Liberty 1890

Norman & Stacey 1910

551

G. Smith 1808

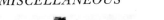

G. Smith 1808

G. Smith 1808

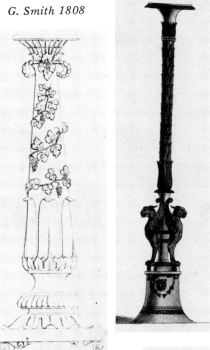

P. & M.A. Nicholson 1826

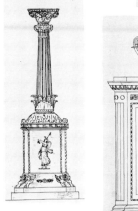

Whitaker 1825

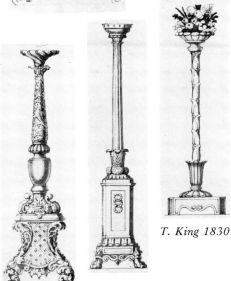

T. King 1830

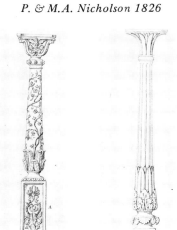

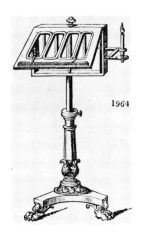

1964

1963

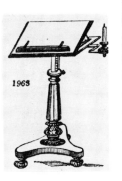

197?

Loudon 1833   *Loudon 1833*

553

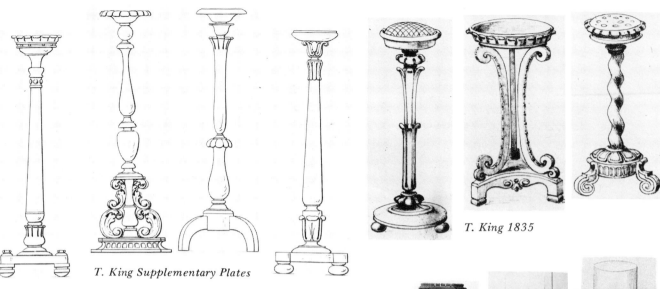

T. King Supplementary Plates

T. King 1835

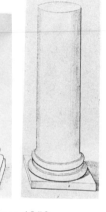

Bridgens 1838

W. Smee & Sons 1850

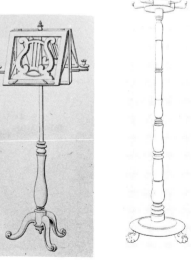
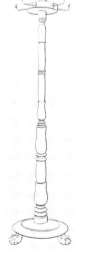
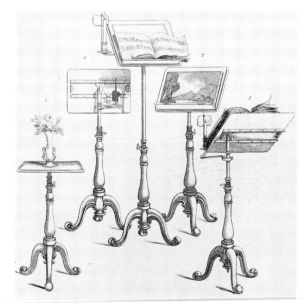

W. Smee & Sons 1850

Braund 1858

Braund 1858

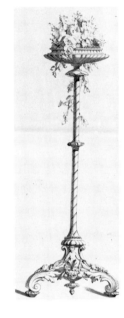

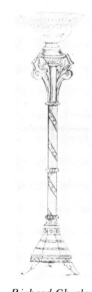

Booth 1864

Richard Charles 1866

W. Blackie 1853

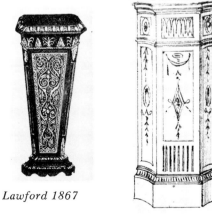

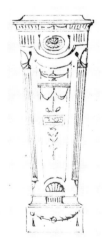

Lawford 1867

Jonquet 1879

No. 30.

Yapp 1879

C. & R. Light 1881

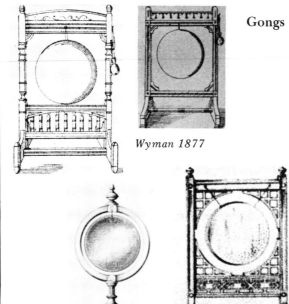

Gongs

Wyman 1877

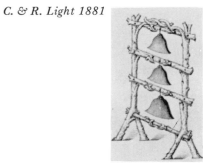

C. & R. Light 1881

C. & R. Light 1881

*Norman &
Stacey 1910*

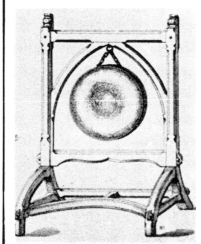

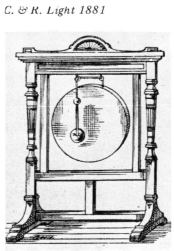

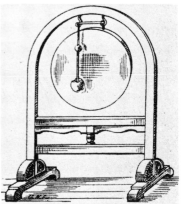

Wyman 1886

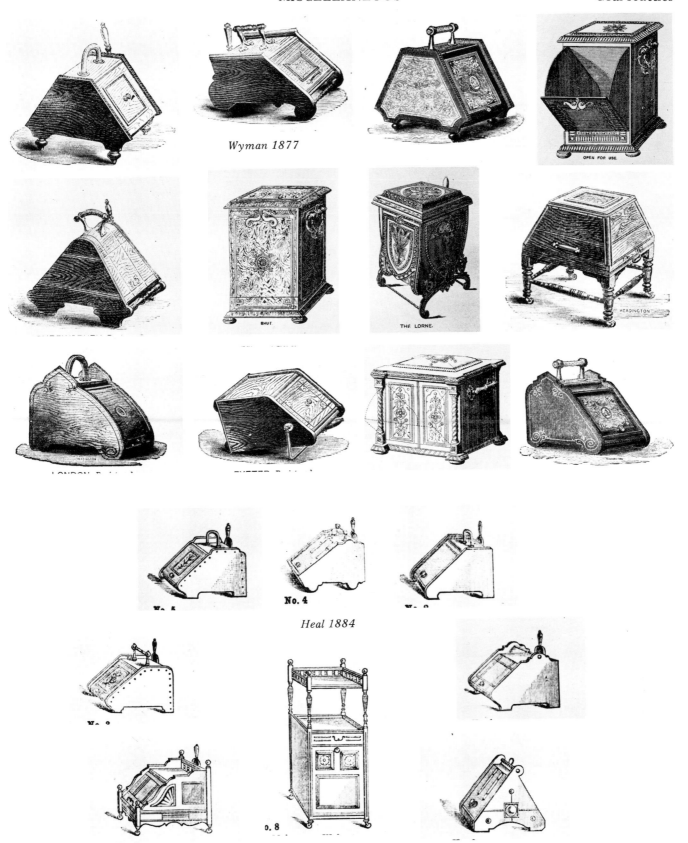

Wyman 1877

Heal 1884

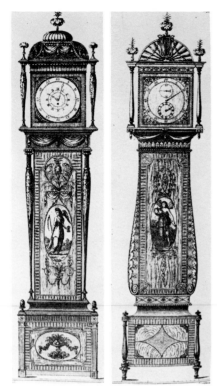

Braund 1858

Sheraton 1802

Loudon 1833

W. Blackie 1853

W. Blackie 1853

W. Blackie 1853

Fig 3

Wyman 1877

Wyman 1877

Yapp 1879

No. 27.

Yapp 1879

Yapp 1879

C. & R. Light 1881

Yapp 1879

Morris 1900

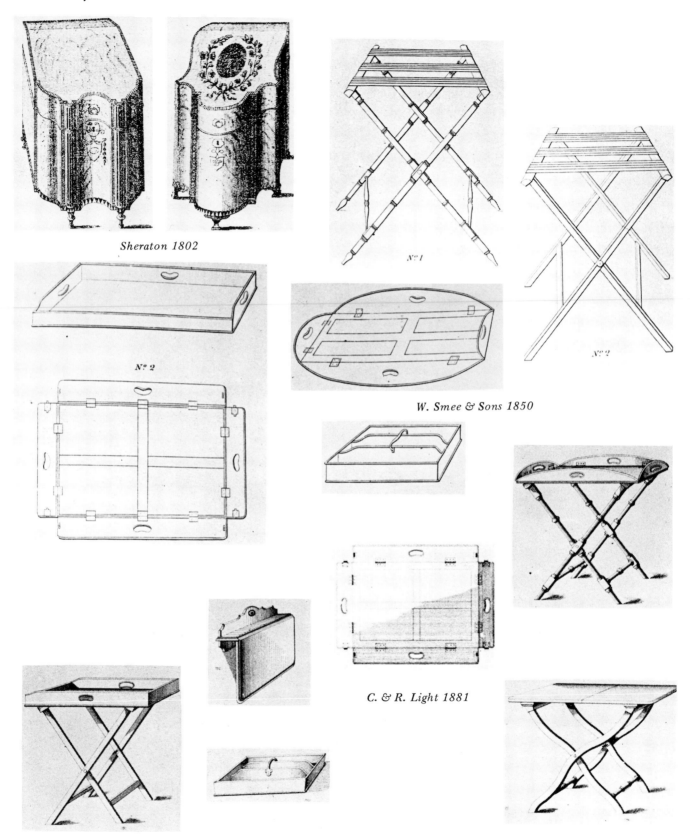

Sheraton 1802

N° 1

N° 2

N° 2

W. Smee & Sons 1850

C. & R. Light 1881

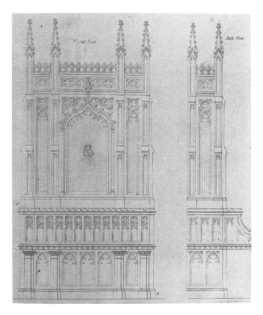

P. & M.A. Nicholson 1826

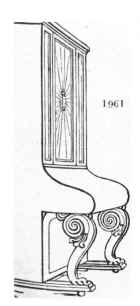

1961

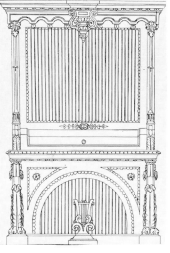

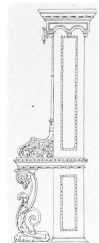

Whitaker 1847

Loudon 1833

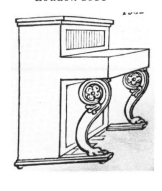

Braund 1858

Waring 1862

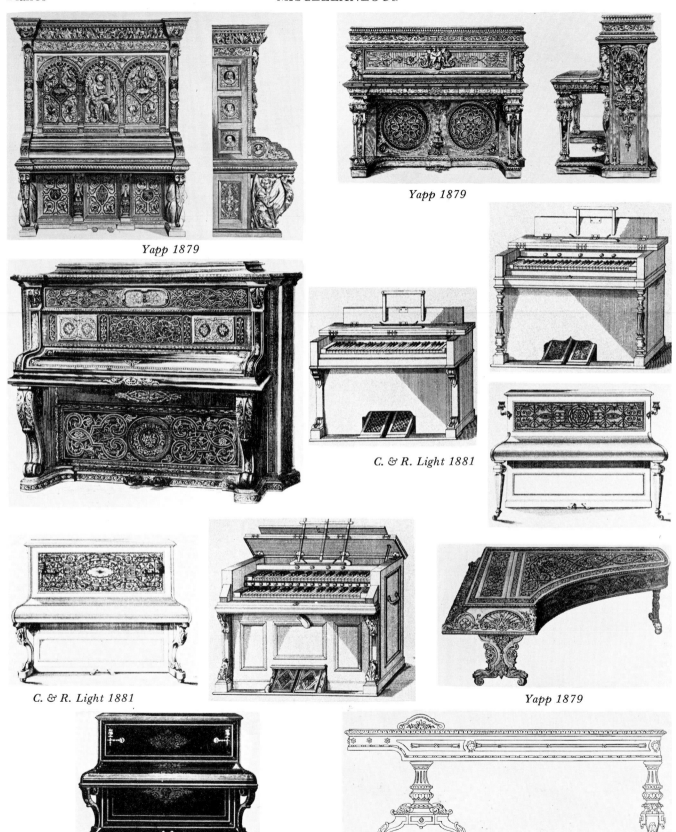

Yapp 1879

Yapp 1879

C. & R. Light 1881

C. & R. Light 1881

Yapp 1879

Whitaker 1847

T. King 1830

Whitaker 1847

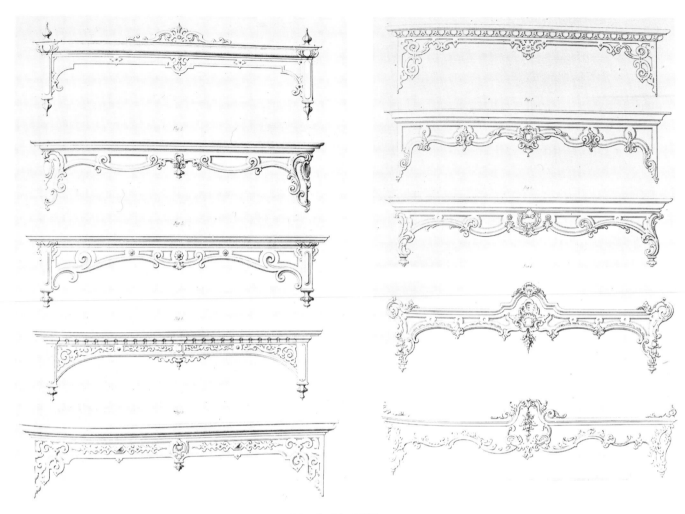

W. Blackie 1853

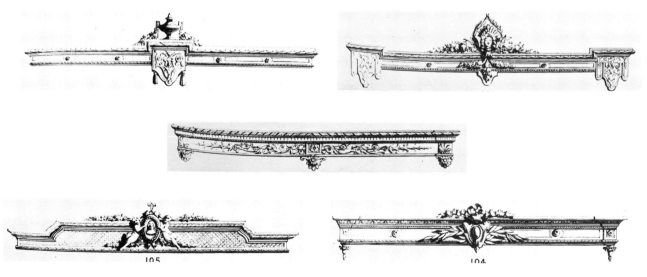

Booth 1864

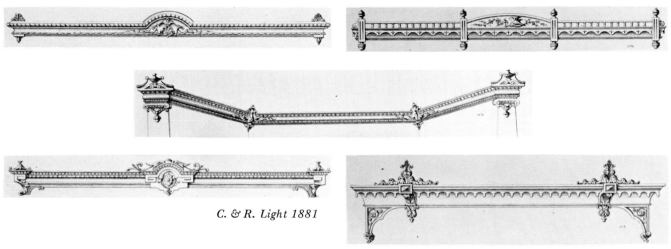

C. & R. Light 1881

With poles   **Window cornice**

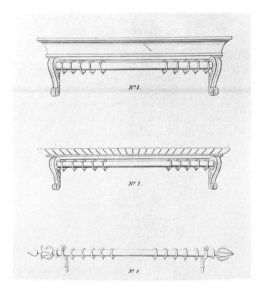

W. Smee & Sons 1850

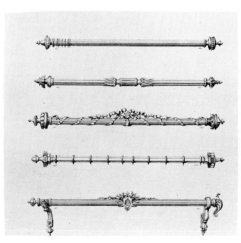

Richard Charles 1866

C. & R. Light 1881

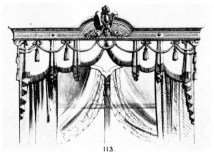

113.

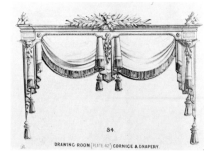

84.

DRAWING ROOM (PLATE 42) CORNICE & DRAPERY.

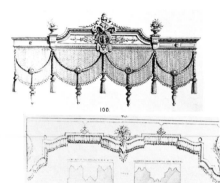

100.

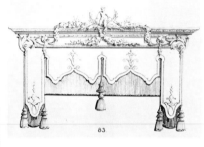

83.

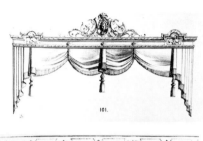

101.

Booth 1864

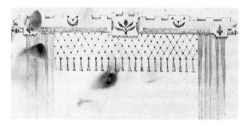

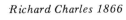

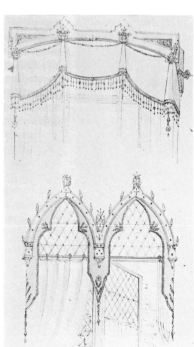

Richard Charles 1866

Richard Charles 1866

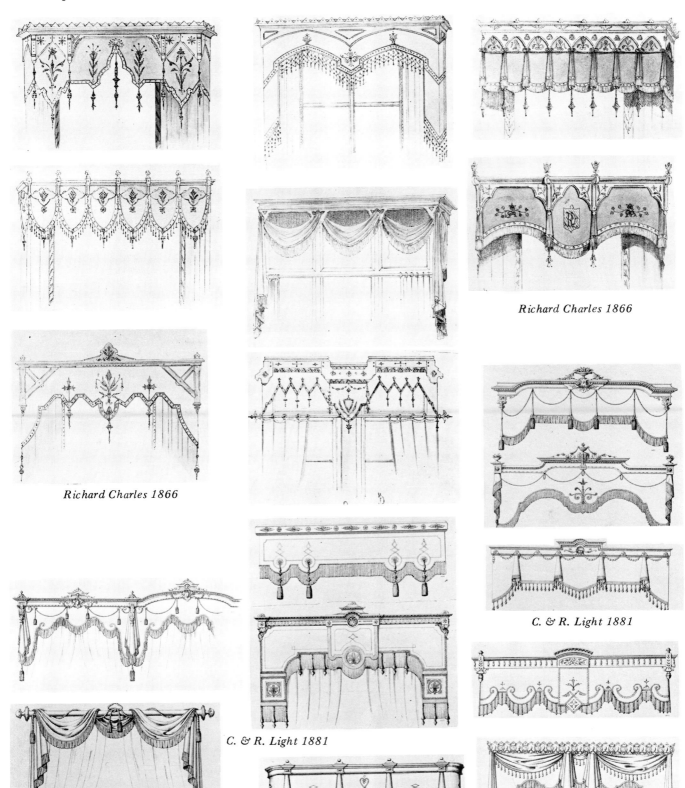

Richard Charles 1866

Richard Charles 1866

C. & R. Light 1881

C. & R. Light 1881

569

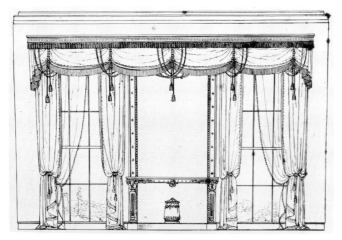

Whitaker 1825

Whitaker 1825

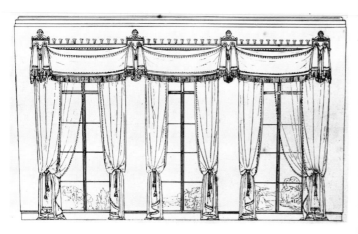

Whitaker 1825

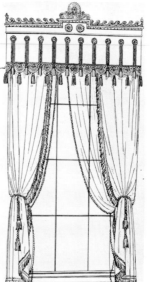

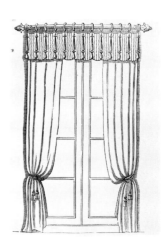

Loudon 1833

G. Smith's Guide 1826

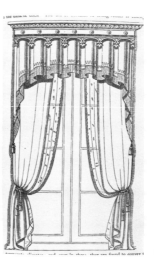

Loudon 1833

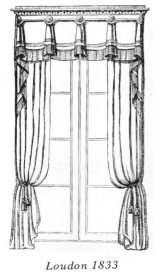

Loudon 1833

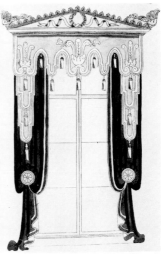

J. Taylor 1850

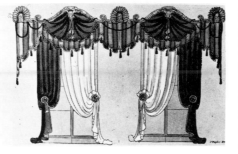

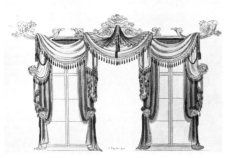

J. Taylor 1850

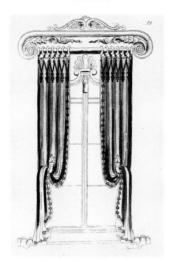

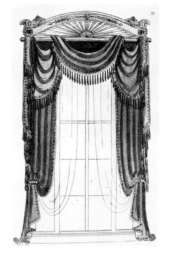

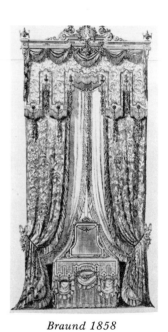

J. Taylor 1850

Braund 1858

Booth 1864

Richard Charles 1866

Bridgens 1838

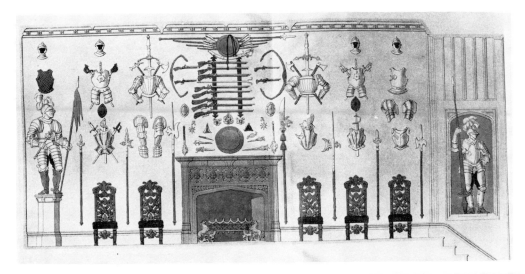

Loudon 1839 edition

Loudon 1839 edition

Loudon 1839 edition

Loudon 1839 edition

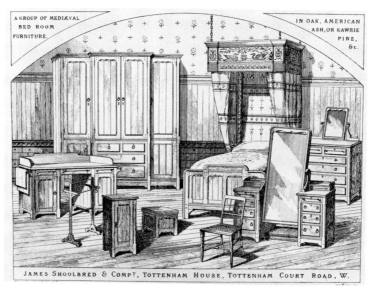

A GROUP OF MEDIÆVAL BED ROOM FURNITURE. — IN OAK, AMERICAN ASH, OR KAWRIE PINE, &c.

JAMES SHOOLBRED & COMPY, TOTTENHAM HOUSE, TOTTENHAM COURT ROAD, W.

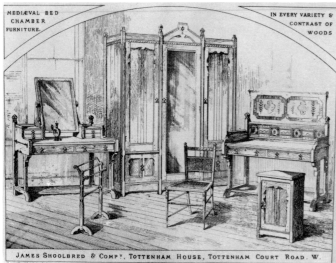

MEDIÆVAL BED CHAMBER FURNITURE. — IN EVERY VARIETY & CONTRAST OF WOODS

JAMES SHOOLBRED & COMPY, TOTTENHAM HOUSE, TOTTENHAM COURT ROAD, W.

GROUP OF "STUART" BED-ROOM FURNITURE IN CONTRASTED WOODS. — DRAWING-ROOM AND DINING-ROOM FURNITURE &c IN THE STYLES OF THE SAME PERIOD

JAMES SHOOLBRED & COMPY, TOTTENHAM HOUSE, TOTTENHAM COURT ROAD, W.

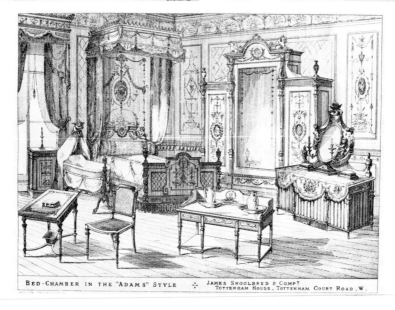

BED-CHAMBER IN THE "ADAMS" STYLE · JAMES SHOOLBRED & COMPY TOTTENHAM HOUSE, TOTTENHAM COURT ROAD, W.

Shoolbred 1876

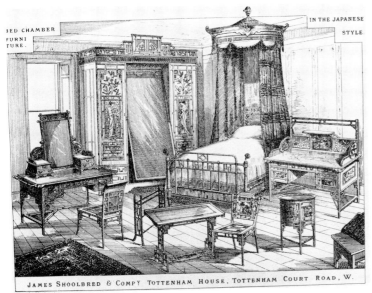

BED CHAMBER FURNITURE.

IN THE JAPANESE STYLE.

JAMES SHOOLBRED & COMPY TOTTENHAM HOUSE, TOTTENHAM COURT ROAD, W.

Shoolbred 1876

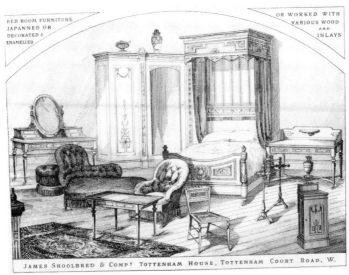

BED ROOM FURNITURE JAPANNED OR DECORATED & ENAMELLED

OR WORKED WITH VARIOUS WOOD AND INLAYS

JAMES SHOOLBRED & COMPY TOTTENHAM HOUSE, TOTTENHAM COURT ROAD, W.

SUITE OF JAPANNED BED ROOM FURNITURE.

OR WORKED WITH VARIOUS WOODS AND INLAYS

JAMES SHOOLBRED & COMPY, TOTTENHAM HOUSE, TOTTENHAM COURT ROAD, W.

MORNING ROOM. ÷ JAMES SHOOLBRED & COMPY
TOTTENHAM HOUSE. TOTTENHAM COURT ROAD. W.

Shoolbred 1876

DRAWING ROOM FURNISHED & DECORATED IN THE OLD ENGLISH STYLE.

DRAWING ROOM IN THE LOUIS SEIZE STYLE ÷ JAMES SHOOLBRED & COMPY
TOTTENHAM HOUSE. TOTTENHAM COURT ROAD. W.

MEDIÆVAL DINING ROOM ❖ JAMES SHOOLBRED & COMPY. TOTTENHAM HOUSE, TOTTENHAM COURT ROAD. W.

Shoolbred 1876

JACOBEAN DINING ROOM. ❖ JAMES SHOOLBRED & COMPY TOTTENHAM HOUSE, TOTTENHAM COURT ROAD, W.

Shoolbred 1876

Shoolbred 1876

580

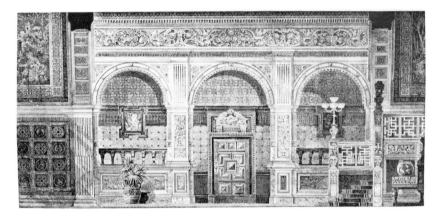

J. Talbert 1876

J. Talbert 1876

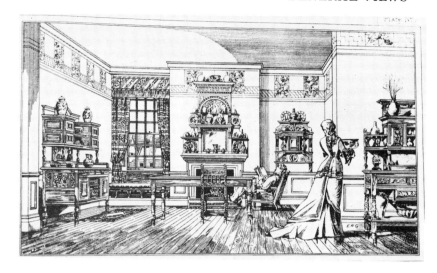

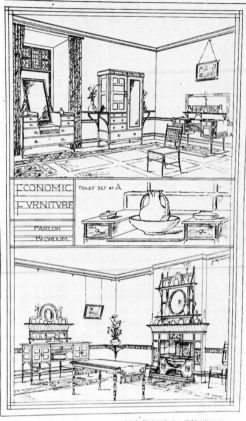

W. Watt 1877

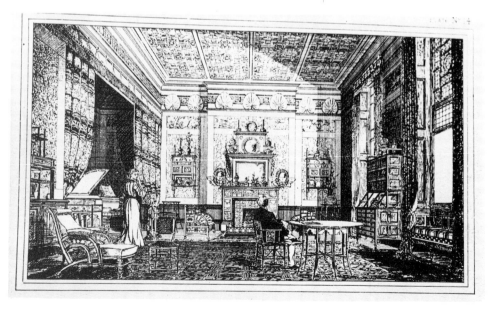

W. Watt 1877

W. Watt 1877

C. & R. Light 1881

Liberty 1890